A Practical Guide to Solving Preschool Behavior Problems

Second Edition

Early Childhood Educators—Select from these other 1990 Delmar publications for the most current coverage of issues:

The World of Child Development: Conception through Adolescence, by George S. Morrison

Early Childhood Experiences in Language Arts: Emerging Literacy, 4th Edition, by Jeanne M. Machado

Creative Activities for Young Children, 4th Edition, by Mary Mayesky

Creative Resources for the Early Childhood Classroom, by Judy Herr and Yvonne Libby

Math and Science for Young Children, by Rosalind Charlesworth and Karen K. Lind

Growing up with Literature, by Diana Comer

Infants and Toddlers: Curriculum and Teaching, 2nd Edition, by LaVisa Cam Wilson

Positive Child Guidance, by Darla Miller

Administration of Schools for Young Children, 3rd Edition, by Phyllis and Donald Click

Developing and Administering a Child Care Center, 2nd Edition, by Dorothy June Sciarra and Anne G. Dorsey

A Practical Guide to Solving Preschool Behavior Problems

Second Edition

Eva L. Essa, Ph.D.

DELMAR PUBLISHERS INC.®

NOTICE TO READER

Cover Credit: Dahl Taylor

Delmar Staff
Associate Editor: Jay S. Whitney
Managing Editor: Gerry East
Project Editor: Marlene McHugh Pratt
Production Coordinator: Karen Seebald
Design Coordinator: Susan Mathews

For information, address Delmar Publishers Inc.
2 Computer Drive West, Box 15–015
Albany, New York 12212–5015

Printed in the United States of America
Published simultaneously in Canada
by Nelson Canada,
a division of The Thomson Corporation

Library of Congress Cataloging-in-Publication Data

Essa, Eva L.
  A practical guide to solving preschool behavior problems.

  Includes index.
  1. Problem children–Education (Preschool)
2. Behavior disorders in children. 3. Social
learning. I. Title.
LC4801.E87   1989   649'.153   89-11619
ISBN: 0-8273-3965-8

Contents

SECTION 4 EMOTIONAL AND DEPENDENT BEHAVIORS

SECTION 5 PARTICIPATION IN SOCIAL AND SCHOOL ACTIVITIES

SECTION 6 EATING BEHAVIORS

SECTION 7 MULTIPLE PROBLEM BEHAVIORS

Preface

One of the rewarding aspects of writing a book such as *A Practical Guide to Solving Preschool Behavior Problems* is hearing from teachers who have used the book. Feedback has conveyed that the format of this book is a useful one. Teachers who have written to me from all parts of the country have indicated that they find the very specific guidelines given for each behavior extremely useful.

The second edition of *A Practical Guide to Solving Preschool Behavior Problems* provides several new features. Based on input from teachers who have used this book, I have tried to incorporate their valuable ideas and suggestions. There are two new introductory chapters that summarize two aspects of the book. Chapter 1 (Why Children Misbehave) offers a discussion of the reasons children misbehave. It is a mistake to assume that children misbehave purely for the attention they gain. There are many reasons that the thoughtful teacher needs to explore. Chapter 2 (Techniques for Dealing with Misbehaviors) provides a summary of the various guidance techniques used in the subsequent chapters. One additional chapter, focusing on the specific behavior of self-stimulation has been included (see Chapter 31).

As with the first edition, this book is intended to help teachers develop appropriate, positive guidance techniques. The text presents a workable method, developed through extensive research, for dealing effectively with children's behavior. The suggested methods match techniques with behaviors.

The text is set up in a practical format. Step-by-step instructions are provided to help the teacher handle specific preschool behaviors. Many texts present theory but leave you on your own to apply it. Here the process is reversed. The applications are given specifically related to a behavior; by applying the suggested methods, you begin to absorb the theory behind them.

One of the main features of *A Practical Guide to Solving Preschool Behavior Problems* is that it focuses your attention first on possible *causes* of the behavior. Before deciding to change a child's inappropriate behavior, you must carefully examine the child's environment to discern which factors might be provoking the behavior. For example, it is essential to learn as much as possible about the child's home life and about any medical factors that may affect behavior. The aim of this book is to help you change behavior; by using this text, you should begin to acquire a clear sense of when and how to apply the techniques suggested here to change behavior.

Working on such a book is never an isolated experience. The specific as well as the indirect input of colleagues and friends provides inspiration and encouragement. My thanks go to Sally Kees Martin, Cynthia Richardson, Syble Solomon, Penny Royce, and Joanne Everts. But my deepest appreciation for his never-failing support goes to my husband, Ahmed Essa.

Eva L. Essa, Ph.D.

ABOUT THE AUTHOR

Eva L. Essa is an Associate Professor of Human Development and Family Studies in the College of Human and Community Sciences at the University of Nevada–Reno. Her undergraduate work in journalism was done at the University of Southern California; her masters in child development/family life, at the University of Nevada–Reno; and her doctorate in child psychology, at Utah State University. Dr. Essa's research on topics related to what affects the behavior of young children has been published in a number of professional journals.

Overview

Since young children are in the process of learning what is and what is not acceptable behavior, a teacher's guidance techniques should be used as guidelines to assist children in their social learning process. The approaches used by teachers should be considered in this spirit. This book is intended as a guide for dealing with specific behavior problems. There are, however, some assumptions about the circumstances and atmosphere in which these suggested techniques should be used.

THE SETTING

The setting in which children are cared for must meet certain minimum requirements. The facility must be child oriented, that is, designed and furnished with children in mind. Careful attention must be given to health and safety factors, and the atmosphere must be conducive to growth and learning. There must be ample materials that are in good condition and appropriate for the ages of the children. Without such a setting, children may misbehave because their needs are not being met.

RULES

Children need to know what is expected of them. Early in the school year, ask the children to help you set up simple, common-sense rules. Most rules for preschoolers should be concerned with safety. Acts that could result in injury to oneself or others must be prevented. When rules are logical, they are easy to follow. Frequent review of the rules and explanations of the reasons behind them help prevent many inappropriate behaviors.

CONSISTENCY

Successful change of unacceptable behavior depends on consistent action. It is extremely important to carry out a plan to change a child's behavior faithfully in order to obtain desirable results. When children behave in a particular way over a period of time, it is because the reactions of people around them reinforce such behavior. To change the behavior, reinforcement must be completely omitted.

If an adult ignores problem behavior most of the time it occurs, but then periodically pays attention to it, the child becomes confused. Inconsistent reactions will be disconcerting, and the youngster may seek the old, expected reactions by increasing the behavior.

CHILD'S CONCEPT OF A BEHAVIOR

Usually children know they are "doing wrong" when they behave in unacceptable ways. However, there are times when children behave inappropriately because they are not aware that their actions are unacceptable. It is important that the adult make the distinction known to the child. If children understand that what they are doing is unacceptable but continue anyway, the adult must systematically work on changing the behavior. If children are unaware of the inappropriateness of their actions, sometimes a simple verbal explanation will suffice. In other circumstances, the expected behavior may have to be taught step by step.

FREQUENCY OF THE BEHAVIOR

Another factor to consider is how often a behavior occurs. The techniques described in this book are intended for use with behaviors repeated consistently. A child may behave inappropriately in isolated circumstances. For example, the child may be tired, a stressful situation may exist at home, or the child may be provoked by a classmate. In such cases, the child should be quietly told that such behavior is not acceptable. At the same time, the cause can be explained. If possible, the situation should be remedied; for instance, you can have the tired child lie down in a quiet area. Not all problems can be remedied, but the child can know that the adult is sympathetic. If the same inappropriate behavior is repeated regularly over a period of time, something in the environment may be reinforcing the behavior. Examine the situation more closely and take systematic steps to remedy it.

THE TEACHER

The teacher's role in dealing with children's behaviors is a vital one. The ability to be thoughtful in assessing children's actions, to understand the factors affecting behavior, and to be consistent in implementing plans for changing behavior are very important. Much is expected of the teacher, who must maintain objectivity and control of emotions. A teacher must be able to see a misbehaving child as a child engaging in inappropriate behavior rather than as a "bad" child. An ability to maintain mastery of the behavior situation encountered is essential.

HOME–SCHOOL COMMUNICATIONS

There are practical needs for parent–teacher interactions. Whenever inappropriate behavior concerns the teacher, it is important to talk it over with the child's parents. Such communication should be honest, but not threatening. The parents may have a similar concern about the behavior. Working on the problem together, parents and teachers may find a combined home–school effort to be effective. It is also possible that the parents feel differently about the child's behavior than does the teacher. In this case, it is important to clarify the underlying values and come to an understanding.

HOW TO USE THIS BOOK

This book is intended to help preschool teachers deal effectively with behaviors that occur in most early childhood settings. If a teacher decides to work on changing a particular behavior that is considered inappropriate, the behavior that most closely fits the situation should be located in the Table of Contents. Some of the most common behavioral situations that occur in early childhood settings are covered in the text. The discussion of each specific behavior is dealt with in a self-contained manner. To work on a particular behavior, study the chapter that is most closely related to the behavior.

All chapters are presented in a standardized format. The following material identifies and explains the sections of each chapter, and discusses how to use the information.

State the Behavior

This section identifies the specific behavior.

Observe the Behavior

Before an attempt is made to deal with inappropriate behavior, all available information about the behavior should be gathered. This section suggests some possible clues as to when, where, how, or why the behavior occurs. Some, but not all, of the suggestions will be relevant to the particular situation. Therefore, to carry out the intent of this section, all teachers in the classroom should carefully watch the child for a few days. Conscious observation often yields some invaluable information and provides the basis for more exact handling of the behavior.

It should be added that not all the suggestions made in this section are related to the outlined program of how to change the behavior. They are presented to help you examine as many aspects of the behavior as is possible.

Explore the Consequences

This section explores what can happen if a problem behavior is not altered. Teachers sometimes react in self-defeating ways when dealing with unacceptable behavior. This may tend to strengthen the problem behavior, establishing a vicious cycle in which efforts to change the behavior only reinforce it.

Consider Alternatives

An important consideration in this book is that inappropriate behavior does not always stem directly from the child. This section examines some alternatives to changing the child's behavior in order to eliminate a problem. Often, the environment encourages a certain behavior. For example, rearranging furniture in a crowded area may eliminate a child's tendency to hit others when in the area. This section should be given careful consideration, after making the initial observation. By no means should you begin to plan behavior change until all other possible alternatives are examined.

State the Goal

The goal for the child whose behavior you want to change is stated in this section. The goal is a suggestion, and may vary according to the child, the setting, the teachers, and the parents' expectations. For one child it may be desirable to completely eliminate a certain behavior. For another child it may be an accomplishment to simply diminish the behavior to a lower level. Have a goal in mind before starting, so that progress can be measured against it.

Procedure

This section presents a step-by-step method for changing the specific behavior addressed in the chapter.

Definition. A concise definition of the behavior to be changed is presented. It is important that all adults who are involved with the child have the same concept of the behavior.

Baseline. Teachers are asked to keep track of the behavior on a simple graph throughout the period of behavior change. Before starting the program, however, it is important to collect baseline data. *Baseline* is simply a base with which to compare later change. It is hard to know if progress is being made unless there is initial information for comparison. Baseline data provides this. It is suggested that baseline data be collected over a three-day period. The baseline period may have to be prolonged if the three days do not provide very consistent information. The section on using graphs discussed later offers more detailed ways of gathering and recording information.

Program. For each program, several consecutive steps or simultaneous procedures are outlined. In some cases a procedure is presented for ignoring an undesirable behavior. A step for reinforcing another, more appropriate action may also be included. In other cases the program involves gradual changes over a period of time, with steps provided for increases in expectation with each specified time period.

In a few cases the program involves a time-out procedure. This is used primarily if the child is potentially or actually harming other children. *Time-out* is a brief period away from the activity, stimulation, and attention within the classroom. The child is asked to sit quietly, without being able to play, in a designated place. Teachers decide the location of a time-out area. It may be a chair in a quiet corner of the classroom or an area outside the room. If it is outside the room, observe safety precautions. The area should be free of hazards to the child, and an adult should be able to observe the child freely. Time-out should last only three minutes at the most. For a very young preschooler, one minute is usually sufficient. It cannot be overemphasized that time-out has to be short. The technique is most effective when used sparingly.

After the situation involving inappropriate behavior has passed, talk with the child and explain what will happen if the behavior resumes. Explain that time-out is a time for the child to think about what happened.

If the child does not stay in the time-out area, as often happens the first few times, be persistent. Return the child to the area each time, and briefly explain that the child cannot engage in classroom activity until the designated amount of time has passed. If a child refuses to remain in time-out, it might be easier to take the child to another area, such as an office. However, it is important that the child not be given undue attention. Remember that time-out is a time away from reinforcement of all kinds.

Maintenance. Once a goal is reached, it is important to maintain it. Suggestions are given to help you keep the appropriate behavior and avoid a setback.

Using Graphs

At the end of each chapter is a Record Keeping Graph which can be reproduced as needed. As you complete them, these graphs provide some basic but very important information. You can see at a glance how often a behavior occurs, how consistent the behavior is, how effective your program to change the behavior is, and how well changes in your program are working.

A graph has two sides, or axes. The vertical axis reflects information on how often the behavior occurs, and the horizontal axis puts the behavior within a time frame.

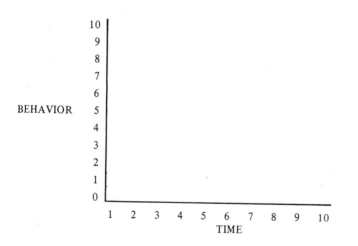

If, for instance, a child has hit other children five times, this information means little by itself. You must know if the child hit five times within a five-minute period, or within an hour, a day, a week or a year. Obviously, each of these circumstances conveys something different. If the child hits five times in one day, record this data on the graph in the following manner:

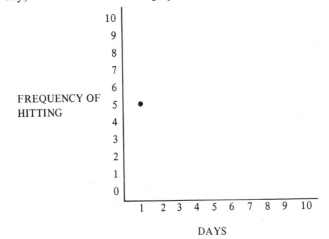

DAYS

This graph is expanded as you collect baseline information. If on Day 1 you count five hits, on Day 2 you count six, and on Day 3 you count five again, your graph will look like this:

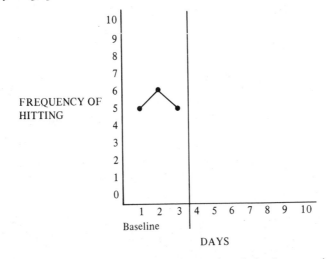

DAYS

Once you begin your program, continue graphing behavior every day. In the case of the child who hits, your goal is to decrease hitting to zero times a day. Often when you change your behavior toward the child, the child tries harder for a while to regain the old, familiar reactions. It is common for negative behaviors to increase at first. Do not give up. With persistence and consistency, the behavior will decrease. If the behavior does not begin to decrease after three or four days, you need to reassess the situation and make changes in your program. Most likely, the undesirable behavior is still being reinforced in some way, and such reinforcement must be removed before you will experience success.

The graph will indicate whether you are succeeding with the program. The following graph reflects a successful program for decreasing hitting. It shows that by Day 16 the program is successful. Measures to maintain the new behavior should now be undertaken.

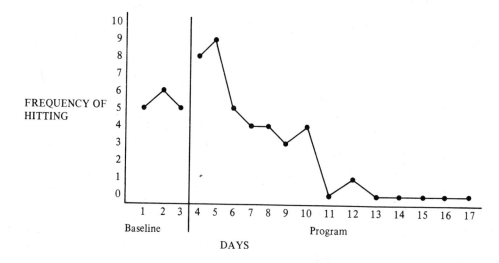

Not all programs focus on decreasing behavior. In some cases, the goal may be to increase a behavior — for example, to increase peer interaction, dramatic play, or large-muscle activity.

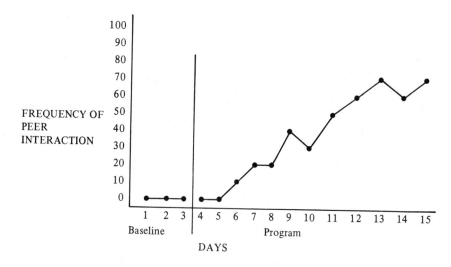

The previous examples show information gathering based on frequency data. *Frequency data* is a tally of how often the behavior occurs in the designated time period. Other ways of collecting information are suggested where appropriate. In some cases, such as whining, it is relevant to know what proportion of the time the child communicates by whining. The behavior is recorded as a percentage rather than as a frequency, as shown in the following graph:

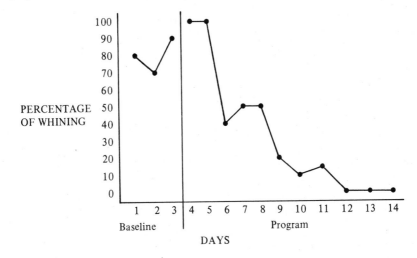

In other instances, the duration or length of the behavior is important. For example, this factor is relevant in a program intended to increase attention span:

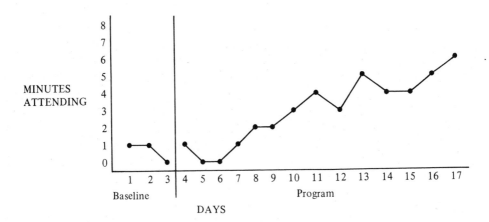

The numbers along both axes of the graph are variable and depend entirely on the child, the behavior, your goals, and how long it takes for the behavior to change. If a child hits five times a day on the average, then you need no more than eight or ten marks on the vertical axis. If a child hits twenty times a day, you have to increase that number. The same holds true for the horizontal axis. The time reflected on the axis depends on how long it takes to reach your goal. Some behaviors can be changed in a few days; other behaviors which are more deeply a part of the child may take longer.

Counting and graphing data may take a few minutes of your time, but you will find the results well worth the effort. The information helps in making the decisions necessary to successfully implement the behavior change program.

CONCLUSION

As you review the instructions for use of this book, you may think that it sounds like a lot of work. It is therefore important to realize that if troubling behaviors are not dealt with effectively, you will have to spend considerable time and energy trying to cope with them. The time and energy expended in this way is taken away from positive interactions with the children in your class.

Management of time resources is important. Even more vital is the effect of misbehavior on the self-concept of the child. Adults' reactions to misbehavior are, in one way or another, negative. The child who receives such negative attention does not develop good feelings of self-worth.

When an undesirable behavior is eliminated, both the teacher and the child benefit. Furthermore, the child learns that appropriate behavior is rewarding.

CHAPTER 1

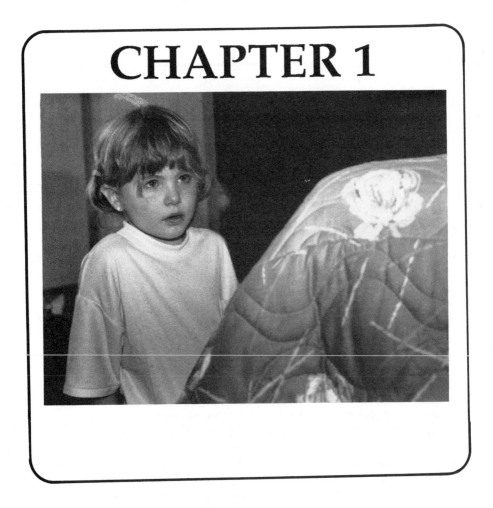

1

Why Children Misbehave

In any preschool classroom there is a wide range of behaviors. Children, as individuals, develop unique ways of responding to what goes on around them. Most of these behaviors are appropriate and develop further when adults or peers show approval. Some behaviors are inappropriate. A preschool class may include a child who hits, another who disrupts the class, one who has difficulty interacting with other children, and one who has frequent toileting accidents. Such behaviors are by no means uncommon but should be of concern. This book provides practical guidelines for helping children learn appropriate behaviors to replace the inappropriate ones.

SOCIAL LEARNING

Before applying the techniques described in this book, it is important to understand how social learning takes place. Behavior, whether appropriate or inappropriate, is learned as children react to their environment and the people in it. As children interact with peers and adults, they learn ways of responding, reacting, and behaving in social situations. They also learn how others respond and react to their social behaviors. As a result, children adopt behaviors that appear to them to meet the expectations of others.

Both adaptive and problem behaviors develop in this way. What children do is either reinforced or not reinforced by those around them. Acceptable behavior continues if it is reinforced. Similarly, problem behavior also continues if it is reinforced. Both kinds of behaviors can be extinguished if they are not reinforced. Many problem behaviors are continued because children are given attention when they so behave. Many appropriate behaviors are discontinued because they are not reinforced.

Inappropriate behaviors exhibited by young children stem either from patterns that have evolved in their past, or from a lack of understanding (caused by limited social experience) of what is expected of them. This is normal. With skill, the adult can systematically change children's unacceptable behaviors to those that are more suitable.

ENVIRONMENTAL CAUSES OF MISBEHAVIOR

Inappropriate behaviors can also be the result of factors in the environment which are beyond the child's control to deal with. It is important for a teacher to consider possible external factors affecting inappropriate behavior—before deciding that it is the child that must be changed— and to try to alleviate the environmental condition. The following section discusses factors that should be given careful consideration.

Inappropriate Expectations for Children's Developmental Level

Adults who work with young children should be aware of the levels of development of the children in the classroom. Each stage of development has unique characteristics, needs, and behaviors. Children may act out because too much or too little is expected of them and as a result they are either frustrated or bored.

Adults' expectations need to be in line with the abilities of each child. The room arrangement, materials, activities, and daily routine should be planned to fit the specific characteristics of the group. Misbehavior can easily occur if expectations or environment are not appropriate for the age of the child. Being familiar with child development helps the teacher plan for and react accordingly to the two-year-old who wants to play with a toy alone rather than share it, the three-year-old who can sit still for only fifteen minutes of show and tell, and the four-year-old who experiments with new words which are sometimes inappropriate.

Health Problems

A child's health can have a definite effect on behavior. Teachers might think about how they react when they are not feeling well—when their nose is stuffed up, when their head throbs, when their stomach aches. Children have fewer resources to handle their behavior when they are not feeling well than do adults. They may not be verbal enough to tell the teacher how they feel, thus they may act out because they are not feeling well. A sick child should not be in school, but some children have chronic health problems or continuous low grade infections that keep them in school but at a lower level of tolerance and functioning. A teacher needs to be sensitive to the child's health status and lower resistance to frustration.

Allergies

Some children's behavior may be affected by food or environmental allergies. As a result they may be overactive, cranky, or have short attention spans. It is important to know the diagnosed allergies of the children in the class and what reactions they have.

Poor Nutrition

A child's behavior can be affected by what he eats or does not eat. A child who comes to school hungry, for instance without breakfast, is vulnerable and likely to be irritable, tired, and cranky. A child whose diet is imbalanced or who lacks certain nutrients will not work to potential and may misbehave. Information on food intake and the eating schedule of children can help detect nutritional problems. If, for instance, children have a long traveling time to school, it may be wise to have a snack available when they arrive rather than an hour or two later.

Sensory Deficits

Behavior can also be affected by hearing or sight problems. A child whose vision is impaired may appear to be insecure, unwilling to try, clumsy, uncoordinated, not able to follow instructions, or even willfully destructive. Similarly, a child who is not hearing well may appear to be overly loud, easily distracted, inattentive, overactive, or disruptive. It is important to watch children carefully for signs of hearing or vision impairment before assuming that their misbehaviors are in their control.

Oversensitivity to Stimulation

A good preschool program is one that is busy, constructively active, and colorful. Most children thrive in an appropriately stimulating environment, but for some the color, noise, activity level, and movement can be overwhelming. It is important to have a quiet area in every classroom, where an overstimulated child can get away for a while.

Family Stress or Change

A child may misbehave because the routine he is used to has changed and he does not understand what is happening. This may mean family discord such as parental separation or divorce, frequent arguments, or money problems. Or the change may involve unusual circumstances such as a new sibling, visiting grandparents, a move to a new house, mother or father temporarily out of town, or any number of other changes. It is therefore important to maintain frequent and open communications with parents to understand what is happening at home and to interpret or even anticipate children's behavioral reactions.

Physical Environment

The physical environment in which children function is very important. The environment itself can encourage or discourage certain behaviors. For example, a large classroom with few dividers to break up space invites running. Materials placed on high shelves require the child to be dependent on teachers. Traffic flow through an activity area may result in disruptive behavior and aggression.

Space is important. A close circle for storytime, a line waiting to get into the bathroom, or any other time when children are crowded can result in pushing or other aggressive behavior. Children's natural activity level combined with too little personal space will result in problems.

The activities and materials provided within the larger environment need to be carefully evaluated. There need to be enough materials so that there is not undue competition or nothing for some children to do. Activities and materials need to be developmentally appropriate and varied enough to provide for growth in all developmental areas. Children's behaviors need to be continually assessed in terms of the environment. Often it is not the child who needs to be changed, but the physical environment.

Inconsistent Messages

Adults may tell children that a behavior is unacceptable on one occasion, but react differently the next time the behavior occurs. When different expectations are conveyed at different times, a child is not given a clear idea of what is acceptable and what is not. Teachers are often not aware of such inconsistencies and need to tune in more consciously to just what they are conveying to children. Similarly, there may be inconsistency between what is expected at home and what is expected at school. Communication with the families to discuss differences is important. If these differences continue, a child can be told, "It is okay to wrestle with your brother at home, but we cannot do this at school." Successful change of unacceptable behavior depends upon consistent action.

Lack of Clear-cut Guidelines

Children need to know what is expected of them and a set of simple but logical rules can help achieve this. Early in the school year, the teacher can ask the children to help set up simple, common-sense rules. Most rules for preschoolers should be concerned with safety to prevent injury to oneself or others. Logical, understandable, easy-to-follow rules can help prevent many inappropriate behaviors.

Attention

Many misbehaviors occur because children have found such behaviors are a good way to get attention from adults. This book focuses on systematic ways of dealing with misbehaviors that seem motivated by an inappropriate bid for attention.

CONCLUSION

Children's misbehaviors are not uncommon. There are many reasons why children misbehave. Before an assumption is made that the behavior is in the child's control, it is important that other factors which might affect the child's behavior be carefully considered. If the misbehavior is in response to a situation that is beyond the child's control, then the teacher needs to try to remedy the situation if possible. If the problem cannot be changed, as, for example, a chronic health disability or parent divorce, then the child can be helped to best cope with the situation through empathic and supportive help from the teacher.

CHAPTER 2

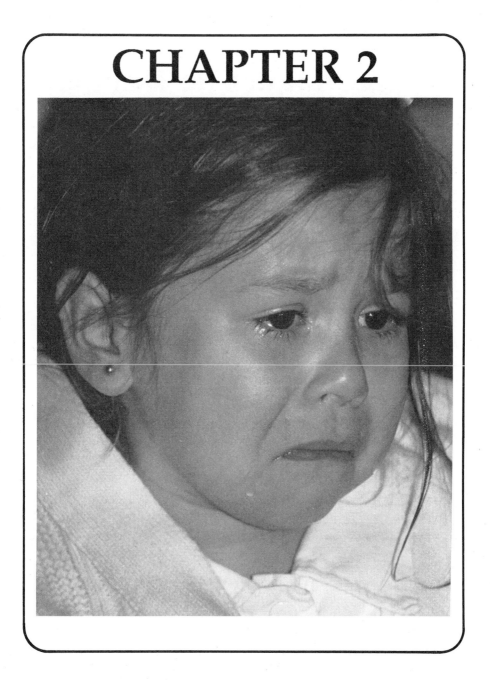

2

Techniques for Dealing with Misbehaviors

Appropriate guidance of young children's behavior is vital. Children's self-concepts are strongly affected by how adults respond to them. Guidance techniques also have a direct impact on the way the class runs, whether smoothly or with frequent disruptions. There are some specific techniques which help maintain positive behavior and eliminate inappropriate behavior. In this chapter, the techniques that are discussed in subsequent chapters of this book are reviewed, particularly in terms of their appropriateness to various situations.

REINFORCEMENT

The first and most important technique to use in dealing with children is positive reinforcement. It should be used often, but at appropriate times. Furthermore, it should *always* be paired with other techniques used to change a child's negative behavior. Appropriate behavior is maintained when children are told that what they are doing is what is expected.

This does not have to be done verbally. Acceptance can be conveyed in many ways, often subtle ones. A smile, a touch, eye-contact, or a hug are just as potent in telling children that adults approve of their behavior as verbal affirmation. In fact, there are times when the teacher does not want to interrupt children's activity but still show approval, and nonverbal reinforcement is the method to use.

It is particularly important to reinforce a child when trying to change a negative behavior. Teachers should keep in mind that when an inappropriate behavior is being changed, something is being taken away from the child, specifically, the attention the child had been receiving for that behavior before. In changing a negative behavior, it is most important to let the child know what *is* acceptable through reinforcement, not just to let the child know what is not acceptable. Every unacceptable behavior has an acceptable opposite which should be encouraged and nurtured through positive reinforcement. If a child frequently hits, that child should be lavishly reinforced for interacting with peers in appropriate ways; if a child whines, that child should be praised for speaking appropriately; if a child tends to disrupt group activities, that child should be told how well he is participating.

Occasionally, very frequent reinforcement might be needed to help a child quickly learn an appropriate behavior. In one example of this use of reinforcement, a three-year-old child's rate of hitting other children was changed from an average of 40 acts of aggression per hour to an average of one. This child did not respond to any of the other techniques that were tried, and thus a program of praise every half minute was implemented. Within two days the rate of hitting dropped dramatically. Over the subsequent weeks, continued though increasingly less frequent reinforcement eventually resulted in no hitting at all. It took much of the teachers' time to carry out this program of constant reinforcement. But in the long run, it was a time saver. Far less time had to be spent in comforting hurt children and dealing with this child.

IGNORING

Ignoring is a very effective strategy, but one which is very difficult to use. When a child repeatedly does something which is irritating to the teachers or disruptive to the class, ignoring is a good technique to use. Ignoring should not be used, however, when children are hurting or potentially hurting themselves or others. Ignoring is especially effective if the child seeks adult attention before the misbehavior. The child who looks to see who is watching before engaging in the misbehavior is overtly bidding for attention.

Total ignoring by all adults every time the misbehavior occurs is difficult but imperative if this strategy is to be effective. Raised eyebrows, sighs, and other nonverbal signs will be read easily by the child, conveying that the misbehavior is "getting to" the teachers and making the strategy ineffective. While ignoring is an important and powerful technique to help eliminate irritating or disruptive behaviors, it is important to keep in mind that this removal of attention needs to be replaced by reinforcement of positive behaviors.

TIME-OUT

Time-out is a technique that has to be used sparingly and carefully. It should be used primarily when children hurt or potentially hurt others or themselves. Agressive behavior needs to be stopped as quickly as possible, and time-out is often, *but not always,* the best method for doing so. Time-out should only be used when a child has repeated the aggressive behavior more than twice and the teacher has already explained to the child that such behavior is not acceptable.

Before deciding to use time-out, teachers need to agree to use this procedure consistently and in the same way. It is important that this be discussed by all involved teachers beforehand to agree on a definition of the behavior for which time-out should be used, the place where time-out is to be carried out, and the actual process of time-out.

This book suggests the following procedure for time-out:

1. Quickly make sure that the child against whom the aggression was aimed is not hurt. If possible, another teacher should attend to the victim.
2. Calmly take the aggressive child by the hand to the time-out area. Firmly but quietly say, "I cannot allow you to hurt other children. You will have to sit here until I tell you that you may get up."
3. Note the time and move away from the child. Do not talk with or look at the child during the time-out.
4. If another child approaches the time-out area, quietly move this child away. Explain, "_____ needs to be by herself for a few minutes. You can talk to her when she joins the class again."
5. At the end of the time, promptly go to the child and say, "You may get up now." Do not lecture. The child knows the reason for the isolation. To channel the child into constructive behavior, you might suggest joining an ongoing activity. Reinforce the child as soon as possible for engaging in appropriate activity.

Keep in mind that time-out is not a punishment. Rather, it is a time for the child to calm down and think about what has happened. Sometimes aggressive behavior is a reaction to a general feeling of anger or anxiety or unease, and time to get away from the stimulation of the class can help the child calm down.

SELF-SELECTED TIME-OUT

One variation of time-out that has been used successfully with some children is self-selected time-out. Some children may, at times, find themselves overwhelmed with the noise, activity level, and general stimulation of the classroom, and may need an opportunity to get away. A quiet, less stimulating area needs to be designated for this. Such an area can be inside or outside the classroom. If it is in the room, it needs to be secluded enough to give the child a sense of being away from the general activity and noise of the room.

A two-and-a-half-year-old boy who was extremely disruptive and aggressive in his class, and who had major tantrums four or five times every morning, did not respond at all to more conventional attempts to change or modify his behavior. One teacher noted that he almost visibly "wound up" before negative behaviors, and the staff began to discuss the possibility that the child could simply not deal with the stimulation level of the class at times. They worked out a new strategy.

The next day a teacher had a talk with him. She told him that she could "see" when he was beginning to feel upset and asked if he knew when he started to feel "mad." He indicated that he did. The teacher then told him that when he started to feel upset he could leave the room and go to a designated area, the office of another staff member. This room was equipped with a small table and chair and a few manipulative toys. He was required to let a teacher in the classroom know, however, anytime he left.

The change in the child was striking. From that same day his unacceptable behaviors decreased dramatically, although they did not disappear completely, and he left the room periodically to go to his designated out-of-the-classroom area. He never abused this opportunity to leave the room, did not go anywhere other than this room, and usually returned within five or ten minutes. He left the classroom several times a day, and continued to do this over a two-year period. The third year that he was at the child care center, he decreased his number of times away from the class, but still maintained the option of leaving. By this time he was also able to verbalize that it made him feel better to be able to remove himself from the classroom when he started to feel upset.

When other methods of dealing with misbehavior seem to fail, you might want to consider this alternative. Self-selected time-out should not be used indiscriminately, but reserved for children who seem to have a hard time handling a stimulating preschool class environment for long periods of time. The cause of the misbehavior, in this case, is external, and this technique gives the child an opportunity to control the environment.

PREVENTION

Stopping a misbehavior before it happens is an excellent technique to use. Using prevention implies, however, that adults have carefully observed the child and have a pretty good idea what triggers the misbehavior. If, for example, the teachers have noticed that a child gets frustrated easily when not successful in an activity and then turns on nearby friends, teachers should look for any occasion when the child might have problems in an activity. This does not mean that they solve all of the child's problems, but that they help the child learn skills and problem-solving techniques. Prevention is especially effective with younger preschoolers who do not yet have the self-control or ability to express themselves that older children have.

REDIRECTION

Another effective technique to use with younger preschoolers, especially two-year-olds, is redirection. The teacher directs the child's attention to another activity or provides a duplicate or alternative toy. Two-year-olds do not yet have the social skills to handle the demands of school and sharing, and teachers need to help them gradually acquire such skills. Redirection should not be routinely used with older preschoolers who need the guidance to solve social problems in effective ways.

DISCUSSION

One technique that works with many older preschoolers is discussion. Often a child of four or five is quite willing to try to solve behavior problems with the teacher. A misbehaving child does not feel good about herself. If the child is seriously interested in changing the behavior, you can discuss this with her and, in effect, become her partner. It is important to find a quiet and private place to discuss such an approach with the child. If she puts forth effort to change, you need to be available to help her until she has mastered the positive behavior.

SPECIAL TIME

A very effective technique to use with a child who engages in excessive attention-getting behavior is to set aside special time. Many families today, with a single parent or two working parents, are very stressed and busy, and often children do not get the attention they need. The result can be mis-behavior and acting out.

If you suspect that a child's misbehavior is a cry for attention—any atten-tion—you might consider special time. This means that the teacher sets aside a few minutes a day, every other day, or even twice a week, when she spends some time just with this child. This is not always easy with a full class of children, but some creative scheduling can help. Early mornings or late in the day before closing time could provide an opportunity. The beginning or end of nap or rest time might also be possibilities. Getting a volunteer into the class, asking the director to come in, or looking at the total staffing pattern could help find a few minutes here or there for special time with one or more children.

Special time should be just for the child alone with a teacher. The teacher can ask what the child would like to do for special time, then use this suggestion. It is amazing how a small time investment can pay off in greatly decreased acting out behavior. In the long run, teachers will spend less time dealing with misbehavior and will create a more positive classroom atmosphere.

STAR CHART

A star chart works particularly well if it helps the child to have a visible, tangible record of progress toward appropriate behavior. It is a visible reinforcer that, for some children and some circumstances, is more effective. A star chart is not meant to be punitive and should never be used to reflect when the child does *not* engage in the appropriate behavior. It should be a record of successes, not failures.

Such a chart is simple to make, with days listed along the side and spaces for a star or other type of sticker when a child performs the appropriate behavior. Stars can be simply added each time a child performs a given behavior, or they can be put on the chart in time-related slots. Length of time will, of course, depend on the behavior.

CONCLUSION

The guidance techniques that a teacher uses are vital in shaping children's behavior. Nine different approaches to changing inappropriate children's behavior were discussed in this chapter. Use of these techniques depends on the child as well as on the misbehavior, and subsequent chapters of this book suggest specific techniques or combinations of techniques for different behaviors.

Reinforcement is a very important technique to use in guiding children and should be used routinely to let children know that what they are doing is appropriate, as well as in combination with any other techniques used to change a child's behavior. The opposite of reinforcement is ignoring, another very effective approach, though one that is difficult to implement. When ignoring a behavior, it is important at the same time to reinforce an opposite, appropriate behavior.

Time-out should be used sparingly and only when children engage in aggressive or dangerous behaviors. Time-out needs to be carefully planned and not considered as a punishment. A variation of this technique is self-selected time-out, where the child has the option of removing himself from the classroom when he feels his behavior about to go out of control.

Careful observation of children can give clues to what triggers some misbehaviors. Prevention is an effective method that teaches the child alternatives by not allowing the misbehavior to occur. This is often effective with young preschoolers, as is redirection. Redirection can help a child whose self-control and language are not yet well developed find a way of dealing with potentially frustrating situations.

Older preschoolers who want to change a misbehavior can participate in discussion of that behavior with you. You are then in a position to become that child's partner in changing the behavior. Special time works well with children whose inappropriate attention-seeking sends the message that they are desperately seeking attention. Finally, a star chart can be helpful by providing a tangible record of progress.

These various techniques are applied to different instances of misbehavior in the following chapters. Their application is suggested based on general knowledge about children and their behaviors. You must use your judgment as to whether the suggested approach fits the child and situation for which you are seeking a solution. Although we can apply some general principles, each child, each teacher, and each situation are unique.

SECTION 1

AGGRESSIVE AND ANTISOCIAL BEHAVIORS

CHAPTER 3

3
Hitting

Patsy, a four-year-old whose mother works full time, has attended the day care center for almost two years. Patsy is a friendly and verbal little girl who enjoys all the activities provided by her teachers. She is imaginative and particularly likes role playing in the housekeeping area, building elaborate block structures, and riding her tricycle on the "freeway" in the play yard. She enjoys being the leader in group play. The other children generally go along with Patsy; when they do not, she hits someone. After she hits a child, she stalks off, saying that no one likes her. At this point, a teacher usually goes to Patsy, tells her that she has hurt the other child, and ends up talking several minutes before Patsy stops pouting and agrees to say "I'm sorry" to the child she hit. The teacher reassures Patsy that the other children like her, but explains that they do not like it when she hits them. Patsy generally protests vigorously and allows the teacher to convince her otherwise only after a period of time. Once the teacher leaves, Patsy quickly rejoins the group play and reasserts her leadership role.

STATE THE BEHAVIOR

The child regularly hits other children.

OBSERVE THE BEHAVIOR

Spend some time observing and gathering information that can give you further insight into the behavior.

A. When does the child usually hit?
- At all times of the day
- At particular times, such as late in the day

- During specific activities or routines
- Indoors
- Outdoors
- When children are in close proximity, such as during group time
- During structured activities
- When children have free choice activities

B. What seems to trigger the behavior?

- A classmate has something the child wants
- A classmate takes something away from the child
- A teacher says no to the child
- The child is not able to accomplish a task
- The child has an argument with another child
- The child is pushed
- The child is close to others
- The child is tired

C. Who is the victim?

- Usually the same child or a few certain children
- Anyone
- Only timid children
- Only assertive children
- Older or younger children
- Bigger or smaller children
- Boys
- Girls

D. What happens when the child hits?

- The child admits hitting
- The child denies it
- The child gets upset when the other child cries
- The child gets hit back
- The child looks to see if someone is watching before hitting
- The child apologizes or tries to make the victim feel better
- The child walks away from the child who was hit
- The child stays nearby

From this informal information gathering you should have some idea of why and when the child hits. There is a difference between children who hit to defend property, children who hit out of frustration, and children who hit to get their own way. Hitting cannot be allowed for any reason, but you can help avert some causes for hitting by being observant and aware.

EXPLORE THE CONSEQUENCES

When a child often hits others, it is easy for the teacher to react in self-defeating ways. Because injury to another child must be avoided if at all possible, a frequent response is to scold and lecture the hitter. The teacher may spend several minutes with the child each time hitting occurs, explaining what was done wrong and why others should not be hit. This attention may be negative, but it is attention nonetheless. Almost invariably, the child who hits is very aware of doing something inappropriate. This awareness is often confirmed by the child who looks to see whether someone is watching before hitting or by quickly apologizing after the episode. Over a period of time, the teacher is reinforcing the child's feeling that an effective way to get attention is to hit another child.

CONSIDER ALTERNATIVES

From your informal observation, you might find a simple remedy for the problem of the hitter. Consider some of the following possibilities.

- If the child always hits one particular child, separating the two should be considered. Very possibly the victim is in some way provoking the other child to hit. Removing one of them from the scene may help. If one of the children can be placed in another classroom, this should be done. If this is not possible, then you should be alert at all times to where these two children are and make efforts to keep them separated. The hitter has no target if the other child is not sitting nearby or is playing in another area of the room.
- Crowded situations tend to provoke hitting in some children. It may help to decrease the times when crowding occurs. Eliminate lining-up times by using different group-management techniques to move children from one activity to another. For example, dismiss a few children at a time to go to the next area. Group times can be less crowded if children are asked to sit in a large circle or semicircle where everyone can see. You can sit next to or between certain children to further avoid potential problems. Say, "I'd really love to sit with you today," or "Will you sit next to me so you can be my special helper?"
- If a child tends to hit when frustrated, you should be more aware of situations where this might happen. For instance, if a puzzle is difficult for a child, sit down with the child and help complete the puzzle or suggest a simpler one. This helps the child to achieve more success, which diminishes frustrations and subsequent hitting.

- Examine the classroom to be sure that available materials and activities are age-appropriate for the children in the group and that there are enough of these. If materials are too simple, too difficult, or scarce, boredom or frustration can lead to undesirable behavior such as hitting.

If the solution to the problem does not lie in one of these suggestions, then you must follow a more detailed approach.

STATE THE GOAL

The goal is for the child to not hit other children.

PROCEDURE

The basic strategy involves three simultaneous procedures:

- Try to prevent incidents of hitting.
- Praise the child for desired social behaviors.
- Use time-out if the child does hit someone.

Definition

Hitting is any instance of deliberate aggression in which a child strikes someone.

Baseline

Before making changes it is important to know how often the child hits another child in the classroom. This information provides a baseline against which improvements can be gauged. Whenever the child hits, take note of the incident by marking it on paper. At the end of the day add up the marks and record the number on the Record Keeping Graph. Keep track in this way for three consecutive days.

Program

After you have gathered the baseline data, begin the following program. It is important that all teachers consistently follow the same procedure.

Prevent Incidents of Hitting Whenever Possible. From your informal observation, you should have some ideas of when to expect hitting. Be especially alert during such times. The old saying "An ounce of prevention is worth a pound of cure" is very appropriate. Prevent hitting by looking for cues. For instance, if a child ends up hitting when playing with blocks, be in the block area when the child is there. Help the child deal with frustration if the blocks fall. Explain the need for sharing blocks and provide the chance to work cooperatively with another child. Model appropriate behavior and facilitate positive social interaction: "Look! Mary wants to play with us in the block area, too. Mary, we're building a barn. Would you help us find this size of blocks for the walls?" In other words, make a positive situation out of something that is potentially negative. In this way the child eventually acquires the skills to deal with situations in ways other than hitting. As alternatives to hitting are learned, the hitting decreases. As hitting gradually disappears, you can trust the child's self-control more and decrease the constant vigilance.

Praise the Child for Desired Social Behaviors. At the same time that you are watching the child for potential hitting, observe positive behaviors. When the child handles a social situation well, say so. Let the child know how pleased you are. Remember, as hitting decreases, so does the negative attention. There are fewer chances to be scolded and lectured. The child still needs and wants attention. Attention given for positive behavior helps ensure that the appropriate behaviors continue. If the child lacks social skills, it is especially important to reinforce behaviors close to the appropriate behavior.

If the Child Does Hit Someone, Use Time-out. If a child hits another youngster, do the following:

1. Quickly make sure the child who was hit is all right. If possible, another teacher should attend to the victim.
2. Calmly take the child who hit to the time-out area. Firmly but quietly say, "I cannot allow you to hurt other children. You have to sit here until I tell you that you may get up."
3. Note the time and move away from the child. Do not talk with or look at the child during the time-out.
4. If another child approaches the time-out area, quietly move this child away. Explain, "Patsy needs to be by herself for a few minutes. You can talk to her when she joins the class again."
5. At the end of the time, promptly go to the child and say, "You may get up now." Do not lecture. The child knows the reason for the isolation. To channel the child into constructive behavior, you might suggest joining an ongoing activity.

Continue Graphing the Behavior. To ensure that change is occurring, continue to record any hitting incidents on the Record Keeping Graph. Progress will probably be gradual. By recording on the graph you will be able to see change, even though the behavior will not be completely eliminated for a while. The decrease in hitting incidents should be encouraging because it means that the behavior is improving.

Maintenance

Once hitting is eliminated, be sure to continue giving attention to appropriate social behavior. Let the child know how much you appreciate her willingness to replace the old inappropriate hitting behavior with new social skills.

RECORD KEEPING GRAPH

CHILD'S NAME _____   AGE _____   DATE _____

GOAL _____

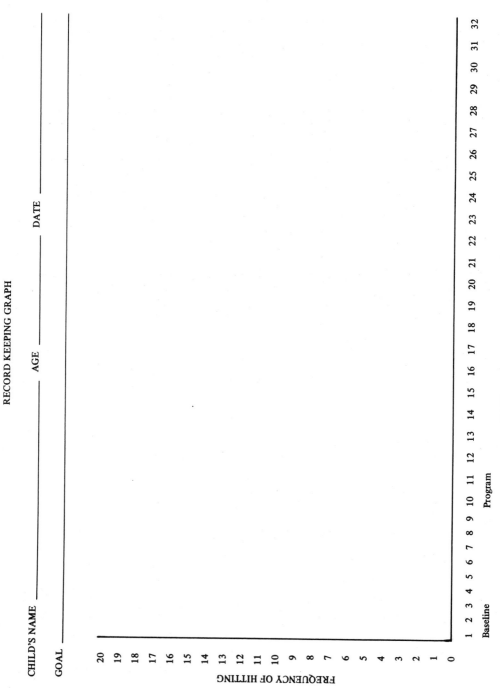

CHAPTER 4

4

Biting

Two-year-old Jason has been in his school only two months. He comes three mornings a week while his mother is in class at the university. Jason is a chunky little brunette who has not yet lost all of his baby fat. He loves school and joins all activities vigorously. He is a very loving child, giving frequent hugs to teachers and peers alike. Jason, however, bites. If someone has a truck or puzzle that Jason wants, he simply bites the person who has the desired item. At other times, he walks up to a child, smilingly puts his arms around his friend, and sinks his teeth into the child's cheek. He has bitten his neighbor at snack time if the crackers did not reach him quickly enough, and in the bathroom while waiting to wash his hands. The teacher's response to Jason's biting has always been to tell Jason how much he has hurt the other child and to scold him for biting. He is reminded that he would not like it if one of the children bit him. Jason is usually very contrite, and apologizes to his victim. His concern does not last long, however. He is back at play quickly. Sometimes he does not bite again for quite a while, but at other times he finds a new victim within a few minutes.

STATE THE BEHAVIOR

The child frequently bites other children.

OBSERVE THE BEHAVIOR

Before taking any steps, observe the child for a few days to gain some insight into the behavior.

A. When does the child usually bite?
- At all times of the day
- During specific activities or routines

- Indoors
- Outdoors
- During group times when children are close together
- During teacher-directed activities
- During free choice activities
- At nap time
- When the child is cranky

B. What seems to trigger the behavior?

- Someone takes something from the child
- Someone else has something the child wants
- The child is tired
- It is close to mealtime
- The child is not able to accomplish a task
- The child is told no
- The child sees another child hurt a peer
- The child is in close proximity to others
- The child is restless and not engaged in a specific activity
- The child has to wait

C. Who is the victim?

- Anyone
- Children of the same age or size
- Younger or smaller children
- Children who grab from the child
- Anyone close by

D. What happens when the child bites?

- The child looks to see if someone is watching before biting
- The child apologizes or tries to make the victim feel better afterward
- The child walks off as though nothing has happened
- The child gets upset when the other child cries

E. Other factors to observe

- Whether the child bites himself
- Whether the child bites objects such as blocks and plastic rings
- Whether the child often puts clothing, toys, or fingers into his mouth

This preliminary observation should give you some idea about when, why, and how biting occurs. Most often the biter is a young preschooler, probably a two-year-old. Biting is a phase many young children go through, but it cannot be allowed because it is dangerous. Therefore, the more clues you have to help you deal with this behavior, the more you can work at preventing it.

EXPLORE THE CONSEQUENCES

Biting is a natural behavior for very young children. Many children, however, do not yet have the social awareness to control this behavior when it is directed against others. The two-year-old is still socially unsophisticated and not well attuned to the feelings of peers and to the finer points of social interaction. Furthermore, teething may be occurring and, like the baby who gums objects, the child may be trying to relieve the discomfort in one way or another. The teacher must be aware that the two-year-old who bites is most likely going through a stage that will soon pass. The teacher cannot allow biting, but can be sensitive to the reason the child is biting and help prevent this behavior. Whenever one child hurts another child, a teacher's natural reaction may be to consider the action as a misbehavior and to scold, lecture, or otherwise punish the biter. The child discovers that whenever he bites, he gets quite a bit of attention. Thus, the teacher's reaction reinforces biting as one way to get an adult to quickly attend. There is confusion for the child, who is held accountable for an act that to the child is not malicious. The child's self-concept suffers when adults get angry about behaviors that he cannot control yet.

CONSIDER ALTERNATIVES

Informal clues might give some ideas of environmental changes that can help the teacher deal with the young biter.

- Crowding may stimulate the two-year-old to bite; classes for this age should be kept small. Groups of eight to twelve children, with two or three teachers, may help decrease this behavior.
- Two-year-olds need many sensory activities. The classroom should be set up to allow for a lot of touching, feeling, smelling, tasting, hearing, seeing, and manipulating. Because objects may be put into the child's mouth, they should be safe and hygienic. Allowing for tasting and biting of objects may help avert the impulse to bite people.
- The classroom environment should have age-appropriate materials and activities within the reach of the children. If materials are not geared for the needs and abilities of two-year-olds, children will experience frustration. Some children may express their frustration by biting their peers.
- The environment should also be arranged in such a way that all teachers can easily see all areas of the room and all the children. Careful supervision of very young preschoolers is especially important and allows for more conscious preventive measures.

STATE THE GOAL

The goal is for the teacher to help the two-year-old child find acceptable alternatives to biting.

PROCEDURE

The approach presented deals with biting by two-year-olds and relies basically on preventive measures by the teacher. If an older child in the class bites, the strategy outlined in Chapter 3 (Hitting) should be used.

Definition

Biting is any occurrence whereby a child sinks his teeth into any part of someone else's body.

Baseline

To be able to effectively evaluate your actions and to recognize when the child begins to get over the biting stage, keep track of all incidents of biting. For three days, mark on paper each time the child bites. At the end of each day, record the total number on the Record Keeping Graph. This information provides a baseline.

Program

After gathering baseline data, all teachers in the classroom should implement the following program.

Ensure that the Classroom Environment is as Effective as Possible. Continually check the classroom arrangement, materials, and schedule to ensure they meet the needs of two-year-olds. The more smoothly the classroom runs, the less the potential frustrations and clashes between children. Two-year-olds tire easily, may need a snack between meals, have a short attention span, and desire immediate attention. They may play near rather than with other children, and may have difficulty sharing. Take these characteristics into account both in your expectations and in how you plan and handle classroom routines.

Prevent Biting by Being Alert to Potential Problem Situations. When you know that a child tends to bite under certain circumstances, you can take preventive steps. Stay near the child and carefully watch him. If he seems about to bite, pick him up and move him. If he fights you, gently restrain him until he stops struggling. If the child accepts being moved, immediately channel his attention to an activity. Do not lecture! Give the child something to bite on if he seems to need to bite.

Reinforce Acceptable Social Behavior. The two-year-old has much to learn about positive peer interaction, including the fact that biting is not an acceptable means of communication. Praise the child for appropriate social behaviors. Let him know that you like what he is doing and help him verbalize his feelings to other children. The more the child learns positive alternatives to biting and other forms of aggression, the more his social interactions will be satisfactory to him and his peers.

If Biting Occurs, Let the Child Know it is Unacceptable. Biting should be decreased through preventive measures, but occasionally a child will still bite. In such a case, do the following:

1. Separate the biter and the bitten child. Say to the biter very firmly, "No! It hurts when you bite."
2. Turn your back on the child who has bitten and attend to the victim. Apply first aid as needed. Give your attention to the child who was hurt, not to the one who bit.
3. Another teacher should, from a distance, keep a careful eye on the child who has bitten to be sure that he does not repeat the behavior.
4. Within two minutes go to the child who bit and give him your attention. If he has not resumed an activity, help him find something to do. Do not discuss the biting incident.

Continue Graphing the Behavior. Use the Record Keeping Graph to keep daily track of the number of incidents of biting. If you find that there is still an excessive number, examine your preventive measures. These may need to be strengthened. With adequate vigilance by all adults in the room, biting should be considerably decreased.

Maintenance

When, over a period of time, the graph shows no more occurrences of biting, the child has probably passed through the biting phase. You can discontinue the deliberate preventive measures. Continue reinforcing acceptable social behavior, because socialization is a long-term learning process.

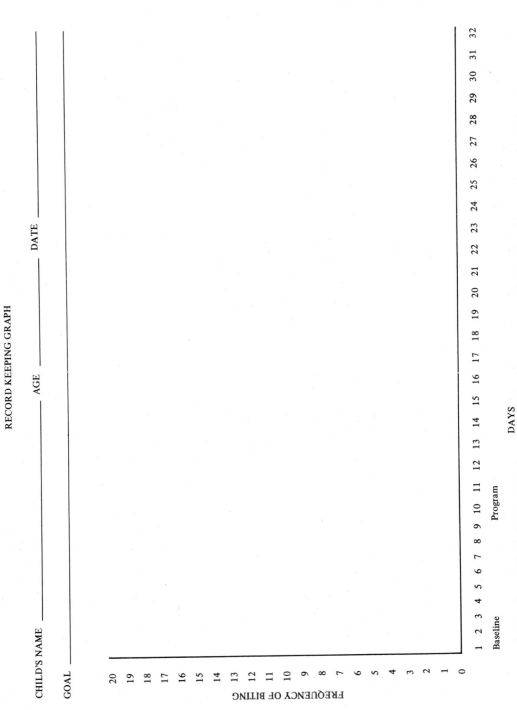

RECORD KEEPING GRAPH

CHILD'S NAME _____ AGE _____ DATE _____

GOAL _____

FREQUENCY OF BITING

20
19
18
17
16
15
14
13
12
11
10
9
8
7
6
5
4
3
2
1
0

1 2 3 4 5 6 7 8 9 10 11 12 13 14 15 16 17 18 19 20 21 22 23 24 25 26 27 28 29 30 31 32

Baseline   Program

DAYS

CHAPTER 5

Throwing Objects at Others

The teachers find that four-year-old Mark is easily provoked to anger. If Mark does not get his way, he loses his temper. The teachers are concerned because Mark has been getting angry over little things more frequently in the last few weeks. When Mark gets angry, he picks up the nearest object and throws it at whoever provokes him. Mark has thrown blocks, puzzle pieces, brushes, dolls, dishes, shoes, stuffed animals, and even scissors and chairs. When he throws, he aims to hit and often does. Luckily no one has been seriously hurt, but Mark has caused several cuts and bruises. The other children in the class have been actively expressing their fear and dislike of Mark, which also angers him. Recently, when Mark hit Amy on the back with a block, her friend Carol shouted, "I hate you, Mark! You hurt Amy." Mark picked up another block and threw it at Carol in response. The teachers have scolded Mark, lectured him, tried to reason with him, and threatened to withhold privileges, but to no avail. Mark still throws objects when he gets angry.

STATE THE BEHAVIOR

The child regularly throws toys and other objects, deliberately aiming these at other children.

OBSERVE THE BEHAVIOR

A few days spent informally observing the child can give you a better idea of what is happening.

A. When does the child usually throw objects?
- Unpredictably, at any time of day
- During free choice activities

- During structured activities
- Outdoors
- Indoors
- Early in the day
- Late in the day
- At mealtimes

B. What usually happens before the child throws an object?

- Another child angers him
- Another child takes something away from him
- Another child has something the child wants
- The child argues with another
- The child is hit by another child
- The child is told no by another child or a teacher
- The child looks to see if a teacher is watching

C. Who is the victim?

- Usually the same child or a few children
- Anyone
- Anyone who provokes the child
- Only assertive children
- Only timid children
- Older and bigger children
- Smaller and younger children
- Boys
- Girls

D. What objects are usually thrown?

- Whatever is in the child's hand
- Any object within reach
- Only hard objects
- Only sharp objects
- Only soft objects
- Only small objects
- Only large objects
- One particular object or type of object

E. What happens after the child has thrown an object at another child?

- The object misses the target
- The object hits the target
- The child is angry if the object does not hit the target
- The child admits throwing the object
- The child denies it
- The child retrieves the object

- The child looks to see if an adult is watching
- The child gets upset when the other child is hit
- The child apologizes or tries to make the victim feel better
- The child walks away
- The child stays nearby

These informal observations should give a more complete picture of when, how, and why the child throws objects. This information helps you to find a solution to the situation.

EXPLORE THE CONSEQUENCES

The child who throws objects at other children is a danger in the classroom. Another child could be seriously hurt from an airborne item, particularly if it is hard or sharp. The teacher may feel an urgent need to stop such potentially dangerous behavior. The teacher thus usually reacts quickly and emotionally to the child who has thrown by severely stating how dangerous the behavior is and what was done wrong. The teacher may even use some form of punishment because of the seriousness of the problem. In whatever way the teacher reacts, this message is conveyed to the child: Throwing things gets quite a reaction out of adults. They get excited and pay particular attention when an object is thrown.

The child relieves anger or frustration by the act of throwing and then gets attention for the action. Almost invariably, when a child aims and throws objects at someone else, it is done in response to anger or frustration. Furthermore, it is often the case that such a youngster is not very verbal or has trouble expressing feelings. The child's inability or reluctance to use verbal expression leads to a physical expression of his anger or frustration. When the teacher talks *at* the child after he has thrown something, the child is given attention for negative behavior, but is not helped to deal with the problem.

CONSIDER ALTERNATIVES

Through observation you might find some clues to the behavior that will help you eliminate it fairly quickly.

- If the child throws only one particular object, remove it from the class-room for a few weeks. If, for instance, the child throws only wooden unit blocks, take these away. After a week or two, you might try substituting larger hollow blocks which would be difficult to throw, or lightweight plastic, cardboard, or homemade milk-carton blocks. After several weeks have passed, reintroduce the wooden unit blocks. Leave them in the classroom if the child has overcome the desire to throw the blocks.

• If one particular child is always the target, this child may provoke the aggression. If at all possible, separate the two children by putting them into different areas of the room. Guide them into separate activities and keep a careful eye on their whereabouts. Removing the target may well remove the problem in this case.

If neither of these suggestions provides a solution to the problem, then continue to the following, more detailed, approach.

STATE THE GOAL

The goal is for the child to not throw objects at other children and to learn appropriate ways of communicating anger or frustration.

PROCEDURE

The basic strategy will involve these simultaneous steps:

• Prevent as many incidents of throwing objects as possible.
• Systematically teach appropriate alternatives to dealing with anger or frustration.
• Use time-out if the child throws an object at someone.

Definition

Throwing objects at others is any deliberate action in which a child attempts to hurt another child by aiming and throwing something at the child.

Baseline

In order to know how often the behavior is occurring, spend three days keeping track of the frequency of object throwing. This must be done before you begin implementing any changes. Mark on a paper each time the child throws something at another child. At the end of each day record this number on the Record Keeping Graph to establish the baseline against which to gauge future improvements.

Program

After gathering baseline data, begin the following program. All teachers must be aware of and cooperate in the program in order for it to be effective.

Whenever Possible, Prevent the Child From Throwing an Object at Someone Else. Based on informal observation, you should have some idea of what provokes the child to throw objects, and when to expect such behavior. Take careful note of any cues. For instance, the child might precede the behavior by clenching his fists or yelling. Or perhaps the only warning is a verbal or nonverbal disagreement between the child and a classmate. Whatever the cues, however, it requires vigilance on the part of all the teachers to recognize these signs, and then to prevent the behavior. When you recognize a cue, follow this procedure:

1. Go to the child who throws things and place yourself in front of him. Block the other child from view by placing yourself between the two children.
2. Get to the child's level and gently but firmly place your hands on his upper arms to limit the freedom of his arms.
3. When you feel the tension going out of his body, release your hold or change it to a hug.
4. At this time you are ready for the next step.

Help the Child Learn Appropriate Alternatives to Object Throwing Through Systematically Teaching Other Ways of Dealing with Anger and Frustration. It is important to prevent the child from hurting others. But it is equally important to help the child gain skills in using acceptable alternatives to aggression. When the initial anger is gone, take a few moments to talk with the child about what has happened. At first, use the following procedure:

1. Ask "What's the problem?" If you have seen what preceded the anger, help the child verbalize the situation. "You are upset because Leslie has the truck you want." Even if you make the initial statement, make sure the child also verbalizes the problem in some way.
2. Once the problem has been stated, say, "I wonder what we can do about it?" Give the child the chance to come up with a suggestion. Praise the child if the suggestion is socially acceptable. If the idea is not acceptable, say, "What else could we try?"
3. If the child has no suggestions, state a way of handling the situation. For instance, say, "We could ask Leslie if you could play with her and the truck. You and Leslie could build a road with blocks for the truck to drive on."

4. Try role playing: "Let's pretend I'm Leslie and you want the truck I am playing with." Pretend you are playing with a truck. Ask, "What will you say to me?" Help the child to phrase an acceptable suggestion. Respond as if you are Leslie. Agree to share the truck.
5. When the role playing is completed, praise the child and then help him find an activity to engage in.
6. It may take several weeks to reach this point, but remember that you are teaching the child a new response to feelings that previously aroused aggression.

When the child demonstrates an understanding of alternative ways of handling anger and frustration and responds naturally to role playing, move to the next step:

1. Ask, "What's the problem?" By this time the child should have had enough practice to tell you why he is angry.
2. Once the problem has been stated, ask the child what he might do about it. Praise him for appropriate suggestions.
3. Now tell the child that you would like him to try his suggestion with the other child involved. For instance, say, "Let's go tell that to Leslie."
4. Go with the child and encourage a friendly solution to the situation. If necessary, use some subtle intervention to structure success. It is important for the child to recognize that the acceptable alternatives you have been teaching really work.
5. Praise both children involved for their cooperation.

As the child demonstrates increased competence in handling anger or frustration in acceptable ways, decrease your role gradually. The child should be able to assume increasing responsibility for his actions. Praise the child frequently; let the child know how happy you are with the new behavior. Also, at any time during the process of teaching new behavior, give lavish praise if the child handles a potential conflict situation in an acceptable way.

If the Child does Throw an Object at Another Child, Use Time-out. If the child throws an object at another youngster, whether he hits his target or not, do the following:

1. Quickly make sure that the child at whom the object was aimed was not hit. If the child was hit, make sure the child is all right. If possible, another teacher should attend to the victim.
2. Calmly take the child who threw the object to the time-out area. Firmly but quietly say, "I cannot allow you to hurt other children. You will have to sit here until I tell you that you may get up."

3. Note the time and move away from the child. Do not talk with or look at the child during the time-out.

4. If this has not been done already, pick up the object that was thrown and replace it in its appropriate place. Do not make an issue of having the child do this, because such a request can easily result in a power struggle. The point you want to make is that it is unacceptable to hurt or try to hurt others, not that objects belong in their proper place. The latter behavior, though an important one to convey to children, should be taught at another time in a different context.

5. If another child approaches the time-out area, quietly move this child away. Explain, "Mark needs to be by himself for a few minutes. You can talk to him when he joins the class again."

6. Promptly at the end of time-out, go to the child and say, "You may get up now." Do not lecture. The child knows the reason for the isolation. Suggest an ongoing activity to channel the child into constructive behavior.

Continue Graphing the Behavior. It is important to continue to graph the number of object-throwing incidents that occur each day. By keeping track you will be able to see at a glance whether change is occurring. You can also get an idea of when to move from one step to the next in your procedure. For instance, before moving the child from role playing with you to actually talking with another child, there should be a substantial decrease in object-throwing. Similarly, before you decrease your role in cuing the child's behavior, the object-throwing incidents should have decreased to zero or near zero. The graph tells you that the child is learning from your efforts.

Maintenance

Once the child has stopped throwing objects at other children, be sure to continue praising the child for using appropriate alternatives to this behavior. What the child has learned has not eliminated situations that anger or frustrate him. These situations continue to occur. The child has learned some acceptable ways of handling his feelings, and should feel satisfaction at having learned to control such emotions. Continued support reinforces the new behavior.

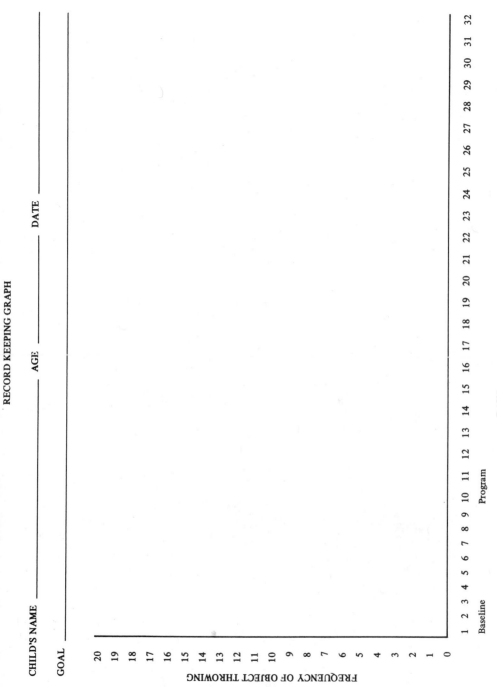

RECORD KEEPING GRAPH

CHILD'S NAME _____ AGE _____ DATE _____

GOAL _____

FREQUENCY OF OBJECT THROWING

20
19
18
17
16
15
14
13
12
11
10
9
8
7
6
5
4
3
2
1
0

1 2 3 4 5 6 7 8 9 10 11 12 13 14 15 16 17 18 19 20 21 22 23 24 25 26 27 28 29 30 31 32

Baseline   Program

DAYS

CHAPTER 6

Hurting Others

Teddy, who first started at the nursery school three months ago, has earned the title of "most aggressive child" from the teachers. Teddy is quickly aroused to anger by other children and then attacks them in an uninhibited manner. He has no single way of hurting other children. He uses whatever means he can to get at them. He hits, bites, pulls hair, punches, slaps, pushes, pokes, knocks others down, and jumps on them. From the beginning the other children in the class have not liked Teddy. When he engages in an activity, he generally plays alone. No one wants to be around him. Even so, Teddy finds ways to pick fights. Sometimes he goes to another child and grabs what the child is working with, saying, "I want that." If the other child resists, Teddy begins a fight. At other times he tries to join a group of children at play. If he is not accepted, he starts a fight. This behavior occurs three or four times every morning. The teachers have talked to Teddy, expressed anger with him and have tried to help the other children include him in their play. Teddy continues in his anger and aggression.

STATE THE BEHAVIOR

The child hurts other children in a variety of ways such as hitting, kicking, biting, pinching, and wrestling. Several forms of aggression are used in unpredictable ways.

OBSERVE THE BEHAVIOR

Get as much information as you can through informal observation of the child.

A. When does the behavior occur?
  • At all times of the day

- During specific activities, such as group times, discussion, or music
- When children are in close proximity
- During transitions from one activity to another
- During structured activities
- During free choice activities
- At outdoor playtimes
- Indoors
- Around mealtime

B. What usually happens before the behavior occurs?

- Another child has something that the child wants
- The child has a verbal argument with another child
- The child is told no by a child or teacher
- The child is close to others
- The child is pushed
- The child appears tired
- The child is provoked by another child
- The child is not able to accomplish a task
- The child does not want to participate in class routines
- There is no apparent provocation

C. Who is usually the victim?

- The same child or a certain few children
- Anyone
- Anyone who argues with the child
- Only timid children
- Only assertive children
- Older or bigger children
- Younger or smaller children
- Boys
- Girls

D. What happens when the child hurts another youngster?

- The child looks around to see if an adult is watching
- The child admits hurting the other child
- The child denies it
- The other child hurts the offender in return
- The child apologizes or tries to make the victim feel better
- The child goes on to hurt other children
- The child stays near the child who was hurt
- The child tries to hurt the same child again
- The child walks away

E. How does the child hurt other children?

- There is a relation between what happened before the child hurt someone and how he hurts that child
- There is a relation between whom the child hurts and how he hurts that child
- There is a relation between where the child is at the time he hurts someone and how he hurts that child

This informal observation period should provide clues to the problem, which will help you implement ways of eliminating such behavior.

EXPLORE THE CONSEQUENCES

The child who hurts other children by using a variety of methods is unpredictable. Such a child is a serious problem in the preschool classroom. When an aggressive child uses hitting to hurt others, the teachers have some idea of how the aggression will be expressed. When the child shows no consistency in method, however, the teachers cannot be sure how an attack will occur. Furthermore, this situation presents more danger of serious injury because often the child who reacts unpredictably has a quick temper and moves swiftly and recklessly. The child gets caught up in feelings of anger, resulting in uninhibited reactions. He may not be aware of how much he may be hurting another child. Admonishing, talking to, and punishing the child are the methods most often used by teachers to change the behavior. These methods, however, do not work. The child has to be told in no uncertain terms that such behavior is not to be tolerated. The child must also be helped to control his temper and reactions to angering situations.

CONSIDER ALTERNATIVES

There is probably no simple solution to dealing with the child who hurts others in varied and unpredictable ways. However, consider the following suggestions.

- If this behavior occurs only during specific activities or times of day, vary the routine. Young children often react negatively to crowding, waiting, or having to stop an activity. It may be such a situation that results in aggression. Crowding can be avoided; designate a larger circle or semicircle at group times. Find alternatives to lining up; have children go a few at a time to the bathroom or to get coats while the rest participate in singing songs or fingerplays. Young children are not able to wait very long. The program should be structured to minimize waits. If the teachers know that a particular child has difficulty waiting, structure the program to minimize such times until the child can wait for longer periods. It is also difficult for a young child to stop an activity in which he is engrossed. Unnecessary interruptions can be avoided. Plan sufficiently large time blocks for activities. Also, let the child know several minutes before the end of an activity that he will soon have to stop.

- If one child is usually the victim of aggression by the child who concerns you, separate the two. If possible, move one of the youngsters into a different classroom. If this cannot be done, keep the two children separated within the class. Encourage them to engage in different activities. Do not let them sit next to each other at group times and mealtimes, and place them in different groups if the class is divided for small group activities. It may require considerable effort and vigilance, but the decreased aggression should be worth it.

In the case of the child who hurts other youngsters through a variety of means, these measures probably will not, of themselves, eliminate the problem. Such aggression is most likely triggered by more than classroom routine or the presence of a certain child. You may combine either of these suggestions with the following program.

STATE THE GOAL

The goal is for the child to stop hurting other children and to find acceptable alternatives for handling anger.

PROCEDURE

Basically, you will eliminate the child's behavior of hurting other children by using several simultaneous steps:

- Prevent instances of aggression whenever possible.
- Praise all positive interactions.
- Systematically teach the child to control the impulse to hurt others.
- Use time-out when the child does hurt someone.

Definition

Hurting others through a variety of means includes all instances of aggression aimed at other children through use of different approaches such as hitting, kicking, biting, and punching. Teachers should agree on what constitutes aggressive behavior and list all forms of aggression that are noticed.

Baseline

Before implementing any changes, take three days to count the number of times the child hurts others. Every time the child hurts another, mark the incident on paper. At the end of each day, transfer the total number onto the Record Keeping Graph. This information is the baseline which you may use to measure later progress.

Program

Once you have baseline data, you are ready to begin. It is important that all teachers cooperate and follow this program consistently.

Prevent Aggressive Incidents Whenever Possible. Informal observation should have given you some idea of when and under what circumstances the child is most likely to hurt others. Using such information, be on the lookout for any clues that indicate the child is about to hurt another child.

If the child's anger is already aroused, do one of two things, depending on the reactions of the child.

1. If the child is receptive to talking, discuss his anger with him.
2. If the child does not respond to talking and simply wants to hit someone, use physical restraint. Put your arms around the child in a way that conveys your concern for him as a person as well as your need to keep him from attacking another child. It is important not to reflect anger in the way you hold him. (If you find that you tend to show anger at the child under such circumstances, it would be better to let another teacher handle the situation. You cannot fight anger with more anger.) Hold the child in this way until you feel the tension leave him. Then give him a hug and tell him, "I'm glad you didn't hurt Luke." Help the child find an activity to engage in.

Preventing situations that might lead to anger and aggression is preferable to preventing aggression once anger has been aroused. Again, use the clues you found in your initial observations and be alert to any potential problems. If there is any consistency as to when, where, or under what circumstances the child usually hurts others, you know when to stay close by and be on the lookout for the behavior.

Praise All Positive Social Interactions. The child needs to learn acceptable ways of dealing with peers. It is important to let the child know when his social behavior is appropriate. Praise positive interactions as often as possible:

- "Thank you for helping Luke. That was very nice of you."
- "I like the way you and Luke are working on that puzzle together."
- "It was really great of you to let Luke help you build that garage with the blocks. I know how much he likes to play with you."
- "Luke is pushing you on the swing. What fun! After you've had a turn, you can push him, right?"

Systematically Teach the Child to Control the Impulse to Hurt Others. It is important to convey to the child that feelings of anger are natural and all right, but that hurting other people in reaction to anger is not acceptable. Set aside a special time each day to discuss feelings with the child and work on acceptable ways of dealing with them. This special time should be one in which you can devote an undivided five to ten minutes to the child. Be prepared to spend more time, however, if the child is really interested and responsive. Take the child out of the classroom if possible to avoid interruptions and distractions. Your discussions with the child should be suited to the child's responsiveness.

1. Begin by discussing situations that evoke different emotions. For instance, "Yesterday I got a new puppy and I was so excited and happy that I felt like dancing and singing. I really felt good inside! What makes *you* feel really happy?" If the child responds, ask for more details; if there is no response, name simple events that make you happy. Go on to discuss other feelings. "Sometimes I feel just the opposite. I get really sad. I had a very good friend and she had to move away. That made me feel terrible. Do you feel sad sometimes?" Again, encourage response in whatever way you can. Discuss anger also. "You know, sometimes I get really angry. I know you must feel angry about things too at times. What makes you angry?" Share some examples of what angers you and help the child verbalize situations that anger him. It may take several days to identify situations that evoke various emotions.
2. Once the child has acknowledged that he feels differently in response to varied situations, focus your discussion on those feelings. "How does it make you feel inside when you are (happy, angry, sad, lonely)?" Help the child put into words the different inner responses to emotions. You should spend some time beforehand thinking about this because

feelings are not easy to describe in words. This way you are prepared to help the child discuss them. Be careful, however, that it is the child who talks about the subject with help from you, not the other way around. Again, this step requires several days.

3. After the child has verbalized how he feels when he experiences different emotions, begin to talk about what the child does to express such feelings. Do not be critical about what he says. If the child tells you that he punches, hits, bites, or otherwise hurts someone who angers him, accept that for the present. Do not express dismay or lecture the child. Again, discuss various emotions in relation to how they are expressed in action.

4. The next step is to tell the child that you want to explore some different ways of reacting to emotions. If the child told you that when he is happy he smiles, ask how else he might express that happiness. Either of you might come up with ideas like clap hands, jump up and down, sing, hop around, or hug someone. In addition to other emotions, discuss alternative ways that the child can handle anger, such as:

   • Talk to the person who angered him.
   • Find something else to do while waiting for the other child to finish with the toy he wants.
   • Pound on the floor or table instead of a child.
   • Talk to an adult to get help in handling angry feelings.

5. Your discussions do not need to be strictly verbal. Use whatever props you want to help you. The use of puppets, clay, or blocks may be helpful in exploring feelings and emotions.

6. With each discussion step, look for opportunities during the day to illustrate what you and the child were talking about during the special time. At first, focus on what event evoked a particular emotion, then switch to discussing how it makes the child feel inside. Next, look for examples of external manifestations of the emotions. Finally, encourage the child to verbalize alternative ways of reacting. Prevention of aggressive incidents provides one opportunity for relating your daily discussions to the child's actual emotions. Do not limit this to negative incidents, however. Find examples of all kinds of emotions and feelings.

If the Child Does Hurt Someone, Use Time-out. Take the following steps:

1. Quickly make sure that the child who was hurt is all right. If at all possible, another teacher should attend to the victim.
2. Calmly take the child who has hurt another child to the time-out area. Firmly but quietly say, "I cannot allow you to hurt other children. You will have to sit here until I tell you that you may get up."
3. Note the time and move away from the child. Do not talk with or look at the child during the time-out.

4. If another child approaches the time-out area, quietly move this child away. Explain, "Teddy needs to be by himself for a few minutes. You can talk to him when he joins the class again."

5. Promptly, at the end of the time, go to the child and say, "You may get up now." Do not lecture. The child knows the reason for the isolation. Channel the child into constructive behavior by suggesting that he join an ongoing activity.

Continue Graphing the Behavior. As you work with the child on changing the aggressive behavior, continue keeping track every time the child hurts someone. Record each day the total number of incidents of hurting other children by whatever means. It is quite possible that progress will be gradual. The graph will reflect even a small change; this will encourage you to continue the task.

Maintenance

Once the child has stopped hurting others, continue praising positive social behaviors and acceptable responses to emotions like anger. Continue to encourage the newly learned behaviors. Remember, at one time the child reacted to anger by hurting others. Also, this aggressive behavior was reinforced while alternative behaviors were not praised. Now that the situation is switched, reinforcement is given for the behavior that is valued and expected.

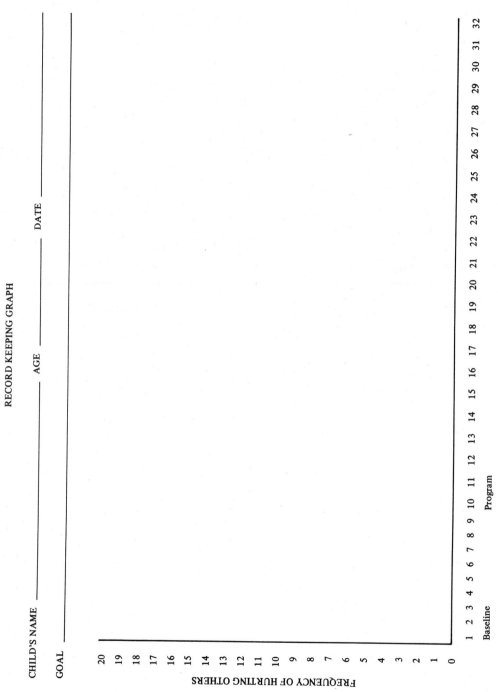

RECORD KEEPING GRAPH

CHILD'S NAME _____ AGE _____ DATE _____

GOAL _____

FREQUENCY OF HURTING OTHERS

20 19 18 17 16 15 14 13 12 11 10 9 8 7 6 5 4 3 2 1 0

1 2 3 4 5 6 7 8 9 10 11 12 13 14 15 16 17 18 19 20 21 22 23 24 25 26 27 28 29 30 31 32

Baseline   Program

DAYS

CHAPTER 7

7

Swearing

Four-year-old Eileen has had considerable experience in day care. Her mother has worked since Eileen was one month old, leaving her first at the infant-toddler center and now at the adjacent day care center. Eileen is the youngest of five children, with two brothers in their teens, a sister in fourth grade, and a brother in second grade. Eileen is assertive and very talkative at school. Recently she has added a variety of swear words to her vocabulary, which is growing increasingly more colorful. When Eileen becomes upset, she uses a swear word to express her feelings. At other times she inserts swear words into normal conversation, usually smiling as she does so. The teachers have conveyed their displeasure with Eileen's language, such as by saying, "Don't use that word, Eileen. It's not nice." This has not, however, affected her behavior. Eileen still swears and some of the other children are now picking up some of her words. The teachers fear that they will soon be hearing complaints from parents.

STATE THE BEHAVIOR

The child uses undesirable language regularly and frequently.

OBSERVE THE BEHAVIOR

It is important to gain an idea of when, where, why, and to whom the behavior occurs. Spend some time observing the child.

A. When does the child usually swear?

- Unpredictably, at any time of day
- During group activities such as story or discussion time
- During free choice activities

- Early in the day
- Late in the day
- During outdoor play
- Indoors

B. What seems to trigger swearing?

- The child is angry
- The child is told no by a teacher or another child
- The child is not able to accomplish a task
- A particular role in role playing
- The child is not engaged in an activity
- The child has a leadership role in play with other children
- The child is in the bathroom
- The child is "silly" and giggly

C. To whom does the child usually swear?

- To anyone
- To one or a few children
- To all children
- To adults
- To good friends

D. What happens when the child swears?

- The child laughs
- Other children laugh
- Other children tell her that she shouldn't say such words
- Other children repeat the word or words
- The child looks to see if an adult has heard
- A teacher tells the child not to say "bad" words
- Adults react in a shocked manner
- Adults laugh

This preliminary observation should give you some idea of the context in which swearing occurs. Use this information in approaching a solution to the problem.

EXPLORE THE CONSEQUENCES

Children acquire language by hearing it used around them, and in the same way they learn swear words. When adults, peers, or siblings swear, children are exposed to and learn such words. For the most part, preschool children do not understand the literal meaning of swear words but they do soon come to realize that these words are somehow special. The child may observe that swear words are usually said only under certain circumstances, such as in anger, and that the words are given special emphasis through voice tone and inflection. Such words become even more special, however, when a child decides to use them. When a child first says a swear word, the reaction is clear. Adults who hear the word usually react in shock or with laughter, reflecting surprise at hearing such language from a little child. This initial reaction is then followed by a question about where the child learned such a word or by an admonition not to use it again. The child learns quickly that use of such words gets attention. When a child uses unacceptable language in the preschool setting, teachers often react in this way. They do not consider swearing to be appropriate for young children, and they try to eliminate it in whatever way possible. In the process they usually call more attention to the problem. Since use of foul language evokes reinforcing responses, it is difficult to eliminate. The situation is further compounded in the school setting by the fact that other children reinforce swearing by repeating the word, laughing, or otherwise paying attention to it.

CONSIDER ALTERNATIVES

There might be a relatively simple solution to the problem of swearing. Examine the information from your informal observations, then see if one of the following suggestions might work.

- If the child swears only under certain circumstances, she might be doing so because of misinformation or lack of understanding. For instance, the child may use undesirable language only when role playing a certain person. Perhaps the only gas-station attendant the child knows swears all the time, and so she generalizes from this experience and believes that all gas-station attendants swear. Discuss this with the child and try to correct the misconception. You may plan a visit to a gas station, or invite a gas-station attendant to visit the class.
- The child may engage in an attention-getting behavior like swearing because of boredom. Consider the information from your informal observations, particularly in relation to when swearing occurs. If you find that inappropriate language happens often during planned or free choice activities, it may be that the child feels unchallenged by the activity and chooses to create her own diversions. Carefully examine what is in the classroom and provide more stimulating materials and activities as appropriate. By providing alternative activities to engage and interest the child, you should soon note a decrease in swearing.

- Sometime during their fourth year, many children tend to go through a phase where they enjoy making up and using "bathroom language." Determine whether the child is imitating adult swearing or is using child-constructed words. The latter will sound like child's language (for example, "pee-pee," "caca," "poo-poo," "potty"). Because use of bathroom language is a phase, children naturally stop using it if you do not pay undue attention. You might, however, find that the use of bathroom terms is getting out of hand. In that case, have a talk with the child or children most involved in using such words, and limit their usage in some way. You could, for instance, agree with the youngsters that such words may be used only in the bathroom and nowhere else.
- If the child who is swearing is a natural leader in the classroom, others may be following her example. It might be possible to enlist her aid in leading the class in a more appropriate behavior. Talk with the child and let her know that you are unhappy that she is using inappropriate language and that others are beginning to use these words. Through discussion, try to come up with an alternative behavior that the child could help the other children learn. This might include using new art media, learning new songs, or playing new games. By reinforcing the child's leadership, it can be channeled into appropriate uses. Praise the child for her successes in teaching new skills to the other children.

If the solution to the problem does not lie in one of these suggestions, proceed with the following detailed program.

STATE THE GOAL

The goal is for the child to stop swearing.

PROCEDURE

To reach the goal, your strategy involves three simultaneous steps:

- Prevent swearing whenever possible.
- Ignore swearing when it does occur.
- Systematically reinforce time periods when no swearing takes place.

Definition

Swearing is any use of language that is inappropriate for a preschool child. This refers to adult swear words rather than to "bathroom words" made up by children. Make a list of the specific words you want to stop to ensure that all the teachers consider the same words as swearing.

Baseline

Before implementing changes, it is necessary to know how often swearing occurs. For three days, mark on paper every instance of swearing. If swearing occurs five or six times an hour, collect information for the total day. If, however, swearing takes place more frequently, such as twenty or thirty times an hour, collect data for only one hour per day.   Select an hour when swearing usually occurs frequently. At the end of each day add up the marks and record the total on the Record Keeping Graph. This record provides a baseline against which improvements can be measured.

Program

A meeting should be arranged with the child's parents to discuss the problem. Unless the child picked up the use of inappropriate language from another child at school, the words were most likely learned from her home or neighborhood. The parents may also have noted the child's swearing and may be concerned about it. Parents and teachers need to discuss how the behavior has been learned and reinforced, and how it can be eliminated. When there is a home-school partnership to change a child's behavior, the change is more effective.

After you gather baseline data and talk with the parents, begin the following program. All teachers should consistently use the same procedure.

Let the Child Know Your Concern and How You Will Deal With Swearing in the Future. At a time when the child is not swearing, take her aside and have a friendly talk with her. Let the child know that you are concerned by her use of inappropriate words. Tell her how you will work with her to help her change this behavior. Be sure to tell the child why you consider use of swear words unacceptable.

Ignore Swearing When It Occurs. Whenever the child swears, whether it is out of anger or because the child wants your attention, ignore it. Do not respond by lecturing or admonishing or even by looking shocked. Such responses provide the attention the child desires. When a child swears, one of two things may happen in relation to the other children in the class:

1. If the other children do not react or take note of the swearing, do nothing. Simply ignore the inappropriate language by turning your back on the child as if nothing was said.

2. If the other children react by imitating, laughing, or talking about the word, divert the others as quickly as possible. Say, for instance, "Jane, Alice, Mike, and Todd, I want to show you a new game over here." Do not include the child who swore and quickly lead the other children away. It is helpful if ahead of time you develop several ideas for such diversions. Do not talk about the fact that the child used an undesirable word, and if one of the children brings it up, say simply, "Yes, I know," and drop the subject.

Prevent Incidents of Swearing Whenever Possible. From your informal observation you may have some clues as to when swearing usually occurs. For instance, the child may use inappropriate language when she is angry or frustrated. If this is the case, be alert to any signs of confrontation with another child. Quickly move to the child and help her express what is bothering her in an acceptable manner. Praise the child for acceptable behavior. In other cases, the child may use swearing not as an outlet for feelings but in a more matter-of-fact manner aimed directly at getting attention. In such a case prevention is not as easy to implement, and ignoring the child is the better way to react.

Systematically Reinforce Time Periods When No Swearing Takes Place. The following procedure will help the child eliminate swearing:

1. From your baseline data, compute the average frequency of swearing. If it occurs six times per hour, then the average frequency is ten minutes (60 minutes ÷ 6). If it occurs thirty times per hour, then the average frequency is two minutes (60 minutes ÷ 30). This average represents not only how often the child swears but also how long she goes without swearing. Your aim is to increase the length of time without swearing until the behavior completely disappears.
2. Make a chart to share with the child. Each vertical column represents a day, and each horizontal column represents a time block within that day. The spaces should be large enough for a star sticker. The chart looks like this:

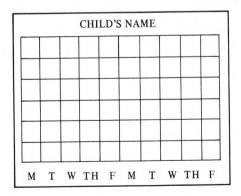

The number of squares within each day is determined by the interval of nonswearing. The shorter that interval, the more squares are drawn on the chart. It might be impractical to keep such a chart all day. In that case, select a shorter time period to fill in on the chart. Be sure the child is aware of when the chart is being used, and be especially alert to positive behaviors at other times so these can be verbally reinforced.

3. Carefully watch the clock and the child during times when the chart is being used. Each time the designated amount of time passes without an incident of swearing, praise the child and tell her that she has earned a star. Give her the gummed star and let her paste it on the appropriate square on the chart.

4. At the end of the day, take the child to the chart again and praise her for the number of stars she has earned (even if she only earned one). Tell the child that you are sure she will earn even more stars the next day.

5. Over the next few days the number of stars that the child earns should increase while incidents of swearing decrease. When the child has earned stars for at least half the squares on two consecutive days, begin to increase the time intervals in which you expect no swearing. This increase should be gradual and paced to ensure success. If at any time swearing increases and the number of stars earned decreases considerably, shorten the time interval. You want to ensure that the child experiences success.

6. When swearing has decreased to zero or near zero, tell the child how pleased you are with her changed behavior. Also tell her that you will discontinue using the star chart because you know she can continue to talk without swearing. Give her the chart to reinforce how well she has done. Most likely, by this time the novelty of using the chart will have worn off and the child will not need the direct reinforcement it offered.

Continue Graphing the Behavior. Continue to count occurrences of swearing each day to keep track of progress. If swearing incidents were counted all day during baseline, continue to count for the full day. If a smaller time block was set, use the same time period to collect data during the program.

Maintenance

Once you have eliminated swearing and stopped using the star chart, it is important to maintain the new behavior. Praise the child when she engages in desirable behaviors of all kinds. If the child occasionally uses a swear word, ignore it. At a later time, tell her how pleased you are when she uses appropriate language.

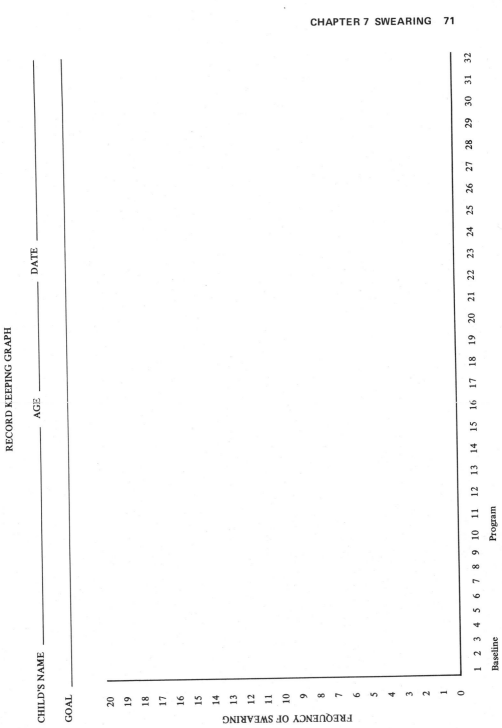

RECORD KEEPING GRAPH

CHILD'S NAME ———————— AGE ———— DATE ————

GOAL ————

FREQUENCY OF SWEARING

20
19
18
17
16
15
14
13
12
11
10
9
8
7
6
5
4
3
2
1
0

1 2 3 4 5 6 7 8 9 10 11 12 13 14 15 16 17 18 19 20 21 22 23 24 25 26 27 28 29 30 31 32

Baseline   Program

DAYS

CHAPTER 8

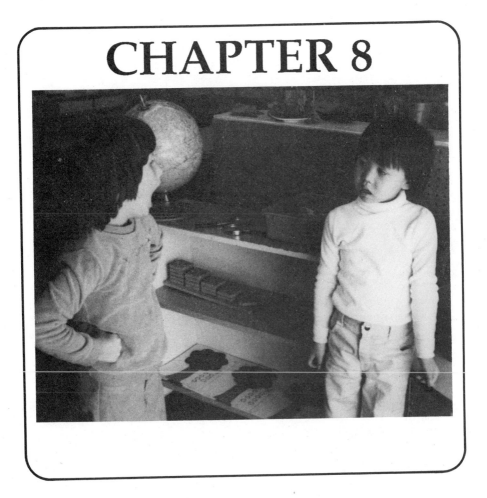

8

Name-calling

"Nancy is a cry-baby! Nancy is a cry-baby!" Nancy, as if on cue, begins to cry while five-year-old Erica smiles and walks away. Such incidents have been happening quite frequently at the Head Start Center, with Erica taunting other children through name-calling. Though a bright and popular child, Erica has been upsetting more and more of the other children by giving them unflattering labels. What particularly bothers the teachers and the other children is that Erica's labels are often based to some extent on real behaviors. Nancy does cry at times. John has a speech problem which prompts, "Johnny is a funny talker!" Randy has a quick temper, so Erica calls him a bully. There are times when the names seem just spiteful, such as "You stupid dummy!" or "You dirty dog!" Repeatedly the teachers have told Erica that it is not nice to call names and upset other children, but Erica continues. After an incident she seems unperturbed by a lecture from a teacher. When Erica is required to apologize, she does so cheerfully. As a rule, she acts as if nothing has happened even though the other child may still be upset.

STATE THE BEHAVIOR

The child provokes and upsets other children by calling them unflattering names or labels.

OBSERVE THE BEHAVIOR

To gain some further insight into this name-calling behavior, spend some time observing the child to gather information.

A. When does the child call other children names?

- At any time of day
- Especially during free choice activities
- During group activities
- During discussion times
- During outdoor play
- Indoors
- At mealtimes
- During toileting times
- At nap or rest time

B. What seems to trigger name-calling?

- Another child does something unusual
- Another child does something of which the teachers do not approve
- Another child angers her
- Another child tells her no
- Another child or a group of children exclude her from play
- No apparent reason

C. Who is being called names?

- Any child in the class
- The same child or a few children
- Girls
- Boys
- Friends of the child
- Timid children
- Assertive children
- Younger children
- Older children

D. What happens when the child calls names?

- The child says the name loudly
- The child repeats it once
- The child repeats it many times
- The child laughs or smiles while she is saying it
- The child is upset when she says it
- The child looks to see whether an adult has heard
- The child looks to see whether other children have heard
- The child tries to get other children to repeat what she said
- The child apologizes
- The child walks away from the other child
- The child stays near the other child

From informal observation you have gained some insight into the circumstances under which the name-calling takes place. Use this information to help find the best way to eliminate the behavior.

EXPLORE THE CONSEQUENCES

Children, like adults, want to feel good about themselves, so anything that does not reinforce a positive self-image is hurtful. The child who calls other children unpleasant names has found a way of hurting them. When the child first begins to put labels on others, there may be no intention of malice. As she notes the other children's reactions and then repeats the behavior to get a similar reaction, she becomes aware of an effective way to influence others. A child's reaction to being called an unflattering name is usually strong. The victim of the name-calling may react in anger or hurt, or by denial, crying, or some other means. In addition to this response, there is usually a reaction from adults as well.

Whether a teacher hears and intervenes or whether the other child calls the teacher's attention to the situation, an adult takes part in the action. Thus, the name-caller is reinforced in two ways. The victim responds very visibly, and an adult pays further attention by talking to the offender or otherwise conveying displeasure. The child has found a good way to get double attention and continues calling names as long as she is reinforced for it.

CONSIDER ALTERNATIVES

You may have some clues from your preliminary observations that can help you come to a relatively simple resolution of the problem. Consider the following suggestions.

- Does the child engage in name-calling only during a specific time period of the day? It might be helpful to restructure the activity or routine during the time when name-calling occurs. A teacher should also stay near the child to help her remain constructively engaged in the activity planned for that time.
- If one child is always the target of the name-calling, separate the two youngsters. Move one child to a different classroom if possible, or keep the two children involved in different areas of the room. The less opportunity for name-calling, the less it occurs.
- If the child engages in name-calling as well as other inappropriate behaviors at school, she is probably not as much involved in classroom

activities as she should be. Carefully check the materials and activities provided for the children for age-appropriateness. It is possible that the child's behavior stems from boredom or frustration. If materials and activities are too simple, too difficult, or insufficient in number or availability, the child may try to keep busy in other, less acceptable ways.

If none of these suggestions helps reduce the behavior, continue to the detailed program which follows.

STATE THE GOAL

The goal is for the child to stop calling other children unflattering names.

PROCEDURE

To stop the child's name-calling behavior, two steps should be simultaneously carried out:

- Reinforce as many positive behaviors as possible.
- Ignore all name-calling incidents in such a way that the child who is the target is also helped to ignore the behavior.

Definition

Name-calling is any incident in which a child gives someone an unflattering label. Teachers should list the labels to be in agreement on what words or phrases fit the definition of name-calling.

Baseline

Before any changes are implemented, it is important to know how often name-calling occurs. For three days, gather baseline information by counting how often the child calls another youngster by an unflattering name. Each time the child calls a name, mark it down on paper. At the end of each day record the total on the Record Keeping Graph.

Program

Once baseline is established, begin the following program. It is important that all teachers use the program consistently.

Reinforce the Child for Positive Interactions with Other Children. Let the child know what behaviors are acceptable. Praise her for them. Whenever the child interacts positively with other children, let her know that you are pleased. Word your praise in such a way as to include the idea that it is nice to make other people feel good. For example, if the child is in the housekeeping area with some other children, say, "I like the way you're playing the mommy. Mommies make daddies and children feel good just like daddies and children make mommies feel nice." Or, if the child is working in the block area with another child, tell her, "You and Paul are building a wonderful tower! Doesn't it make you both feel great to be working so well together?"

When the Child Name-calls, Ignore It and Help the Child Who is the Target to Ignore It Also. The child who name-calls is getting reinforcement for this behavior from the target child and an adult. It is relatively simple for the adult to ignore name-calling, but it is more difficult for a child not to react when given an unflattering label. Therefore, the adult needs to help other children to ignore incidents of name-calling, or at least to minimize their reactions.

When you hear the child call someone a name, do the following:

1. As quickly as possible get to the two children involved. Physically place yourself between them. Face the child who has been called the name and turn your back to the one who did the name-calling.
2. Put your arm around the child who was called the name (if the child reacts positively to physical contact from adults). Do this to reassure this child of your understanding. If possible, move away from the name-caller, taking the victim with you. This should only take a few seconds.
3. As you move away with the child who was called a name, talk about something unrelated to the incident. Ask for help in an activity such as feeding the rabbit or mixing paint, or show the child something of interest.
4. If the child complains about the name-calling incident, say simply, "I know, it's not nice to be called such a name. We have to help Erica learn to give better names to her friends." Acknowledge that such labels are not pleasant but at the same time enlist the victim's help in changing such behavior. Also establish that you do not want to create a disturbance over name-calling.
5. You may not be successful in decreasing the target child's reaction. Your aim in such a case is to get the victim away from the name-caller so the behavior will not be reinforced by the victim's reaction.
6. The child who has done the name-calling is given as little reinforcement as possible for this behavior. A few minutes after the incident, make a point of going to the name-caller and giving attention and praise for an

appropriate behavior. Convey the message that it is the undesirable behavior, not the child, that you disapprove of. Reinforce the fact that socially acceptable behavior gains your attention.

Continue Graphing the Behavior. Continue to count the number of name-calling incidents and record them on the Record Keeping Graph. Your control over the victim's reaction to name-calling is not complete. You can only influence, but not dictate, how youngsters who are victims of name-calling react. Therefore, the name-caller's behavior will receive some reinforcement, and it may take a while before change is evident. Be persistent. Eventually you will be rewarded with a decrease and the disappearance of this undesirable behavior.

Maintenance

Maintain interaction without name-calling by continued praise of appropriate social behaviors. Help the child recognize that it is more rewarding to be pleasant to others than to be negative. If an occasional name-calling incident occurs, treat it as you did during the program.

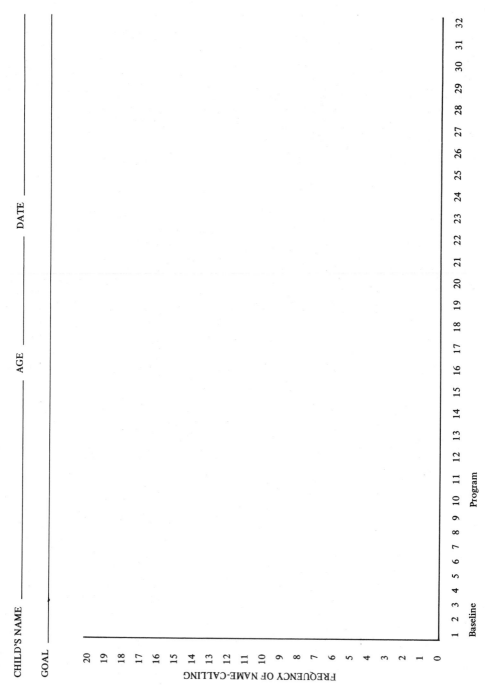

RECORD KEEPING GRAPH

CHILD'S NAME _____ AGE _____ DATE _____

GOAL _____

FREQUENCY OF NAME-CALLING

20
19
18
17
16
15
14
13
12
11
10
9
8
7
6
5
4
3
2
1
0

1 2 3 4 5 6 7 8 9 10 11 12 13 14 15 16 17 18 19 20 21 22 23 24 25 26 27 28 29 30 31 32

Baseline   Program

DAYS

CHAPTER 9

Nonsharing

"These are mine! I had them first!" The teacher turns around to see four-year-old Monica fiercely protecting some blocks she has been building with. Monica puts her arms around as many blocks as she can reach. Ricky stands by rather bewildered, then says, "I want to play, too." Monica replies, "You can't! I need all of them and you can't have any!" The teacher puts her arm around Ricky and says in a low tone, "Come on now, Monica. There are plenty of blocks. Let Ricky play with some." "No!" shouts Monica. "They're mine!" Ricky decides to take matters into his own hands. He picks up several stray blocks that are out of Monica's reach and starts to stack them. Monica kicks over the blocks Ricky just stacked, screaming, "You can't have any! They're mine!" The teacher becomes stern and lectures Monica about sharing. A few minutes later, she forcibly takes some blocks from Monica and moves these and Ricky a few feet away. Monica gets up and stamps away, crying, "I hate you! You took my blocks!" The teacher is unhappy with this outcome, but does not know what else to do. Monica is always unwilling to share.

STATE THE BEHAVIOR

The child refuses to share school or personal items with other children.

OBSERVE THE BEHAVIOR

Take a few days to observe the child to get an idea of the circumstances under which the child will not share.

A. When is nonsharing most likely to take place?
- Most times of the day
- Early in the day, soon after arriving

- Later in the day
- During show and tell
- During free choice activities
- Around nap or rest times
- During transition times
- At cleanup times

B. What items does the child not want to share?
- Whatever the child is using
- Only personal items, such as toys from home
- Housekeeping area items, such as dolls, dishes, or clothes
- Blocks
- Art materials, such as paper, paint, or clay
- Manipulative materials, such as puzzles, tabletop blocks, or Legos
- Sand or water play implements
- Books
- Outdoor equipment and materials

C. With whom does the child refuse to share?
- Any other children
- Only one or a few children
- Boys
- Girls
- Older and bigger children
- Smaller and younger children

D. How does the child refuse to share?
- The child verbally tells other children that the items she is using belong to her and no one else
- The child hits another child who asks for or tries to take an item
- The child calls for a teacher to come help
- The child screams or cries out
- The child hoards the items by putting her arms around them
- The child moves to an isolated area where she is less likely to be disturbed
- The child grabs other items if another child approaches
- The child tells other children she does not want to play with them
- The child refuses to take turns if suggested

E. How does the child react if another child does not share with her?
- The child becomes angry
- The child cries
- The child calls a teacher to help
- The child forcibly takes or attempts to take what she wants from the other child

Use these observations to gain insight into the behavior so you can best help the child change it.

EXPLORE THE CONSEQUENCES

Before children can share with other people, they must feel secure with their own possessions, knowing that no matter who uses them, the items belong to them. It is only after children experience ownership from their own point of view that they can begin to understand someone else's right to ownership. Young children do not yet grasp the meanings of "mine" and "yours." They fiercely protect what is theirs and at the same time want what belongs to someone else. This is a normal stage in development, very typical of two-year-olds. The situation becomes more complex in a preschool setting where few items are "mine" or "yours" and most are "ours." Young preschoolers have to learn that they have the right to play with an item, but the other children have the right as well. Later this simple rule becomes expanded when consideration is also expected.

Four- or five-year-olds must recognize the rights of others, and must also at times be encouraged to give up or share their rights when another person wants to use an item they have. *Sharing* is a concept which needs a great deal of practice and the help of adults. Sharing means that children cannot always have exclusive use of whatever toys they want. Sometimes they may not be able to use the toys they want, or they may be asked to give up a toy because other children have been waiting to use the toys for a long time. Sometimes they can use toys together with other children in ways that often enhance rather than detract from play. Sharing requires a measure of social understanding and development. Children should learn the concept and use it at least part of the time. Preschoolers should exercise sharing by three and a half or four years of age.

CONSIDER ALTERNATIVES

Your expectations, understanding, and classroom arrangement can facilitate sharing by the children. One of the following suggestions may provide a solution to the problem.

A. Remember that nonsharing is a stage most children go through. Do not expect sharing on the part of two-year-olds or of some three-year-olds. Understand the child's need to develop a firm sense of "mineness" before "yourness." This understanding is necessary to set the stage for the later learning of sharing. One way a classroom of very young preschoolers can accommodate the nonsharing stage is in the materials available. It is better for a class of two-year-olds to have several of the same few items than many different toys. Thus, rather than having forty distinct toys, it would be better to have eight or ten different items, but four or five exact copies of each. This way, if one child plays with a duck pull toy and another child wants that same toy, there will be a toy just like it to give to the second child. Such availability of duplicate items avoids the need to share.

B. Preschoolers share school items much more readily than their own personal toys. It is not unusual and is quite natural for children to feel possessive about something that is theirs. If a child brings a treasured item to school and it is lost or broken, this situation does not help the child learn about sharing. It is, therefore, wise to establish and maintain some rules about personal belongings such as toys brought from home. Some suggested rules are as follows:

- There should be a special place where children can keep their belongings. A coat cubbie or bin should suffice. Otherwise provide storage for special items from home. Separate home and school toys throughout the day.
- Establish a specific daily or weekly period for sharing personal toys. Such a sharing time can be carefully supervised to ensure the safety of such items as well as safety of the children. Remember that home toys are often not as durable as school items. Materials made specifically for the preschool are constructed to withstand considerably more wear and tear. Be alert to toys that seem especially fragile or brittle and watch how they are handled. Put time limitations on the sharing period (a definite beginning and end), and have the children put away their toys when the time is over.
- With the children, discuss bringing in objects from home. With the children's help, establish some rules for handling personal belongings. Stress the need for respect of others' property. If the children are involved in setting guidelines and know the appropriate ways to share personal belongings, they will be much more inclined to follow such rules.
- You may have experienced problems when children bring in items from home. You may have found that items are broken or lost or children are unwilling to share. In this case you might consider not allowing children to bring such items to school for a time. Let the children and parents know of this decision and why it was made. Then enforce the decision.

C. If you have found that sharing school items is difficult for the children, examine your classroom to see if the difficulty arises from lack of availability of materials. If there are not enough materials for all of the children to be simultaneously involved, there will likely be problems in sharing. In a class for about twenty children, the basic classroom interest areas should be stocked so as to keep at least five or six children supplied at any given time. This includes such areas as blocks, dramatic play, manipulative toys, books, art, sensory play, cognitive games, and any other areas that are in your classroom. In addition, for any activities that you provide on a daily basis, there should be enough materials for all children who want to participate. Nonsharing can result if children feel that they have to compete for available materials. This does not mean, of course, that there has to be one of each item for each child. There should be enough materials for all the children to be constructively engaged at any given time. Situations will arise when more than one child wants a certain item. If these happen in an environment where items are plentiful, sharing will be facilitated.

D. Sometimes children are attached to a very special item which gives them a feeling of security. A child should not be expected to share a security item such as a stuffed animal, doll, or blanket. If necessary, the teacher should protect the child's right to the security item.

If none of these suggestions provides a solution to nonsharing, continue on to the following detailed program.

STATE THE GOAL

The goal is for the child to share school materials with other children at least two-thirds of the times that the child is asked to share. Two-thirds is a reasonable goal since preschool children should not be expected to share all of the time but should share a reasonable amount of time.

PROCEDURE

The basic strategy to eliminate nonsharing involves several procedures:

- Make environmental changes to facilitate sharing.
- Provide systematic help to learn why and how to share.
- Reinforce spontaneous sharing.
- Deal with situations in which the child is not willing to share.

Definition

Nonsharing means that the child is unwilling to allow other children to use materials the child is using, or even materials that are simply nearby. For example, the child may be playing with only some of the blocks but tells others that they are all hers.

Baseline

Before starting the program, gather baseline data for three days. Keep a pencil and paper handy in the classroom. Divide the paper into two columns. Title one column Sharing and the other Nonsharing. Carefully observe the child throughout the day. Whenever anyone asks the child to share, record the child's reaction in the appropriate column. Also, if the child voluntarily shares with another youngster, record this under Sharing. At the end of each day, compute the percentage of sharing opportunities in which the child actually shared. Use this formula:

$$\frac{Sharing}{Sharing + Nonsharing} \times 100 = \% \text{ of sharing}$$

Thus, if the child had twenty opportunities to share and your record shows five checks in the Sharing column and fifteen in the Nonsharing column, your computation would be as follows:

$$\frac{5}{5 + 15} = \frac{5}{20} = 0.25 \times 100 = 25\%$$

Record the percentage on the Record Keeping Graph. Your daily score tells you what percentage of opportunities for sharing the child actually used to share. The higher the percentage, the greater your progress.

Program

After gathering baseline data, you are ready to begin the program. It should be stressed that this program is not intended for very young pre-schoolers.

Facilitate Sharing Through the Environment. To help the child feel more positive about sharing with peers, provide as much help as possible through classroom setup, routines, and activities.

1. Classroom arrangement can facilitate sharing. As previously mentioned, the class should have ample materials so that children are not competing for a few available materials. Also, examine the space provided in each interest area. There should be enough room for several children to work

comfortably together or independently without getting in each other's way. Be sure, too, that the various interest areas are set off from each other, with boundaries defined by furniture, storage, or other dividers. Sharing is easier for children if they are not constantly in each other's way and thus feel they must defend their space and materials.

2. Teacher supervision is a controllable factor that can facilitate sharing. Problems in sharing will be less likely in activities where each child has a separable item, such as a puzzle. When several children are building with blocks or making collages from a central supply of materials, problems related to sharing are more likely to occur. These activities need careful teacher involvement.

3. Specific projects for activity times may be planned to encourage sharing. There should be ample supplies for all the children for art activities. Materials such as paint, glue, or glitter should be provided in several small containers rather than in one large one so the children have fairly quick access to what they want. Cooking activities should be selected to allow each child who participates to have some active involvement in the process. Another way to avoid sharing problems is to consider whether certain activities should be limited to a specific number of children. If, for instance, the cooking activity involves adding and stirring six ingredients, allow no more than six children to participate at a time. The activity can be repeated with groups of six until all the children who want to cook have a turn.

4. A school usually has a few items for which there is more demand than supply. Swings are an example. Often there are more children wanting to swing than there are available swings. In such a case sharing has to take place or there will be some unhappy children. There are some techniques you can use to encourage sharing if the children are reluctant to let someone else have a turn. A definite time limit, agreed upon by the children, can be used. You can either have a timer on hand or refer to a clock or watch. When the specified time is up, it is the next child's turn. Another way of handling the use of swings (or any other equipment that lends itself to being timed) is to specify a number of times the child can swing back and forth. After the child reaches that number, it is the next child's turn. The child on the swing, the children waiting, and the teacher can count together to add another dimension to this activity.

Systematically Help the Child Learn to Share. Use this step if the child rarely or never shares. The other steps should suffice for a child who shares at least some times (at least twenty percent of the time according to the baseline data).

Implement the following sequence of steps. Because of the nature of this procedure, it may be helpful if only one teacher works with the child.

1. Begin by structuring situations for the child to experience sharing. At least once a day, find a cooperative and even-tempered child who is involved in an activity that is suitable for sharing. Go to the child who has problems with sharing at a time when that child is not overly involved in an activity (for example, soon after a child-selected activity time begins). Take the child by the hand and go to the other child, and ask, "Can we play with you? We'd like to share the toy you're using." Stay with the two children for a few minutes. Make several comments about sharing and how nice it makes one feel. Stress the positive value of sharing.

   Continue this step daily for one to two weeks, until you feel the child who has difficulty sharing has begun to understand your message.

2. The next step requires that the child be the one who shares. At least once a day find a situation where the child you are concerned about is involved in an activity that lends itself to sharing. Go to the child and say something like, "Can I play with you? I'd like to share the toys you're using." Choose your approach carefully to encourage the child to answer "yes." Join in the activity and let the child know how much you appreciate her sharing with you. If the child answers "no," simply say, "All right. Maybe we can work together later." Leave the child alone. Do not lecture or scold. Convey that sharing is a positive experience, not something one is forced into.

   This step may take a few days or weeks. Allow enough time for the child to understand what you are conveying by setting up these situations. Once the child is sharing with you and enjoying the experience on a regular basis, move on to the next step.

3. When you feel the child is ready to share with someone other than adults, shift the focus to children. At least once a day, when you see the child engaged in an activity that lends itself to sharing, find another child who is not involved in an activity at the time, and invite that child to share with you. Go to the child whose sharing difficulties you are concerned about and say, "Ricky and I would like to share with you. Will you share with us?" If the child says "yes," then join in the play. Be involved only to the extent that is necessary. Let the two children take the major role in the play. Verbalize how nice it was of the child to share her activity with a friend.

   If the child says "no," don't make an issue of the matter. Tell her that perhaps another time she will feel like sharing.

   When the child is sharing with another child on a regular basis, after at least two weeks move on to the next step.

4. This step is similar to Step 3, except that the teacher's role is lessened. Approach the child with another youngster, and say, "Ricky would like to share the blocks with you." Allow the children to work out the

details of the play. Retreat once the two have agreed to work together. Periodically reinforce them by your attention and praise.

5. When the child consistently shares at least two-thirds of the times that you approach her with another child, begin to withdraw your involvement further. Use Step 4 every other day, then every third day, and so on until it has been phased out. At the same time, the child should be sharing spontaneously and increasingly more often. This will be reflected in the Record Keeping Graph.

Reinforce Spontaneous Sharing When it Occurs. The procedure described gradually helps the child share more freely. Be on the lookout throughout the day for situations in which the child shares. At such times be lavish in your praise. It is important to let the child know that you value this behavior. When you first begin this program, offer praise every time the child shares. Later, when sharing takes place more frequently, decrease your rate of reinforcement gradually. Eventually you should only have to give reinforcement intermittently, at about the same rate as you reinforce the other children in the class.

Help the Child Handle Situations in Which She is not Willing to Share. There will be times, at first quite frequently, when the child is unwilling to share with other youngsters. Your handling of such situations will have a considerable effect on the child's future attitude toward sharing. Sharing has to originate from inside the person who shares, it cannot be forced. Therefore, it is important to present sharing as a positive experience. Whenever a situation arises in which the child is refusing to share, do the following:

1. Go to where the two children are as soon as you notice a problem or a potential problem related to sharing. Be sure that your manner is calm and quiet at all times.
2. Ask the children what is happening. Restate what they verbalize as the problem. For instance, "Cathy, you would like some of the cookie cutters to use with the clay. Monica, you had the cookie cutters first and want to keep them. Is that right? What can we do here?"
3. If the children are not too upset by the situation, encourage them to suggest some alternatives. Especially urge the child who is unwilling to share to come up with suggestions. If a good idea is brought up that both children are happy with, implement it, and praise them for sharing so well. Point out the merits of working together and helping each other.
4. If one or both children are overly upset by the situation and are unwilling to compromise, do not make a fuss over the situation. Say simply, "Cathy, Monica is not ready to share right now. Why don't you come with me, and we'll see if we can find something else for you to use with

the clay." Look for an alternative acceptable to the other child. Also reassure this child that you will see that she gets a turn with the desired object soon.

5. Once the child has refused to share under any conditions, move away from her. You do not want to make an undue fuss over her attitude; you also do not want to give more attention than necessary. Above all, do not lecture and scold. That will not change the mind of a chronic nonsharer but will only reinforce the behavior.

6. Such nonsharing situations provide good timing for creating a sharing experience. If possible, set up a structured sharing situation within five or ten minutes. The type of experience you provide depends on which step is currently being used. By doing this, you provide a positive experience in sharing as a contrast to the nonsharing that was just taking place.

Continue Graphing the Behavior. As you implement this program, continue to keep daily track of sharing and nonsharing, as you did during baseline. Record the percentage of sharing done each day on the Record Keeping Graph. This provides information on progress and shows when the goal is reached.

Maintenance

When the child consistently shares at least two-thirds of the time, you can discontinue the procedure and record keeping. However, do give periodic praise for sharing. Once the child realizes that sharing is a positive experience that has its own rewards, the child will continue to share on her own. Do keep in mind that preschool children still have much to learn about social behaviors. Your help and guidance in sharing situations continues to be needed.

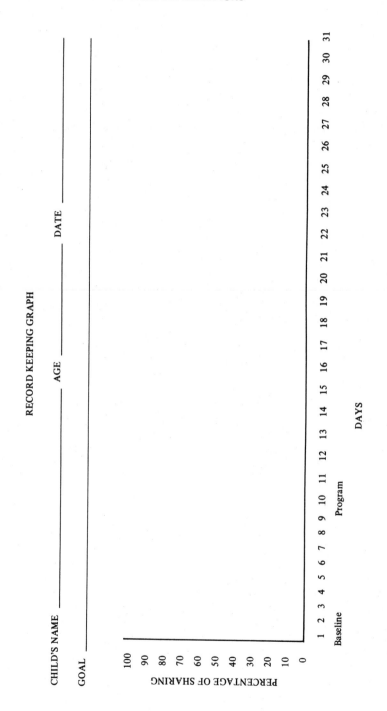

RECORD KEEPING GRAPH

CHILD'S NAME _____   AGE _____   DATE _____

GOAL _____

PERCENTAGE OF SHARING

100 90 80 70 60 50 40 30 20 10 0

1 2 3 4 5 6 7 8 9 10 11 12 13 14 15 16 17 18 19 20 21 22 23 24 25 26 27 28 29 30 31

Baseline   Program

DAYS

CHAPTER 10

10
Bribery

"Larry, I'll give you some of my Halloween candy if you let me have your flashlight," whispers Sherrie, age four. Larry, who brought his father's big flashlight for show and tell, replies, "No way!" Sherrie, undaunted, ups her offer. "I'll give you all my candy, okay?" Larry considers this, asking for an accounting of what Sherrie got for Halloween. Ultimately a teacher puts a stop to the bartering by mentioning that the flashlight is not Larry's to give away and moving it to the director's office for safekeeping. At lunch that day, Sherrie notices that Carmen has a peanut butter sandwich in her lunch box. "I'll give you my tuna sandwich for your peanut butter sandwich." Carmen shakes her head, takes a determined bite of her lunch and turns to the child sitting at her other side. Later still, Sherrie tells Brent and Candy, "I have some money in my coat. I'll give it to you if you let me play." Both children say, "I don't want to play with you," and move elsewhere to continue their game. The teachers have noted that when Sherrie wants something from another child, she invariably offers some kind of bribe to get it. She is usually unsuccessful. The other children react negatively to her approach. There are times, however, when she has a taker to her offers and "buys" friendship, food, and other items in this way.

STATE THE BEHAVIOR

The child frequently uses bribery to win friendship or favors from other children.

OBSERVE THE BEHAVIOR

Spend a few days observing the behavior to gain further insight into how it takes place.

A. When is the child most likely to use bribery?

- During free choice activities
- During sharing times when children have personal toys from home at school
- During outdoor play
- During mealtimes
- Usually early in the day
- At any time of the day

B. What does the child try to gain through bribery?

- Friendship
- The right to join in the play of another child or group of children
- A turn with a toy that another child brought from home
- A chance to take a personal toy home
- The gift of another child's personal toy
- A turn with a school toy
- Part or all of another child's meal
- A piece of gum or candy that another child has

C. What does the child offer in exchange for the favor requested?

- To play with the other child
- Food
- Money
- A toy
- The chance to cut ahead in line for something children are taking turns for
- Friendship
- An outlandish offer ("I'll give you a million dollars")

D. To whom does the child offer bribes?

- To any other child
- Only certain children
- Girls
- Boys
- Younger and smaller children
- Older and bigger children
- Outgoing children
- Quiet children

E. What happens when the child bribes another youngster?

- The other child accepts the offer
- The other child does not accept the offer
- The other child discusses the request
- The other child ignores the briber and walks away

- The other child gets upset
- The other child calls a teacher

F. Does the child fullfill the offer in exchange for the favor?

Use the information from these observations to help you deal more effectively with the problem.

EXPLORE THE CONSEQUENCES

Children, like adults, develop a variety of techniques to get something they want from another person. Most of these are based on a socially acceptable system of give and take. It is quite common for children to offer something in return for what they ask. It is an area of concern when this method is the only one used by a child. The child who consistently uses bribery has a limited repertoire of social techniques. There are several concerns about such behavior. First, the child is not developing to full social potential. Appropriate social development means that the child must acquire many techniques for obtaining what she wants. Second, other children and adults have a negative response to a child who uses frequent bribery. Ultimately the child's self-concept suffers because others respond negatively. Such a child needs help in learning a range of ways to get what is wanted or needed from other people. Otherwise, the child will continue to try using bribery to get things. In the long run, the child has unsatisfactory social relations, at the expense of self-image.

CONSIDER ALTERNATIVES

Consider whether one of the following suggestions might provide an answer to the situation.

- Be sure that what you consider to be a problem is indeed a problem. All children, at one time or another, use the trade-off technique to gain what they want. In a preschool class you may often hear, "If you ..., then I'll ..." If a child occasionally uses such a format, this is acceptable. It is only when the child uses it exclusively that you should be concerned. Watch and listen. If the child employs other means to get things, do not be too concerned. To decrease bribery (especially of material and unrealistic objects), make a point of reinforcing other ways of asking for what the child wants.

- A child may feel a need to employ bribery because there is undue competition for available items in the classroom. Examine the facilities. There should be ample materials and variety to constructively engage all children at all times. If there are a few popular items of limited quantity, work out a method for sharing so that everyone may have a turn.
- When items that are not normally a part of the classroom are present, problems may result. This can happen when a child brings a highly popular or unique toy from home or when a child has candy, gum, or other treats that are not a part of the school's usual menu. Such items may cause a child to try bribery to gain the favor of the child with the treats. If this situation is the root of the problem, set up some rules to control it. You may want to ban food items other than what is part of the normal menu unless there are enough treats so everyone can have one or because they do not meet your school's nutritional standards. You may need to set up regulations to convey how toys from home are to be handled. (See Chapter 9, Nonsharing, for suggestions.)
- If the child's bribes are often unrealistic, you can help the child see how outlandish the offers are. Point out that the child does not have "a million dollars" or whatever was promised. Suggest alternatives. Be sure that when you interfere in such a situation, the children are not engaged in a humorous conversation or "tall tales" contest, but that the bribe is being made in earnest.

If none of these suggestions helps deal with the problem, move on to the following detailed program.

STATE THE GOAL

The goal is for the child to use a variety of ways of getting what is needed and wanted from others instead of bribery.

PROCEDURE

The basic method for eliminating overuse of bribery involves these steps:

- Develop a systematic program to help the child acquire other techniques for getting things.
- Reinforce the use of other techniques.
- Ignore bribery when it occurs.

Definition

Bribery is a situation in which a child tries to win friendship, favors, or material objects from others by promising something in return. To be defined as a problem, bribery should occur at least 50 percent of the time that the child wants something from someone else.

Baseline

Spend three days gathering baseline information with which to compare later progress. Select a one-hour period or two half-hour periods per day during activities when you expect bribery to occur, according to your earlier informal observation. Keep a pencil and paper in the classroom for your record keeping. Draw a line down the middle of the paper and label the columns Bribery and Other. For the period of observation make a mark in the Bribery column each time the child uses bribery. Make a mark in the Other column when the child uses another technique to get something.

The following is a list of techniques other than bribery that a child might use to get something from other children:

- *Asking* for the desired item. This means that the child goes to another youngster and simply states that she wants something the other child has. The child might say,

   "Let me try!"
   "Can I have a piece of gum, too?"
   "Can I play with that?"

- *Sharing* the desired thing with another child. Here the child expresses her desire to have or use something, but she suggests that she and the other child share. The child might say,

   "Can I have a turn now?"
   "Let's do that together, okay?"
   "Can I help you?"

- *Offering* something in the hope that the other child will share or offer the desired thing. In this case the child does not come out and express her desire, but tries to gain it more subtly by offering something that she thinks will induce the other child to share or give up the desired item. Here the child might say,

   "Would you like to play with this?"
   "I'll give you a piece of my candy."
   "I've got the doll buggy. Do you want to use it for your baby?"

- *Waiting* for an invitation to use or share the desired thing. This means that the child stands by passively, neither asking nor offering something in exchange, in the hope of being given a turn or being asked to share the desired item. The initiative may be taken by the other child or by a teacher who is standing nearby.

- *Substituting* the desired item with something else. In this instance the child decides to find a substitute for the desired item. She may decide to play with a similar toy, join another child in play, or in some other way be satisfied with something else.
- *Foregoing* the desired item. Rather than trying to gain the desired thing, either actively or passively, the child decides to get along without it.

Not all of these techniques are apparent to the observer. For instance, the decision to forego or substitute may occur in the child's mind without your knowledge. Therefore, count only those techniques that are readily recognizable.

When using bribery, the child may combine a number of techniques. For example, the child might say,

"I'll give you the cookies from my lunch if you let me play with your doll."

"Can I play with you? You can drive my truck on the blocks."

"If you give me your candy bar, I'll bring you a million dollars tomorrow."

At the end of each day, total the marks in the two columns. Then compute a percentage of bribes in relation to total techniques, as follows:

$$\frac{\text{Bribes}}{\text{Bribes} + \text{Other Techniques}} \times 100 = \% \text{ of Bribes}$$

Record this percentage on the Record Keeping Graph.

Program

Now that you have established a baseline, you are ready to begin the program. All teachers should be aware of it and implement it as appropriate.

This program is for a child who uses bribery to the exclusion of other techniques for getting what she wants. If the child uses bribery occasionally but also uses other methods, do not worry.

Implement a Systematic Program to Help the Child Acquire Other Techniques for Getting What is Desired. Use the information gathered from informal observation to determine when bribes are most likely to be offered. Then be on the lookout for such situations to implement your program.

1. At least five times a day try to stop the child before she offers a bribe. Look for signs of wanting an object, a playmate, or a favor. Such signs might include the child stopping what she is doing, looking around the room, or looking at a specific object or person.

2. Go to the child and say, "What would you like?" Encourage an answer. If you are fairly sure what the child wants and she does not tell you, ask specifically: "Would you like the blocks?"

3. Now suggest that you and the child try to get what she wants. Recommend a very specific approach, using the techniques previously mentioned. The following are examples of what you might say:

   - *Asking*

     "You want to play with the new blocks? Let's ask Nancy if you can use them now."

     "You'd like to run Tracy's truck. We'll ask him to let you use it, okay?"

   - *Sharing*

     "Since you want a turn on the swing, we'll see if you can push Christine for awhile, and then she can push you."

     "You really want to play with Claude and Tiffany, right? Let's ask them if you can join their tea party."

   - *Offering*

     "It would be fun to be a firefighter with them. Let's find a hose and see if they'd like you to join them."

     "You can take this sifter to the sand box. Maybe Rachel will let you use the funnel when she sees it."

   - *Waiting*

     "Would you like me to ask Kyle to let you use the hammer when he is finished?"

     "Let's stand by the table and watch. Maybe they'll ask you to play Bingo when they've finished this game."

If, for some reason, these techniques are not appropriate or do not get the desired response, suggest that the child find a similar alternative or that she forego the thing she wants. Use these techniques only if the others are not possible.

4. If the first techniques work for the child, state this success verbally. Say, for instance, "See, you got to use the blocks by asking!" or "Suggesting that you share the swing and push each other worked! You got to swing."

5. Continue using this program as often as possible, at least five times per day. When you begin to see a decrease in the percentage of bribes used (indicating an increase of other techniques) on the graph, you know the program is working. Gradually cut back on the number of times you

lead the child through this process. If you note a slowdown or reversal in the rate of improvement, you may be withdrawing your support too quickly. By the time you have reached the objective, you should be helping the child employ other techniques only periodically.

Reinforce the Use of Other Techniques When These are Used Spontaneously. Throughout the day, watch for times when the child receives things by spontaneously using alternative techniques. Whenever you see this, go to the child and give reinforcement. You may do this by praising the child, by simply being there, or by commenting on her success. It is important to let the child know that you approve of such acts. Once the child uses these techniques fairly frequently, gradually cut back on the rate of reinforcement. Eventually you should be reinforcing these techniques no more frequently than you do with other children.

Ignore Bribery When It Occurs. Offering something in exchange for a desired item is a legitimate means of getting that item. Because the child already has this well-developed technique in her repertoire of behaviors, there is no need to reinforce it. Simply pay no attention when the child uses this technique to get what she wants. As you expect other techniques to increase, this one will automatically decrease. By ignoring it, you will help this process.

Continue Graphing the Behavior. Keep daily track of bribes and other techniques. Compute the percentage and record it on the graph each day. As you implement this program, count only spontaneous use of other techniques. Do not count the situations in which you help the child gain what she wants through alternative techniques. You may decide not to use the systematic procedure during the hour that you are counting behaviors. The graph reflects progress and tells when to decrease the systematic teaching of alternatives, and when to cut back on reinforcement of spontaneous use of these alternatives.

Maintenance

Once the child has learned and freely uses various ways of getting what she wants, continue to give periodic reinforcement for the alternative methods. The child should gain intrinsic satisfaction from use of these different methods as other children respond more positively. As a result, the child gets what she wants more frequently without constantly using bribery.

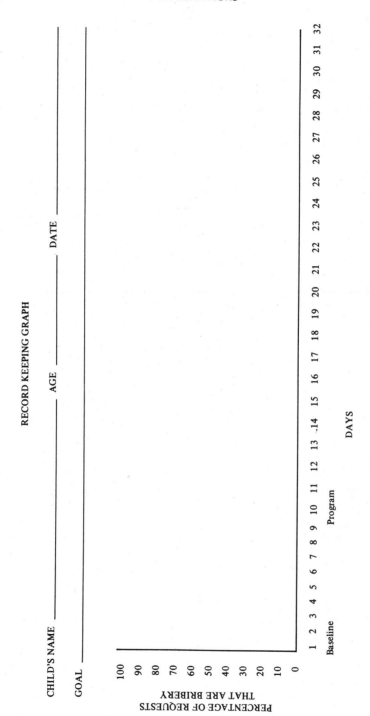

RECORD KEEPING GRAPH

CHILD'S NAME _____ AGE _____ DATE _____

GOAL _____

PERCENTAGE OF REQUESTS THAT ARE BRIBERY

100 90 80 70 60 50 40 30 20 10 0

1 2 3 4 5 6 7 8 9 10 11 12 13 14 15 16 17 18 19 20 21 22 23 24 25 26 27 28 29 30 31 32

Baseline   Program

DAYS

CHAPTER 11

11

Stealing

"Andy took my car, teacher!" yells Patrick. Andy digs his hands deeper into his pockets and says "Did not!" when questioned by Mrs. Lyle. "Let me see what's in your pocket, Andy," she coaxes. Andy resists and begins to cry when Mrs. Lyle forces his hands out of his pocket. She pulls out a bright blue car. "That's my car," states Patrick. "No, it isn't. It's mine," cries Andy. Mrs. Lyle gives the car to Patrick while Andy continues to insist tearfully that the car is his. Mrs. Lyle sighs and again talks to Andy about taking things that are not his. Almost daily such incidents occur where Andy has taken a toy belonging to another child and claimed it to be his own. In addition, lately there have been mysterious disappearances of small classroom items. No one has seen Andy take these items, but the teachers strongly suspect that he did. They are at a loss about what to do because Andy always denies stealing, even when confronted with the evidence.

STATE THE BEHAVIOR

The child takes items which belong to someone else or to the school.

OBSERVE THE BEHAVIOR

For a few days observe the behavior to gain further insight. Because stealing is usually done surreptitiously, this requires very careful observation.

A. When does the child steal?

- Unpredictably, at any time
- During planned activities
- During free choice activities
- During group times

- When children are getting or putting away coats or other belongings in their cubbies
- During cleanup times
- During transitions
- During lunch or snack times
- At nap time

B. What precedes stealing?

- The child talks about liking a particular toy
- The child plays with a particular toy
- The child keeps coming back to the admired item
- The child asks if he can keep the item
- The child is not allowed to handle or play with the item by the child to whom it belongs
- The child stays near the child to whom the item belongs

C. What happens when the child steals?

- The child looks around to see if someone is watching
- The child puts the item in his pocket
- The child holds the item in his hand
- The child hides the item somewhere in the classroom
- The child takes it to his cubbie
- The child denies taking the item if asked
- The child insists the item belongs to him
- The child gets upset when he is found to have the item
- The child claims he has the item by accident
- The child returns the item to its rightful owner
- The child refuses to return the item

D. What does the child steal?

- Small items that fit into a pocket
- Larger items
- Toys that other children bring from home
- School toys or materials
- Parts of larger items (such as a puzzle piece)
- Any type of item
- One specific item or type of item
- Food

Use these informal observations to gain greater understanding of when and how stealing takes place. This information will be used in implementing the program to eliminate the behavior.

EXPLORE THE CONSEQUENCES

When a young child takes something that does not belong to him, he usually does this simply because he wants the item in question. A preschooler is still developing a sense of ownership which eventually becomes part of a broader sense of ethics and morals. An understanding of property rights is still unclear. Sometimes the desire for something appealing combined with the young child's natural impulsiveness becomes more important. So, the child takes the item. The child needs to learn that it is wrong to take something that does not belong to him. He learns this, along with what other behaviors are socially acceptable and unacceptable, through the long-term process of socialization. When the child is taught through gentle guidance what ownership means and why it has to be respected, he adopts values that include consideration for others' belongings. If, however, the child is made to feel shame and guilt when he takes something that does not belong to him, he becomes resentful.

Everyone has some desires that are out of reach. Young children have to be helped to understand such desires and alternative ways of dealing with them. Stealing cannot be allowed in the preschool, but it can be handled in a way that does not make the child feel badly about himself.

CONSIDER ALTERNATIVES

Some relatively simple steps may help minimize the opportunity for stealing. Consider whether one of the following suggestions might work.

A. When children bring toys or other belongings from home to share at school, problems can arise. The owner of a desirable item gains a certain amount of power, because the owner can say who may or may not play with the toy. If another child is prevented by the owner from using the item, that rejected child may become very resentful. At the same time, the item becomes even more desirable because he cannot have it. Such a situation may invite stealing. Consider these alternatives to allowing children to bring toys from home to school:

- Items from home can be completely banned. If you decide to do this, write a letter to the parents explaining that home toys are creating a variety of problems. Enlist the parents' help in enforcing the new rule. If a child still brings something from home, stop the child from taking the item into the classroom right at the beginning of the day. After admiring the object, remind the child of the new rule and ask the parent to take it back to the car. If this is not feasible, tell the child you will take the item to the office and will return it when the child goes home.

- Limit the time for sharing items from home at school. You might designate one day of the week as "sharing day." Or you may set aside a limited time each day when children can share home items. Provide a place where toys from home can be kept safe at other times of the day.
- Set some rules on how personal toys are to be shared. Children can help in deciding on appropriate rules. They may decide, for example, that everyone is given at least one turn with the toy.

B. Another way of discouraging children from taking items is by keeping the classroom neat and well organized. When school materials are stored in a haphazard way, no one quite knows what is in the classroom or where it belongs. When everything in the room has its place and is clearly visible, the message is that all items in the room are important and contribute to the class. It is not as easy to take a toy that clearly belongs in a specific place as it is to take a toy that has no particular place.

C. If the child takes only one specific item or type of item from the class-room, you can do one of two things. You may remove the item from the room for two or three weeks, if such a move would not be too limiting to the functioning of the class. Or you can keep a close watch on this item to prevent the child from taking it.

If none of these suggestions serve as a solution to the problem, then continue to the following program.

STATE THE GOAL

The goal is for the child to stop taking items that do not belong to him.

PROCEDURE

To eliminate stealing, the basic strategy involves these procedures:

- Reinforce appropriate handling of classroom materials or items belonging to peers.
- Make environmental changes.
- Prevent stealing.

Definition

Stealing involves any incident in which a child deliberately takes and keeps an item that does not belong to him, whether the item belongs to the school or to another child. Such behavior occurs regularly. All teachers should discuss and agree on what behaviors will be considered as stealing (such as putting an item in his pocket or placing an item in his cubbie).

Baseline

To compare later progress, it is important to know how often the child steals before starting the program. For three days count the number of stealing incidents that occur. It will require considerable vigilance to collect this information because the child probably does not steal openly. This information may not be as precise as it could be, but try to be as accurate as possible. Make a mark on paper each time the child steals something, and transfer the total to the Record Keeping Graph at the end of each day. These three days provide a baseline.

Program

Once baseline data are collected, you are ready to begin the program to change this behavior. It is important that all teachers follow it consistently.

Reinforce Appropriate Handling of Classroom Materials or Items Belonging to Peers. If the child is still learning respect for property that is not his, he needs to be told what he is doing well. Therefore, whenever the child appropriately handles classroom materials or items belonging to peers, he should be verbally reinforced:

"I like the way you are holding Paula's doll so carefully. Thank you for helping her take good care of it."

"I'm so glad that you put all the pieces back in the box. If everyone helps take care of them like you do, we won't lose any."

"You remembered to put the tricycle in the shed! Here it won't rust, so everyone can enjoy riding it when they want to."

Discourage Stealing Through Appropriate Changes in the Environment or the Routine. Examine the organization of the classroom in relation to stealing. It is not as easy to take an item off a shelf that is neatly arranged, with the item displayed clearly. It is much easier to take something that is part of a haphazard jumble. Convey your respect for classroom materials, as well as an awareness of what is in the room, through careful arrangement and storage.

Consider whether children should be allowed to bring items from home to school. Set specific rules and limitations on when, how, and under what circumstances personal items are to be shared. Such guidelines should also discourage stealing.

Prevent Stealing Without Shaming the Child. The following is a procedure to help prevent children from taking home items that do not belong to them. It is done through a "pocket hunt." Follow these steps:

1. Explain to the children in a group time that classroom items and children's belongings have been disappearing. Acknowledge that it is easy to put a toy in one's pocket accidentally. Enlist everyone's help in preventing such losses in the future.
2. Just before the children leave school, conduct a pocket hunt to find items that belong to the school or to children. It is important that no one child be singled out. Everyone must participate, including the teachers. Provide a box into which items are deposited. Have everyone empty their pockets, and put anything that does not belong to them into the box. An adult might periodically contribute a crayon or other small item to the box to avoid placing a stigma on children who do have things in their pockets. Whatever is in the box should then be returned to its rightful place or owner. Handle this hunt as a game, not as an inquisition. Minimize reactions and conduct the activity in a matter-of-fact manner. Never shame a child or accuse him of stealing. Simply point out that items need to be replaced in their proper locations or returned to their owners.
3. The timing of the pocket hunt is important. If all the children leave at the same time, as in a preschool or in a program where the youngsters board a bus together, the hunt can be carried out just before everyone leaves. If the school is a day care program where children leave at different times, however, a different arrangement needs to be worked out. Plan the pocket hunt for a few minutes before the child who has posed the stealing problem leaves. In this way you minimize the recurrence of stealing in the time between the pocket hunt and the time the child leaves, while still involving a group of children in the process.
4. If the items stolen are primarily the personal belongings of other children, keep closer track of ownership of such toys. At the beginning of each day, as you greet youngsters, ask them if they brought something special to school. If they did, record the item and its owner on a list. In this way you can double-check that all children have their own belongings after the pocket hunt at the end of the day.

Continue Graphing the Behavior. The conditions under which you kept track of stealing during baseline will differ to some extent from your measurements during the program. Nonetheless, continue counting items the child has which do not belong to him. This can be done more easily during the pocket hunt. Simply record the number of items the child empties from his pockets that do not belong to him. Use the Record Keeping Graph. The pocket hunt itself should decrease stealing, so expect a fairly rapid drop in total once you begin. Draw a vertical line after the baseline data, then record each day's total on the graph.

Maintenance

Continue the pocket hunt even after the child no longer takes objects that do not belong to him. After an additional two weeks, begin to decrease the hunts gradually to every other day, then to every third day, then to once a week. Discontinue the hunts when you see no recurrence of stealing. However, continue praising the child periodically for handling materials with care. Similarly, keep on evaluating the environment so that it discourages stealing by the way it is arranged.

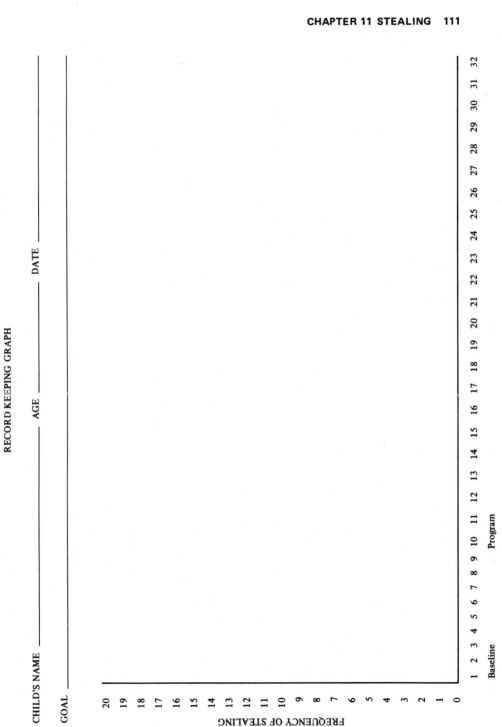

RECORD KEEPING GRAPH

CHILD'S NAME _____ AGE _____ DATE _____

GOAL _____

FREQUENCY OF STEALING

20
19
18
17
16
15
14
13
12
11
10
9
8
7
6
5
4
3
2
1
0

1 2 3 4 5 6 7 8 9 10 11 12 13 14 15 16 17 18 19 20 21 22 23 24 25 26 27 28 29 30 31 32

Baseline   Program

DAYS

SECTION 2
DISRUPTIVE
BEHAVIORS

CHAPTER 12

Disrupting Group Time

"I'd like to share a book with you about a special little train," says Ms. Sylvester as she opens the reading selection for group time. The children quiet down, and eighteen expectant faces turn toward the teacher from the circle. Halfway through the second sentence of the story, the teacher is interrupted by a thud. Ms. Sylvester resumes reading, but several children turn toward the noise. As the teacher turns to the second page, there is a giggle from the same part of the circle, followed by some whispering. Ms. Sylvester stops reading. "Brian, you need to sit quietly and listen now." Brian, aged three and a half, wiggles back into place, smiles at Ms. Sylvester, then sits quietly with hands folded in his lap. The story is continued. Thirty seconds later a loud, "Ouch! Brian kicked me!" is heard from Brian's neighbor. "Brian, let's keep our feet to ourselves, please!" Again Brian smiles. The story is resumed. Almost immediately Brian starts wiggling, then moves to another area of the circle. Ms. Sylvester continues reading, though she throws Brian an annoyed look. Brian is now sitting by the block shelf. He reaches slowly behind him and pulls out a unit block. He examines it carefully, then turns to Cindy next to him and declares loudly, "Look what I got." A nearby teacher says, "Shhh!" Brian reaches for another block and begins banging the two blocks together. Several children laugh, and most turn to look toward him. Ms. Sylvester tells Brian to put the blocks away immediately, but Brian continues banging them together. One of the other teachers gets up, goes to Brian, and tries to take the blocks away. Brian resists, crying, "They're mine! They're mine!" A struggle ensues. All the children watch this interchange at first, but soon some begin talking and a few get up to go elsewhere. Ms. Sylvester closes the book and announces the end of group time. The teachers feel discouraged because Brian disrupts group times more and more in this way.

STATE THE BEHAVIOR

The child disrupts group activities such as storytime and music.

OBSERVE THE BEHAVIOR

Take a few days to observe the child's disruptions and gain greater insight into this behavior.

A. How does the child disrupt group activities?

- The child talks or whispers to other children
- The child giggles
- The child talks or whispers to no one in particular
- The child pushes or shoves other children
- The child brings toys to the group and plays with them noisily
- The child moves from place to place in the circle
- The child gets up and walks away from the group
- The child plays noisily with other objects elsewhere in the classroom

B. With whom does the child disrupt the group?

- The child acts alone
- The child is disruptive only when sitting next to a particular child or a few children
- The child tries to involve any other children in disruptive activities

C. What activity is underway when the child disrupts?

- Music
- Creative movement
- Discussion
- Storytime

D. What happens before the child disrupts group activities?

- The child pays attention to the activity
- The child is distracted from the activity
- The child squirms and wiggles
- Another child distracts the child
- The child sits near an adult
- The child sits away from adults
- The child sits by a friend or friends
- The child looks to see if adults are watching before he disrupts the activity

E. What happens after the child is disruptive?

- Other children look toward him
- Other children laugh
- Other children join in
- The child continues disruptive activity when asked to stop
- The child quiets down when asked

- The child gets upset when asked to quiet down
- The child engages in increasingly more disruptive activities as the group time progresses
- The child denies being disruptive

Utilize the information from these informal observations to help you deal with the situation.

EXPLORE THE CONSEQUENCES

Group activities are planned into the curriculum for several reasons. There is usually a concept or skill that is being conveyed. Group time may serve to reinforce or strengthen a concept presented to the children during another part of the curriculum. Group activities also foster enjoyment of music, literature, and dance. Finally, group times provide practice in group social behaviors such as sitting quietly, listening, waiting a turn, and consideration for others in the group. These behaviors are learned gradually, but by the time children leave preschool, they have acquired some of the skills required in kindergarten or elementary school.

With very young children, group time lasts only a few minutes. As children get older these time periods are expanded. Whatever its length, however, group time must be stimulating and exciting enough to hold the interest of all the children in the group. Because teachers carefully plan group time to fulfill a variety of objectives, it is dismaying when one child disrupts the activity. This affects not only the child who is disruptive, but also the other children who miss the lessons planned for the group. Adults feel frustrated and angry as well. The child learns that being disruptive gains him considerable attention. Adults talk to him, sit by him, and otherwise pay attention only to him every time he talks, pushes, or makes other distracting noises. The child finds the individual reactions he is getting from adults, even if these are negative, much more enjoyable than what is happening during group time. Unfortunately, all the teachers' attempts to stop the behavior only serve to reinforce it. The more the child disrupts, the more teachers react, and the more the child realizes that disruption is a behavior that gets attention.

CONSIDER ALTERNATIVES

Examine the information from your informal observation to see if there are some clues for a simple solution to the problem.

- Group activities, because they are directed at a relatively large number of children at one time, are not easy to plan. The youngsters in a group have a range of interests, abilities, and attention spans. Consider whether group activities are stimulating enough for all of the children or if one or more youngsters are disruptive because the planned activities bore them. Try a change of pace. Introduce new activities, provide new types of activities, or shorten the length of group time. If the usual pattern for group time is to do two fingerplays and then read a story, change the pattern. Try to tell rather than read a story, use flannelboard props instead of a book, or let the children act out a familiar story. Listen to music, dance, have a Round-Robin story, or let the children tell a story while you write it down. There are many ideas for group time available in resource books. With age-appropriate activities, the right balance of repetition and novelty of activities, and an appropriate length for activity time, you can hold the interest of the group.
- It may be difficult to plan group time if the children have a wide variety of attention spans and interests. Try breaking up the class into two or three more homogeneous, smaller groups, with one teacher for each. In this way, what goes on in group time can be geared more directly to the youngsters in each group.
- If a child is disruptive in group only when sitting next to a particular child or children, separate these youngsters. You might assign places for all the children in the group. For instance, write everyone's name on a large card, place the cards in a circle, then let the children find their places. If there are two children you want to separate, say, "I'd like to sit with you two today. How about making a little space between you where I can sit?"
- Examine the area in which group time is held. Are there distracting items within close reach? If so, consider moving either the items or the location of the group activity.
- Examine the timing of the group. If it is preceded by quiet or structured activities or a period when the children are required to sit, they may not be able to sit quietly for yet another activity. Restructure your daily schedule so that quiet and active times are alternated.

If none of these suggestions provides a solution to the problem, continue on to the following program.

STATE THE GOAL

The goal is for the child to stop disrupting group activities.

PROCEDURE

The basic strategy to eliminate disrupting group times involves three steps:

- Evaluate and restructure group times to maximize interest by the children.
- Reinforce appropriate group behavior.
- Remove the child from the group, after one warning, if the child is disruptive again.

Definition

Disrupting group activities includes any deliberate actions that upset group times, such as making noise or causing other interruptions in the activity. The teachers, as a group, need to identify specific actions that they consider disruptive to agree on a definition of the behavior.

Baseline

Before beginning on the program to eliminate the behavior, it is important to establish a baseline. Your aim is to eliminate disruptions during group time. Work toward achieving this goal by trying to increase the time between disruptions. To provide a measure that will be consistent during baseline as well as later during the program, count the number of disruptions up to two only. Thus, your count will be zero, one, or two. (The reason for this limit will become evident later.)

Time the period that elapses before the child makes his first interruption after group time begins. Define the beginning of group time as when the lead teacher begins the first activity.

Consider each group time as an individual event, and record the information for each time separately on the Record Keeping Graph. This information should be gathered over a minimum of two days. Include only those group times in which the child is regularly disruptive.

Program

Once you have gathered baseline data, you are ready to begin implementing your program. It is important that all teachers follow the procedures consistently.

Evaluate and Restructure Group Times to Maximize Interest by the Children. Examine group activities carefully. Watch all the children's reactions to determine whether they show enjoyment, interest, boredom, or distraction. If a number of children are not involved in the activities you provide, it is time for a change. Make any necessary changes in the activities, types of activities, and/or length of group times.

Reinforce Appropriate Group Behavior. During implementation of this program, it is extremely important that you sit next to the disruptive child during all group activities. This is most important to the success of this program. At the same time, another teacher should be conducting the group activities so that you can be relatively free to attend to the child as needed. Reinforce the child as unobtrusively as possible when he is sitting quietly and attentively. Turn and give him a smile. Whisper in his ear, "I'm proud of the way you're sitting quietly." Give him a squeeze if you have an arm around him. However you do it, let him know you are pleased with his behavior.

When you begin this program, provide reinforcement frequently. From your informal observations and baseline data, you should have some idea of how often the child has been disrupting the group. If the behavior occurs on an average of every two minutes, reinforce good behavior about every minute. If it occurs every ten minutes, reinforce every five minutes. Praise the child before he has the chance to misbehave.

As disruptive behaviors decrease, gradually decrease reinforcement. This individual reinforcement can be completely eliminated once the disruptions have stopped. Continue praising appropriate behavior in the entire group. You might say, "My, you are all listening so carefully today!"

If the Child is Disruptive, Give One Warning and Then Remove the Child From the Group. Disruptive behavior occasionally occurs during group activities. On the first day of the program, before the first group time, have a friendly talk with the child. Tell him that you are concerned about his behavior during group time and why it bothers you. Then tell the child what will happen in the future if he does disrupt. Let him know that he will get a warning the first time and will be required to leave the group if he disrupts a second time. Emphasize, however, your positive expectations and that you will help him stop disruptive behavior at group time. During group times sit by the child to give intermittent reinforcement. If the child is disruptive, do the following:

1. When the first disruption of group time occurs, say to the child in a quiet tone, "You may not [specify the behavior]. The next time you interrupt, you will have to leave the room."
2. If the child stops, praise him within thirty seconds for being attentive to the activity.
3. If a second disruption takes place, get up, have the child get up, and leave the room with him as quietly and quickly as possible. Outside the room,

in a quiet area, seat the child on a chair you have placed there for that purpose. Say, "You will have to stay here until group time is over." Stay nearby, but do not pay attention to the child. You might have some reading materials on hand to occupy you while you wait. If the child is within view of another responsible adult, go back into the classroom. This other adult must be briefed beforehand, however, about the situation and what is to be done and not done.

4. As soon as group time is over, have the child return to the class. Do not lecture or scold. Simply say, "You may go back in now."

Continue Graphing the Behavior. As you follow through with the program, continue counting disruptive incidents as you did during baseline.

Because the child is removed from the classroom after the second disruption, you can only count up to two on this measure. You will know that the warning procedure is effective when you can consistently record one disruption on the graph. You know that your entire program is effective when the count reaches and stays at zero.

Much improvement can be reflected in the measure between two and one and between one and zero. Therefore, record the length of time until the first disruption. Increases in the length of time indicate that you are on the right track.

Draw a line after the baseline data on each graph. Measure behavior only during the same group times that you included in the baseline. The two graphs give enough information to evaluate the success of the program. The first improvements should be reflected in the time measure, while later changes and final success will be evident from the information on both graphs.

Maintenance

Tell the child periodically that you appreciate how well he behaves in group activities. Continue to evaluate group times to ensure that they are appropriate for and interesting to all the children in the class. The child may on occasion disrupt group time again. In this case remind him gently that he is disturbing the class and that he will have to leave if he does it again.

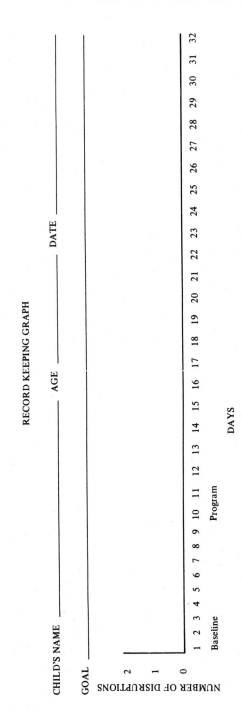

RECORD KEEPING GRAPH

CHILD'S NAME _____ AGE _____ DATE _____

GOAL _____

NUMBER OF DISRUPTIONS

2

1

0

1 2 3 4 5 6 7 8 9 10 11 12 13 14 15 16 17 18 19 20 21 22 23 24 25 26 27 28 29 30 31 32

Baseline   Program

DAYS

RECORD KEEPING GRAPH

CHILD'S NAME ——————— AGE ——————— DATE ———————

GOAL ———————

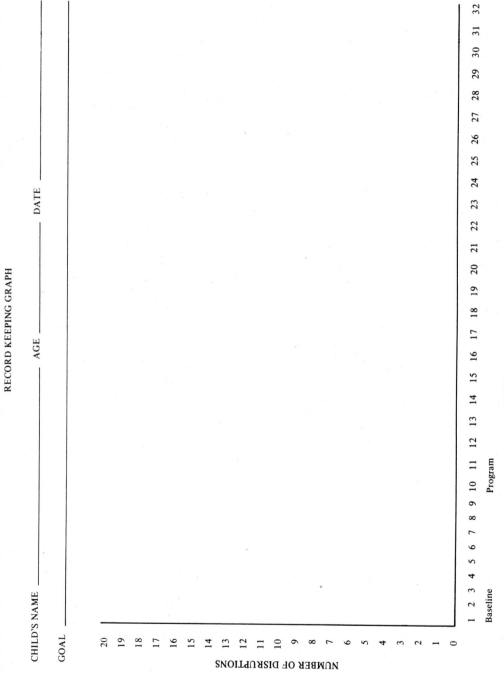

CHAPTER 13

13

Leaving the Classroom

"Where is Annette?" All the teachers take a quick count and, by un-spoken signal, Ms. Turner goes out the door and down the hall. There she finds four-year-old Annette sitting in her coat cubby, looking glum. Ms. Turner gets down to Annette's eye level, saying, "Hey, Annette, we missed you. Where have you been?" No answer. "Annette? You know what? We're going to be dancing to the new record we got yesterday. Don't you want to hear it?" No answer. "Come on. Let's go back inside, Annette. Here, take my hand." Annette sits on her hands. After several more minutes of coaxing, Ms. Turner and Annette go back into the classroom. A half-hour later Annette is gone again. This pattern of frequently leaving the classroom has been going on for several months. The teachers have tried patient coaxing, have expressed their frustration, and have talked with Annette, but to no avail. When Annette first began leaving the room, she treated such occurrences as a silly game, laughing and teasing and running from the teachers as they tried to get her back. After a while, however, the teachers became angry with this repeated behavior, and Annette's reactions changed to the pouting she displayed with Ms. Turner. The adults feel at a total loss as to what to do with Annette.

STATE THE BEHAVIOR

The child frequently leaves the classroom without a legitimate reason.

OBSERVE THE BEHAVIOR

To get a better idea of when and why the child leaves the classroom at in-appropriate times, spend some time observing this behavior informally.

A. When does the child leave the room?
- Unpredictably, at any time of day
- When the child first arrives at school

- Later in the day
- Before a specific activity or routine
- During activity times
- During free choice time
- During transitions

B. What happens before the child leaves the room?

- The child is not engaged in an activity
- The child is engaged in isolate play
- The child is playing with another child or group of children
- The child verbally expresses a dislike for an activity
- The child is told no by a teacher or another child
- The child is wandering aimlessly around the room
- The child has an argument with another child
- The child is not able to accomplish a task
- The child cries and asks for her parents

C. What does the child do when she leaves the room?

- The child looks to see if an adult is watching before leaving
- The child announces that she is leaving
- The child leaves quietly
- The child encourages other children to accompany her
- The child gets upset when asked to return to the class
- The child laughs when asked to return
- The child plays "hard to get" when an adult tries to bring her back
- The child returns to the class by herself

D. Where does the child go when she leaves the room?

- The child stays right outside the door
- The child stays within fairly close range to the classroom
- The child goes to the school kitchen
- The child goes to the playground
- The child leaves the school building
- The child goes into a street
- The child walks toward home
- The child heads in a specific direction (such as a nearby park or store)

Use these observations to help you work on eliminating this behavior.

EXPLORE THE CONSEQUENCES

The child who walks out of the classroom may do so for one of two reasons. The child may genuinely want to be somewhere else, or the child may be seeking attention by frequently leaving the room. If the child really wants to be somewhere else, it is important to work on remedying her unhappiness with the situation. It is the latter case, attention-seeking, which is the focus of this chapter. As with any attention-seeking behavior, the child has learned that adults pay attention when she leaves the classroom. Teachers of preschoolers are given the responsibility of caring for the children in the absence of the parents. Any time a child is out of sight, there is a danger that something unexpected can happen. Therefore, adults react very quickly when a child leaves the classroom. The child is followed and brought back into the classroom as soon as possible. It is this very act which reinforces the behavior. Every time the child seeks attention by leaving the class, a teacher obliges by giving such attention by following, chasing, talking to, coaxing, and bringing the child back. A vicious cycle is created which does not eliminate the behavior but only reinforces it.

CONSIDER ALTERNATIVES

Before deciding to change the child's behavior, think about whether some simpler changes might not resolve the problem. Carefully consider the following suggestions.

- A child may walk out a door simply because the door is open. Perhaps keeping the classroom door closed will take care of the situation.
- A child may want to leave the classroom because she does not want to be there. If this is the case, the child will show signs of distress at other times. For instance, a child to whom the school experience is new may not want to be at school. Knowing that her parents went out the door, she may try to leave the same way.
- If school is not offering activities and materials that are challenging enough for a child, she may decide to find a better way of keeping busy. Leaving the room may represent an adventure or more exciting things to do. Carefully examine the classroom's arrangement and contents to be sure they are appropriate for the child's abilities and interests. Introduce some new, more stimulating activities into the curriculum. If the child finds enough of interest in the classroom, she may not need to seek challenge elsewhere.
- If coats and personal belongings are kept outside the classroom, such as in a hall or entryway, a child may be leaving the room for this reason. A coat, sweater, blanket, or other item in her cubbie may be the reason the child frequently leaves, particularly if that child feels insecure without the item. In such a case let the child keep the security item with her in the classroom. Once she no longer needs its security, the item can go back into the cubbie.

- A child may leave the classroom because of curiosity. She may indicate this by asking questions. Plan a tour through the school building and its surroundings. Such a tour should provide satisfaction for the child's curiosity as well as the possibility for a wealth of related activities.

If none of these suggestions presents a solution to the problem, continue to the following detailed program.

STATE THE GOAL

The goal is for the child to stop leaving the classroom at inappropriate times.

PROCEDURE

To change this behavior, the basic strategy involves the following simultaneous procedures:

- Arrange the classroom and its contents and plan activities to encourage staying in the room.
- Prevent the child from leaving the room whenever possible.
- Praise the child for engaging in activities in the room.
- Provide opportunities for the child to leave the room legitimately.
- Ignore inappropriate departures, if at all possible.

Definition

Leaving the classroom includes any occasion when the child goes out of the classroom without legitimate reason. Such behavior occurs on a repeated and frequent basis.

Baseline

It is important to know how often the child leaves the classroom to be able to recognize progress when the child begins to decrease the behavior. For three days, count the number of times the child leaves the room inappropriately. Each time she leaves mark it down on paper. At the end of each day record the total number on the Record Keeping Graph. These three days provide a baseline.

Program

Begin implementing the program. It is important that all teachers follow it consistently.

Arrange the Room and the Program to Encourage the Child to Stay In the Class. Provide the child with good reasons to stay in the class. It is easier to remain in the room if it provides interest, challenge, and stimulation. Consider the following ideas:

1. Rearrange classroom furnishings to provide renewed interest in the class. If possible, provide a new area or convert an old area to a new purpose. You might add a science table, a cooking area, a music center, or a sensory area. Similarly, you could convert the housekeeping area to a pretend airport, store, or restaurant.

   As you rearrange the room, take into account preventive measures. Arrange the room in such a way that a teacher can be stationed near the door. The activity area that is nearest the door should be one that generates a good deal of interest. An alternative idea would be to have a table near the door and provide activities there.

2. Be sure that the materials stored in the classroom are of high interest to the children. Introduce some new materials if your school is equipped to rotate items. Materials in the room should be appropriate for the abilities of the children and available in ample amounts for everyone. Also examine storage spaces. Classroom items should be attractively displayed, uncluttered, and easily accessible to the children.

3. It may also be time to plan some different activities. It is easy to become unimaginative in relation to curriculum planning. For new ideas, scan some of the many preschool activity books available. Both the teachers and the children will feel a renewed interest in school with some new ideas.

4. The daily schedule might also be due for a change. Rearrange the order of events. Lengthen or shorten time blocks. Add or subtract activities. Take into consideration that the children have changed since school began. They are older and have learned and experienced many things.

These suggestions should be discussed by the entire staff. They are not meant for a classroom that has only been in session a few weeks. They are intended to provide a possible change of pace where the room arrangement, materials, curriculum, and schedule have been the same for two or three months or more. Periodic change can be stimulating, but change that occurs too often and too quickly can be confusing.

Prevent the Child From Leaving the Room Whenever Possible. Several things can be done to make preventive measures effective. It is possible to prevent the child from inappropriately leaving the classroom altogether if vigilance is carried out well.

1. Keep the classroom door closed. In this way you are placing an obstacle between the classroom and the outside that will take extra time for the child to overcome.
2. Provide an added cue for yourself to inform you if the child does try to leave. Fasten a bell or other signaling device toward the top of the door. Whenever anyone opens the door, the bell will ring. If you hear the bell at a time when the door should be closed, it is easy to quickly check.
3. An adult should be near the door during structured and unstructured activities. This teacher will have a dual role. The teacher will be involved in an activity that is ongoing in the class, and will be on the lookout for the child who frequently leaves the class.
4. From your informal observation you should have an idea of when the child leaves the classroom and what she usually does before this happens. Be on the lookout for such cues. If the child usually wanders aimlessly around the room before she exits, help her become involved in an activity. If she walks out after she becomes angry or frustrated, help her deal with those feelings more effectively.
5. If the child is already at the door and about to walk out, stop her. Put your arm around her, close the door, and turn back to the class. Tell the child that you want her to choose an activity. Help her become involved in one. If she struggles, keep a gentle but firm hold on her until she calms down. Do not discuss the situation at length; simply say, "You may not go out."
6. If the child usually leaves during group activities, you will need a different approach. One teacher should be seated with the child during group times. The child can either sit on the teacher's lap or next to the teacher. If the child tries to leave, the adult should restrain her by gently but firmly holding on to her until she stops struggling. (See Chapter 12 if the situation is one where the child regularly disrupts group time.)

Praise the Child for Engaging In Activities In the Classroom. The aim of this program is to get the child to remain in the classroom and to constructively engage in activities. Let the child know that you are pleased when she does so. Make a point of reinforcing her frequently through verbal praise, a smile, a pat, or a hug. Once the child decreases the attempts to leave the class, gradually cut down on the reinforcement until you are praising her at about the same rate as the other children in the group.

Provide Opportunities for the Child to Leave the Class Legitimately. Let the child know that there are appropriate reasons to leave the class, but these have to be approved by a teacher. The child may be sent on errands to the office or to another classroom. The responsibility of conveying a message helps the child feel important and trusted. The child should not be sent on an errand for at least half an hour after she has tried to leave the room. Such a responsibility should be given on a day when she has stayed in the room and was constructively involved.

Being able to send children on errands depends on the facility. Examine your building and surroundings to be sure such activity is suitable and safe. Take into account the age of the child in your class. Two-year-olds and young three-year-olds should not be sent out of the room alone. Older preschoolers enjoy such responsibilities and may be trusted.

Another way of legitimately leaving the room is through planned class activities. You might visit other classes, walk around the building, or visit the kitchen periodically.

Ignore Inappropriate Departures, If At All Possible. Your preventive measures should eliminate or considerably reduce the behavior. On occasion, however, the child may still leave the room. You have one of two options, depending on your facility:

1. If at all possible, ignore the child's behavior. The child is seeking the attention that usually follows her exits. The less attention given, the better. To ignore such behavior, prepare some safety precautions beforehand. The child should not be able to leave the school premises. Other adults in the building should be able to keep an eye on her once she is out of the class. Teachers in other classes, office personnel, and the kitchen staff should be alerted to the situation, asked not to give attention to the child, and requested to watch her carefully. Eventually the child will return to the class. At this point say nothing about the fact that she was gone. Tell her what activities are available, then praise her for being involved soon thereafter.

2. If, for safety reasons, you cannot let the child leave the room, redouble your preventive efforts. If on occasion the child does leave the room, follow her. With a minimum of fuss and attention, return the child to the class. Do not even give the child eye contact as you walk back with her. Once you are in the room, tell her, "You may not leave the classroom because it is not safe for you to be outside alone." Hold the child gently but firmly until she stops struggling, if this is the case. Help the child find an activity to engage in and give her praise once she is involved.

Continue Graphing the Behavior. Each day, keep track of the number of times the child actually leaves the room as well as the number of times she tries to leave. Define what indicates an attempt to leave so that all the teachers agree on what this means. An example might be that the child attempts to open the door. Because preventive measures should eliminate or nearly eliminate actual exits, it is necessary to include attempted departures in the daily count. You will not achieve your goal until the child voluntarily remains in the room. Recording only incidents where the child actually leaves the room may not give an accurate picture of the behavior.

Draw a vertical line after the baseline data and record each day's count as follows:

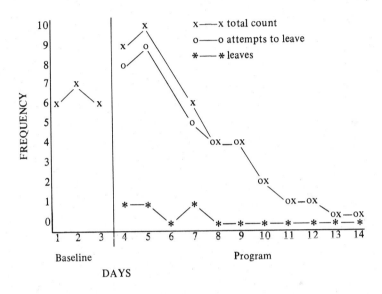

There should be few incidents of actual departures from the class. If there are many, examine the preventive measures. When the total is at zero for several days, the program may be considered successful and can be discontinued.

Maintenance

Continue praising the child for involvement in classroom activities. Also continue to examine all aspects of the environment to ensure that it is as stimulating as possible to the children. Once you interest the child in school, she should feel no need to leave the room.

CHILD'S NAME

AGE

DATE

RECORD KEEPING GRAPH

GOAL

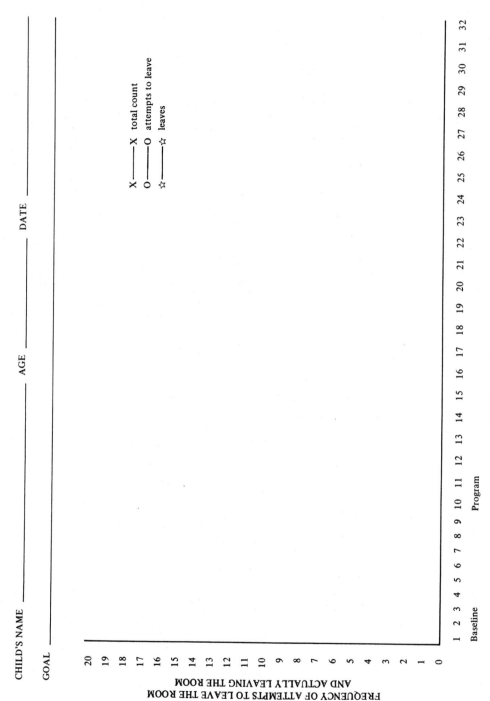

X——X total count
O——O attempts to leave
☆——☆ leaves

FREQUENCY OF ATTEMPTS TO LEAVE THE ROOM
AND ACTUALLY LEAVING THE ROOM

20 19 18 17 16 15 14 13 12 11 10 9 8 7 6 5 4 3 2 1 0

1 2 3 4 5 6 7 8 9 10 11 12 13 14 15 16 17 18 19 20 21 22 23 24 25 26 27 28 29 30 31 32

Baseline   Program

DAYS

CHAPTER 14

Running Aimlessly
Around the Classroom

It is activity time. The teachers have prepared and introduced several activities for the children. The children have selected the area in which they want to work. Three-year-old Sylvia chooses to go to the easel. She picks up a brush saturated with paint and makes a quick line down the center of the paper. She repeats with another such line, allowing the paint to drip down the paper and onto the floor. Sylvia returns the brush to the paint jar, flings off her paint smock, and shouts, "I'm done, teacher!" She walks to the block area, watches a few seconds, then goes to the manipulative table where several children are working. She takes out a puzzle, empties the pieces out of it, then walks away. After a quick look around the room, Sylvia runs to the bathroom. She quickly dashes out and darts back to the art area. Within a few seconds, Sylvia is running around the room, distracting children, interrupting play, and knocking over the block tower that Jimmy carefully built. Mrs. Anderson sighs. This is a typical day with Sylvia running aimlessly around the classroom. Mrs. Anderson catches Sylvia and says, "Stop running around, Sylvia. You need to find something to do." Sylvia smiles and walks over to the block area. Within half a minute she starts running around again. Again Mrs. Anderson asks Sylvia to stop, but succeeds in only a few more seconds of calm. The third time Mr. Gomez restrains Sylvia by holding her arms, saying, "Come on, Sylvia, let's find something for you to do." He takes the child by the hand and leads her to the sand table. Mr. Gomez collects several implements, stands by Sylvia for a couple of minutes, and talks with her while watching her play. He then walks away from the sand table area. A minute later, Sylvia is again on the run. The teachers feel exasperated. Sylvia's behavior continues in spite of their efforts.

STATE THE BEHAVIOR

The child runs around the classroom aimlessly rather than engaging in planned activities.

OBSERVE THE BEHAVIOR

Observe the child for a few days to gain insight into the behavior.

A. When does the behavior occur?
   - During planned activity times
   - During free choice activities
   - During group times such as story, discussion, or music
   - At cleanup times
   - During transitions

B. What seems to cause the behavior?
   - The child finishes an activity
   - The child plays with a particular child or a few children
   - Another child or several children exclude her from joining them in play
   - The child is not able to complete a task
   - The child is asked by a teacher to do something
   - The child expresses dislike for the planned activities
   - A teacher does not attend to the child when she asks for help or attention

C. What happens when the child engages in the behavior?
   - The child looks to see whether an adult is watching
   - The child runs right by one or more adults as she goes around the room
   - The child tries to get other children to join her
   - The child runs randomly through the various areas in the classroom or follows a specific route
   - The child makes noise as she runs around the room
   - The child runs around the room quietly
   - The child responds to a teacher trying to interest her in an activity

These preliminary observations should give you an idea of when and under what circumstances the child runs aimlessly around the classroom. Use this information to implement your plan.

EXPLORE THE CONSEQUENCES

Disruptive behavior is usually motivated by a need for attention. The child who engages in a disruption such as running aimlessly through the classroom is saying, "Hey! Look at me!" For one reason or another the child has found that she does not get adult attention as often as she needs it. She probably does not get enough reinforcement for appropriate behavior. The child also finds that adults pay attention to her when she is disruptive. As soon as she runs around the room, a teacher talks to her, attempts to stop her, scolds her, and tries to interest her in an activity. Running around the room results in adult attention. If this attention is not given quickly enough, the child increases the behavior to get a reaction from an adult. A teacher may provide the expected reinforcement, and thus cause a self-defeating pattern to emerge. The more a teacher tries to stop the child's aimless running about the room, the more the child is reinforced for engaging in this activity. Your informal observations may lead you to another conclusion, that the child has a very short attention span and, therefore, is unable to stay with an activity for any length of time. If this is the case, turn to Chapter 39, Short Attention Span. This chapter focuses on aimless running around the classroom used as an attention-seeking behavior.

CONSIDER ALTERNATIVES

Disruptive behaviors are often a response to the classroom environment. Examine the school carefully for potential problems before attempting to change the child's behavior.

- Take a critical look at classroom arrangement. The arrangement depends on the shape and size of the room and on the furnishings and equipment available. The arrangement should be related to the ages, total number, interests, and special needs of the children. Examine the placement of furniture, storage spaces, and equipment. Open spaces invite running. Poorly defined interest areas are not conducive to engagement in defined activities and can lead to frequent interruptions. All staff members should be involved in discussion and arrangement of the classroom.
- Another cause of disruptive behavior such as running about the classroom can be lack of availability of activities and materials. A child may become frustrated if activities are too difficult. She may become bored if activities are too simple, or frustrated if there are not enough materials for everyone. She may create her own diversions through disruptions. Carefully examine what is in the room in relation to the child's developmental level, needs, and interests. If only one child is reacting disruptively within the environment, consider whether another classroom might be more appropriate for her.

If aspects of the classroom environment do not seem to be the cause of the problem, continue on to the following program.

STATE THE GOAL

The goal is for the child to stop running aimlessly around the classroom and to engage instead in the activities planned for that time.

PROCEDURE

The basic strategy to eliminate aimless running around the room involves three simultaneous steps:

- Arrange the classroom environment to discourage such behavior as much as possible.
- Reinforce all occasions when the child is constructively engaged in activities.
- Ignore any running that may take place.

Definition

Running aimlessly around the classroom includes any incident in which the child runs about the room with no evident purpose instead of taking part in a game or activity.

Baseline

To know how often, on the average, the child runs about the room aimlessly, count the number of such incidents over a three-day period. If this behavior occurs only at specific times rather than throughout the day, decide on a specific time block to do the counting. Consistently use that same time period for all future counts. Mark down on paper each incident of aimless running when it occurs. At the end of each day, record this number on the Record Keeping Graph. These three days of counting before you implement any changes will provide a baseline.

Program

Start using the following program after collecting the baseline data. All teachers must follow these procedures at all times to provide the needed consistency to change the behavior.

Rearrange the Classroom to Discourage Running. All teachers should participate in a brainstorming session to arrange the classroom more effectively. The aim is to discourage running by eliminating any straight, empty stretches that exist in the room. Do not block exits or place small obstacles in the direct path of traffic, but use furniture and materials as effective dividers and definers of space.

The two illustrations show the same furnishings arranged differently in the same room. In Room A, the length of the room is open to running. Although furnishings are grouped by interest areas, the spaces surrounding these are not well defined. Children playing in different areas can easily get in one another's way. These problems are solved in Room B. Much of the running space is eliminated because the furniture arrangement uses all of the space in the room, not just the edges. Interest areas are defined. Each group of furnishings defines its own, contained space. Children can work without outside interference.

If a child in the classroom spends too much time running aimlessly around the room rather than engaging in constructive activities, carefully examine the room first. Rearrange it to best facilitate the behavior you want. Once you have made room changes, continue to evaluate the classroom and make appropriate changes. There is no one right way of arranging a classroom, but some arrangements are better than others.

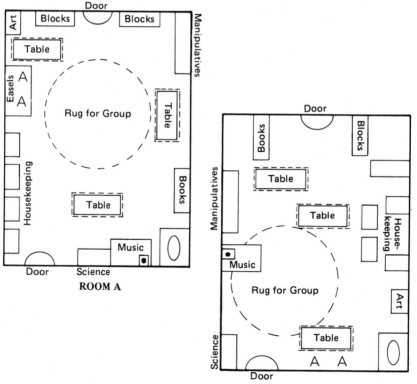

Reinforce the Child For Being Constructively Engaged In Activities. You want the child to replace aimless running around the room with constructive participation in planned or self-selected activities. Reinforce this behavior when it occurs. Whenever the child is constructively engaged, tell her you are pleased. Praise her socialization, her work, her technique, her product, or whatever else is appropriate. Time such reinforcement to maximize its effect:

1. At first, praise the child every time you see her engaged in constructive activity. If she stays with an activity, reinforce her about every two minutes.
2. As the child decreases aimless running and increases activity involvement, gradually decrease the frequency of praise.
3. Finally, once the child's behavior has reached the goal, cut back reinforcement. Praise this child with about the same frequency as you praise the other children in the class.

If the Child Does Run Around the Room, Ignore the Behavior. It is difficult to ignore the child when she is running around the room, because such behavior is very disruptive to classroom functioning. However, it is important that all teachers completely ignore this behavior when it occurs. For the first few days this behavior may be more intense than usual. The child may await the customary adult reactions. Once the child realizes that there is no reinforcement forthcoming for such aimless running, the behavior should quickly disappear.

Continue Graphing the Behavior. Continue recording the number of running incidents that occur each day on the Record Keeping Graph. Collect this information during the same time period that baseline data were gathered. This graph provides the information you need to decide when to decrease reinforcement for positive behaviors.

Maintenance

Continue reassessing the room arrangement in relation to the behavior of all the children, even after the running problem has been resolved. Continue giving intermittent praise for the behaviors you expect. These measures should prevent any further incidents of aimless running since the child realizes that she will not be getting further attention for them.

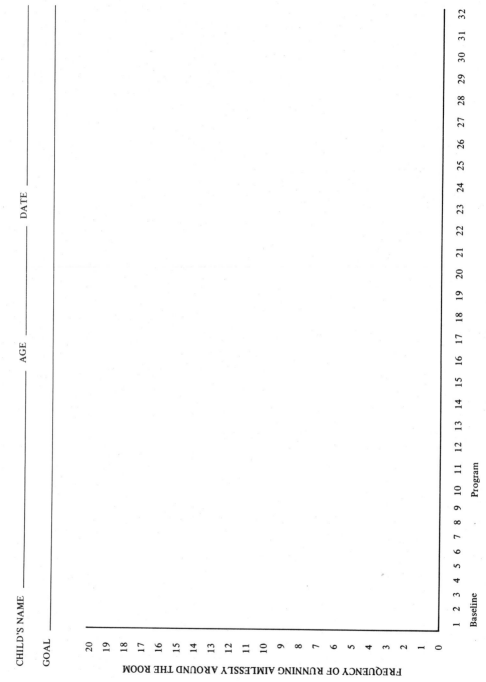

RECORD KEEPING GRAPH

CHILD'S NAME _____ AGE _____ DATE _____

GOAL _____

FREQUENCY OF RUNNING AIMLESSLY AROUND THE ROOM

20
19
18
17
16
15
14
13
12
11
10
9
8
7
6
5
4
3
2
1
0

1 2 3 4 5 6 7 8 9 10 11 12 13 14 15 16 17 18 19 20 21 22 23 24 25 26 27 28 29 30 31 32

Baseline   Program

DAYS

CHAPTER 15

Shouting in
the Classroom

A piercing whoop interrupts the normal noise level of the class of four-year-olds. "Stop that, Charles!" says one of the teachers, while the other two turn toward the source of the noise and grimace. Charles gives them each an engaging smile, then continues with his play. A few minutes later Charles gives an extended Tarzan call, and soon thereafter he shrieks with an ear-splitting intensity. Statements like, "Stop it, Charles!" and "Charles, you're really bothering everybody!" are accompanied by sighs, ear-covering motions, and scathing looks from the adults. Charles, who is physically small for his age but bright and verbal, has been making noisy interruptions since school began two months ago. They occur primarily indoors and during activity times, storytimes, singing, and group discussions. The teachers are bothered by Charles' disruptions, which interfere with the smooth functioning of the class.

STATE THE BEHAVIOR

The child makes unnecessarily loud noises in school at inappropriate times.

OBSERVE THE BEHAVIOR

Take some time to observe the child informally to gain insight into the behavior.

A. When does the behavior occur?
- At any time of day
- At times when children are expected to remain relatively quiet
- During outdoor play
- Indoors

- During self-selected activities
- During activity times
- During group activities such as music, story, dance, or discussion
- At nap or rest times
- During transitions

B. What seems to precipitate the behavior?
  - There is general quiet in the classroom
  - There is an overall high noise level in the classroom
  - The child is engaged in solitary play or activity
  - The child is involved in social play
  - The child is involved in spontaneous role-playing activity
  - Others talk during group activities
  - The child plays with a particular child or group of children
  - The child is asked to do a particular task, such as help with cleanup time

C. What happens when the child shouts?
  - The child looks around to see if an adult is going to react
  - The child repeats the noise one or more times
  - The child seems upset
  - The child smiles
  - The child tries to get other children to join in the noise
  - The child becomes upset when reprimanded by an adult
  - The child seems unconcerned about adult reactions

You should now have an idea of the circumstances under which the child makes unnecessary noise in the classroom. Use such information to find a solution to the problem.

EXPLORE THE CONSEQUENCES

Probably at some point in the past, the child found that adults react very quickly to loud noises. The louder and more piercing the noise made by the child, the greater the reaction. Such response from adults only reinforces the behavior. The child shouts, and an adult reacts. The next time the child wants adult reaction he shouts and an adult reacts, and thus the cycle perpetuates itself. Because loud noise above the normal volume in the classroom is disruptive, teachers feel compelled to react quickly when it happens. Teachers reinforce shouting, and the behavior continues as long as adults pay attention to it.

CONSIDER ALTERNATIVES

There might be a simple solution for dealing with the child who shouts unnecessarily. Carefully consider the following suggestions.

- Examine your expectations for the children to be sure that they are appropriate for the age and developmental level of the class. Young children should not be expected to remain very quiet. They are exuberant and enjoy making noises appropriate to their play. An active and productive preschool classroom is not always a quiet place.
- It is possible that a child whose voice level is slightly louder than that of the other children has been repeatedly asked to "keep it down." The child concludes that making noise is a good way to get attention. In such a case, faulty adult expectations have led to inappropriate behavior. Work on eliminating shouting, but keep in mind that the child normally speaks loudly.
- A child who is frequently loud may have a hearing problem. Young children are susceptible to ear infections, which sometimes cause blockages and result in hearing loss. Consider such a possibility carefully. The child may be loud or make loud noises simply to reassure himself that he can be heard. If you suspect a hearing problem, try a crude test. Make various noises behind the child and watch for reactions. If the test confirms your suspicion, ask the parents to have the child's hearing tested.
- Examine your schedule to see whether it is too restrictive for the children. The youngsters may react to an overly structured situation by disruptive means such as shouting. You may be expecting the children to listen, engage in activities where they are given no choices, or sit quietly for periods that are too long. If this is the case, rearrange your daily schedule. Alternate quiet and active times. Alternate teacher-directed and child-selected activities. Decrease the length of group times as appropriate.
- Be sure that the child who shouts understands your expectations. Tell him that he may shout outside as much as he wants, but that indoors his voice level needs to be kept down. If the child cannot abide by such a rule, then move to the following program.

STATE THE GOAL

The goal is for the child to keep his voice at an appropriate level in the classroom.

PROCEDURE

Essentially, the strategy to eliminate disruptive shouting involves these steps:

- Give attention to appropriate classroom behaviors.
- Provide for a "noisy time."
- Ignore incidents of shouting.

Definition

Shouting includes all instances where the child raises his voice well above what is acceptable in the classroom. In addition to shouting this may include yelling, shrieking, whooping, and other annoying loud noises.

Baseline

Before working on changing the behavior, take three days to count the number of daily shouts. This will provide baseline data against which you compare improvements. If a child makes unnecessary noise mostly during a specific time period, use only this period in which to count shouts. Specify an hour to use consistently every day to gather data. Keep a pencil and paper handy for marking down each time the child shouts. At the end of each day record the total on the Record Keeping Graph.

Program

Once you have gathered baseline data, you are ready to begin. It is very important that all teachers follow this program consistently.

Reinforce Appropriate Classroom Behaviors. Whenever you try to eliminate a behavior, it is also important to let the child know what behaviors you expect and value. Therefore, make a point of praising the child frequently for appropriate behaviors. This should include keeping voice level down as well as engaging in activities and social play, and contributing to discussions. At first, reinforce such behaviors as often as possible. Later, as the frequency of shouting decreases, gradually decrease such praise. Give praise for such behaviors at about the same rate as you give it to other children in the class.

Provide For A Daily "Noisy Time." Make a clear distinction between appropriate and inappropriate places in which one can make noise. Tell all the children in the class that there will be a noisy time when they go outside. Encourage them to "save" noises for this occasion. Design the noisy time to what you are comfortable with. You might, for instance, let all of the children together make as much noise as possible for a few seconds. (You may have to forewarn people who work or live nearby.) Another approach is to have the children take turns sharing noises.

The reason for the noisy time is to provide a legitimate outlet for the urge to make noise and to designate appropriate and inappropriate times and places to make noise. As with any novelty, the children will probably enjoy this for a while. When their interest wanes, you can discontinue this activity. By that time the child who was making inappropriate noise in the classroom should have substantially decreased or completely stopped the behavior.

Ignore Incidents Of Shouting When They Do Occur. Whenever the child shouts, do not react in any way. It is important that all adults in the classroom act consistently in this matter. The child receives considerable reinforcement through the reactions of adults whenever he shouts. Therefore, when all attention is withdrawn, expect the behavior to increase. You will probably have to tolerate quite a bit of noise for the first day or two of ignoring. Once the child realizes that no one is paying attention, he will quickly decrease, then stop, the behavior. Other youngsters may call your attention to the noise. Simply say, "I know," then go on to talk about something else. Use any opportunity to praise the child for appropriate behaviors. Make your message as clear as possible. The child gets attention for acceptable behaviors, but is ignored for shouting.

Continue Graphing the Behavior. As you implement the program, continue to count and record behaviors on the Record Keeping Graph. Record the total count each day. Most likely the count will increase on the first day or two. It should drop quickly to zero if the program is consistently followed.

Maintenance

After the rate of shouting is at zero for a few days, consider the program successful. Continue praising desired behaviors periodically, as you do with all the children. If, on occasion, the child does revert to shouting, ignore it completely.

RECORD KEEPING GRAPH

CHILD'S NAME _____ AGE _____ DATE _____

GOAL _____

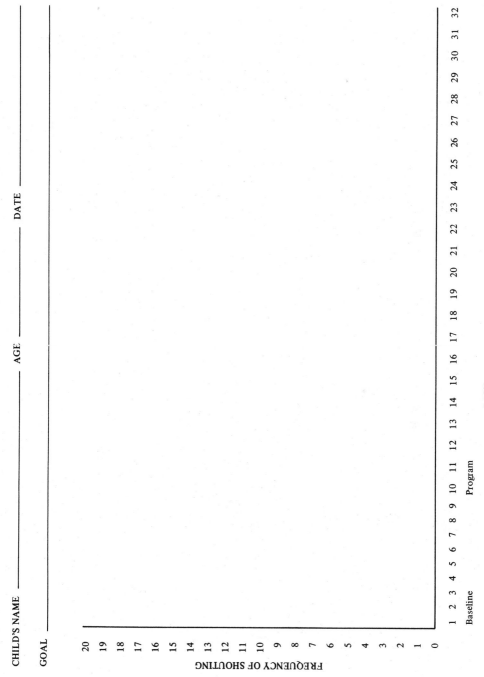

FREQUENCY OF SHOUTING

20 19 18 17 16 15 14 13 12 11 10 9 8 7 6 5 4 3 2 1 0

1 2 3 4 5 6 7 8 9 10 11 12 13 14 15 16 17 18 19 20 21 22 23 24 25 26 27 28 29 30 31 32

Baseline   Program

DAYS

CHAPTER 16

16

Dropping Objects to Create Noise

Crash!! The adults and children look toward the source of the noise. Five-year-old George is standing next to the overturned wooden refrigerator in the housekeeping area. It is apparent that he dropped the refrigerator simply to make noise. Earlier in the day, George collected a number of blocks, placed them on a shelf, then climbed on the shelf to drop the blocks, one by one, onto the linoleum below. Two teachers ran toward George. One teacher lifted him off the shelf and put him on the floor. The other rescued the blocks. Both adults conveyed their displeasure about the incident to George. During all this time, George's face reflected pleasure about the event. He nodded when asked if he would please not do that again. George put away the blocks and righted the refrigerator in response to a teacher's request. The teachers feel frustrated because they know, from past history, that George will again drop objects for the sake of making noise.

STATE THE BEHAVIOR

The child deliberately drops objects onto the floor or another surface for the purpose of making noise.

OBSERVE THE BEHAVIOR

Observe the child for a couple of days to gain an understanding of the circumstances under which deliberate dropping of objects takes place.

A. When does this behavior usually occur?
  - At any time of day
  - During free choice periods

- During activity times
- During structured activities
- During activities when children are required to listen, such as story or music times
- At quiet times like rest or nap times
- During cleanup time
- During transitions

B. What happens before the child drops an object?

- The child is involved in play with other children
- The child is involved in solitary play
- The child looks around to see where adults are
- The child collects objects
- Another child or a teacher says no to him
- The child cannot complete a task
- The child is asked to keep quiet

C. What happens when the child drops an object?

- The child tries to make it look like an accident
- The child makes a point of showing that it was a deliberate act
- The child voluntarily picks up and replaces the object
- The child picks up the object when asked to by a teacher
- The child refuses to pick up the object
- The child gets upset by a teacher's reaction
- The child shows no concern

D. What objects does the child drop?

- Anything
- Usually the same object or same type of object
- Large items
- Small items
- Wooden, metal, plastic, or cardboard items
- Breakable items
- Nonbreakable items
- Items that make noise on impact

E. Where does the child drop objects?

- Anywhere
- On cement
- On wood
- On tile
- On linoleum
- On carpeting
- On tables or shelves

This preliminary observation should give you some clues about the behavior. Use these clues when you implement the program to eliminate the dropping of objects.

EXPLORE THE CONSEQUENCES

Children who engage in being disruptive do so because they enjoy the attention such behavior brings. The child who deliberately drops objects for the sake of the noise this creates is no different. Such behavior quickly brings adults to the spot for several reasons. First, the noise from the dropped object is irritating. Second, although preschool materials are made to be sturdy, rough handling through deliberate dropping can result in damage. Finally, this behavior is potentially dangerous because someone could be inadvertently hurt. For these reasons, adults respond swiftly and give considerable attention to the child who has deliberately dropped something. Not only do teachers lecture and scold the child for such behavior, but they insist that the child pick up what has been dropped. At this point the child may well prolong the attention by changing the issue. He may refuse to clean up. The resulting power struggle between the teacher who says, "Yes, you will pick up these items" and the child who responds, "No, I won't" can ensure several more minutes of attention. Consequently, the child receives satisfaction by dropping objects for the sake of making noise. Meanwhile, the adults are frustrated. Their reactions reinforce rather than eliminate the behavior.

CONSIDER ALTERNATIVES

Consider the following ideas carefully. One may provide a solution to the behavior.

- The child may have a hearing problem. A child who has trouble hearing may be trying to reassure himself that he can be heard by making deliberate noises. Conduct a crude test by making various noises behind the child and checking for reactions. If this procedure confirms your concern, talk to the parents and recommend that they have the child's hearing checked.
- The child may drop objects because of a physical disability. An eye problem may cause the child to bump into and knock over objects frequently. Similarly, poorly developed eye-hand coordination can result in objects being dropped more often than normal accidents would warrant. If you

suspect such a problem, recommend further medical testing to the parents.

- The room environment may invite such behavior. For instance, interest areas in which play is usually noisy should be carpeted. The block area must contain some kind of soft floor covering. The housekeeping area might also benefit from carpeting if it is available. When hard objects are placed on hard flooring, noise occurs naturally. This may well present the original idea for disruptive behavior to a child. Noise which results from dropping a hard object on a hard floor gets adult attention. This behavior may become a repeated one.

- If the child's behavior is focused on turning over large items, such as housekeeping furniture, rearrange these. You might place these items against a wall so the child cannot get behind and push. You could back the items against the rear of another piece of furniture, such as shelves or storage units.

- If the child drops only one particular object or type of object, consider removing it temporarily from the classroom. If, for instance, the child repeatedly drops dishes from the housekeeping area on the floor, remove the dishes for a while. You might convert the area into a store by replacing the dishes with empty food cartons, a cash register and paper bags. After two or three weeks, try replacing the removed items.

- Be sure that the child understands the purpose of the various materials and equipment in the classroom. Systematic help in learning how to use them may stop the disruptive behavior of dropping things. A child will respect the equipment more if he understands it.

If none of these suggestions helps in providing a resolution to the problem, continue to the following program.

STATE THE GOAL

The goal is for this child to stop dropping objects for the purpose of making noise.

PROCEDURE

To reach this goal, your basic strategy will involve three simultaneous procedures:

- Prevent the dropping of objects whenever possible.
- Reinforce appropriate use of materials and equipment.
- Ignore the behavior when it occurs.

Definition

Dropping objects to create noise includes any incident in which the child deliberately drops an object on the floor or other surface, for the purpose of making noise. Objects may be dropped or thrust downward from any height onto the floor or any other surface.

Baseline

Before you begin to implement changes, take three days to gather baseline data. Mark on paper every time the child deliberately drops something. At the end of each day transfer the total number to the Record Keeping Graph. The information from these three days gives a count against which to compare later change.

Program

Now begin the following program. It must be followed by all the teachers in the class consistently.

Prevent the Dropping of Objects Whenever Possible. From your informal observation you should have some clues about what precedes the behavior. Use these clues to prevent the child from carrying out his intention. For example, if the child usually collects objects before dropping them, watch for such behavior. When you see him collecting items, go to the child and engage him in a situation where these items will be used appropriately. Say, "I see that you've gathered some puzzle pieces together. Let's put them into the puzzle frames where they belong." Or, you might have noted that the child looks around for a few seconds to find an object to drop. If you see this, go to the child and direct his interest elsewhere.

It is possible that dropping of objects occurs whenever the child plays with certain other youngsters, with a particular toy, or in a particular interest area. When you see the child in a situation that often precedes dropping objects, stay nearby and guide the situation to avoid such behavior.

Reinforce Appropriate Use of Materials. Because dropping objects is an inappropriate way of handling classroom materials and equipment, let the child know that you are pleased when he uses objects properly. Convey to the child the need for respect of the items through your reinforcement. Say, for instance,

"You are really using the paints carefully."
"I like the way you're turning the pages of that book so they won't tear."
"Thank you! You certainly stacked those pots and pans nicely."
"What a great way to use those blocks! First you built a road and now you're using the small blocks as cars."

At first, reinforce appropriate use of materials as often as possible. When the child's rate of object-dropping decreases, cut back gradually on the amount of praise you give. Eventually, reinforce the child's careful handling of materials as often as you would praise such behavior in the other children.

Ignore the Dropping of Objects If It Does Occur. The child is reinforced by teacher attention when he drops objects. Withdraw that attention to stop the behavior. It is difficult at first to ignore dropping of objects since the behavior will probably increase before it decreases. But once the child gets the message that no one will pay attention to the behavior, he will stop it. If the child does drop an object, none of the adults in the classroom should react in any way. Act as if nothing has happened. If another child calls your attention to the noise, simply say, "I know," and change the subject. Do not make an issue of forcing the child to pick up the dropped item. If it does not present a safety hazard, leave it where it is. If someone might stumble over it, wait a minute, and then quietly move it out of the way. If an object was broken and presents a danger, sweep up the pieces without saying anything about the incident to the child. When cleanup time comes, treat the dropped object like all the other items that need to be put away.

It may seem natural to insist that the child pick up and put away the dropped item. Ask him only once, in a matter-of-fact manner, to pick it up. If he does, praise him. If he does not, turn away. Such a situation can easily lead to a confrontation which, in turn, provides attention from you. Use other opportunities to teach the need to clean up.

Continue Graphing the Behavior. Each day of the program, continue counting incidents of deliberate object-dropping. Record the data on the Record Keeping Graph. Draw a vertical line after the baseline data to differentiate between before- and after-program implementation scores. It is likely that once the child realizes there is no attention forthcoming for dropping objects, the behavior will quickly decrease and then disappear.

Maintenance

To ensure that object dropping will not happen again, continue giving periodic reinforcement for proper use of materials and equipment. If the behavior recurs, ignore it the same way you did in the program.

RECORD KEEPING GRAPH

CHILD'S NAME _____ AGE _____ DATE _____

GOAL _____

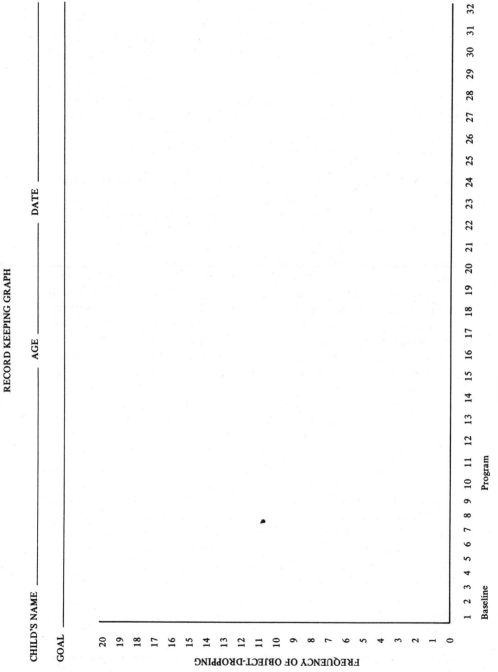

SECTION 3
DESTRUCTIVE BEHAVIORS

CHAPTER 17

17

Tearing Books

A soft sound catches Ms. Larkin's attention. She turns to find Jamie with the ripped page of a book in his hand. The two-and-a-half-year-old recently began attending the day care center and is still discovering the do's and don'ts of school. "Oh, no, Jamie! That's a library book!" Ms. Larkin rushes to Jamie, takes the book from him, and looks in dismay at the ripped page. She sits down by Jamie, tells him that he may not tear books, and explains why. Jamie listens and nods when asked if he will not do that again. Ms. Larkin is not hopeful because this is the third book Jamie ripped today. Over the past two weeks Jamie has damaged several books. The teachers talk to Jamie and have him help repair the books with tape. Last week the director talked to Jamie's parents to tell them they had to assume the cost of replacement of library books. Jamie's father told Ms. Larkin that Jamie got "a good paddling" for what he did. Jamie has continued to tear books.

STATE THE BEHAVIOR

The child regularly and frequently tears the pages of books deliberately.

OBSERVE THE BEHAVIOR

To gain more information about the behavior, spend a few days observing the child.

A. When does the behavior occur?
- During free choice activities
- During planned activity times
- During group times when a teacher reads books
- After storytime

- At cleanup time
- During transitions
- During nap time

B. What happens before the child tears a book?

- The child looks through a book
- The child plays alone
- The child plays with another child or group of children
- The child is excluded from play by a group of children
- The child is frustrated with a task
- A teacher or a peer tells the child no
- The child wanders aimlessly around the room

C. What does the child do when he tears a book?

- The child looks to see whether an adult is watching just before he tears a page
- The child looks to see whether a teacher heard or saw just after tearing
- The child continues tearing pages
- The child puts the book back on a shelf
- The child leaves the book lying on the floor or on a table
- The child walks away from the torn book
- The child calls attention to the torn book
- The child laughs about what has happened
- The child gets upset because the book is torn
- The child apologizes for the damage

Such observations should give you some idea of the circumstances under which the child tears books. Use this information to help eliminate the behavior.

EXPLORE THE CONSEQUENCES

Acquiring respect for material objects is one of the things children learn during the preschool years. The equipment, games, toys, and other items in the school need to be treated with care so they can be enjoyed and used by others. Most preschool materials are made to be very sturdy, but some items, like books, are more fragile. Children who have been around books usually understand that they need to be handled carefully. Occasionally, however, a child treats books disrespectfully, damaging them in the process. The reason for such behavior may vary. The child may, for instance, damage books because he has never been taught that books need special care. Or the child may lack the physical coordination to turn the pages without tearing them. Finally, the child may have learned that damaging a book brings attention from the teachers, and therefore continues to do it. Whenever the child rips the page of a book, adults get very excited, talk to him about his behavior, and may even engage him in helping to fix the book. There is a great deal of adult attention for the child who tears a book, and he may tear pages more often to earn this attention. When a child repeatedly tears pages of books, he is telling you that he has found a definite way of gaining teacher attention.

CONSIDER ALTERNATIVES

There may be some environmental changes that can help you eliminate the tearing of books. Carefully consider the following suggestions before moving on to the program for changing the child's behavior.

- The concern a teacher has for the items in a classroom is conveyed through the way they are arranged in the room. If books are haphazardly strewn around the class, it is an unspoken message that books are not really very important. Examine the way books are stored. They should be arranged attractively in a quiet area of the class. If possible, the book area should be somewhat enclosed to discourage unnecessary traffic. A few carefully displayed books are more attractive than many cluttered books on a shelf. Consider arranging five to ten books so that the fronts of the books face out rather than having forty books packed into the shelf with only the spines showing. Rotate the books frequently to introduce new ones as the children are ready for them.
- If the child who tears books is in a class of very young children, the books you provide may be inappropriate. Very young preschoolers are just beginning to learn how to handle books carefully. Furthermore, their small motor control may not be developed enough to turn thin paper pages properly without tearing them. For a class of primarily two-year-olds, provide toddler books. Such books are made more durably of cardboard or cloth. They are also designed for very young children by portraying common objects, using simple designs, showing bold colors, and telling a simple story. As two-year-olds graduate to older classrooms, they become more adept at handling books.
- A young child may tear books because he enjoys the experience of tearing. Supply paper for this purpose in the art area. Invite the child to engage in a tearing activity by providing different colored papers and old magazines. The products of the tearing activity may be used for a collage.

If none of these suggestions is appropriate for solving the problem, continue to the following program.

STATE THE GOAL

The goal is for the child to stop tearing books, while learning to use them appropriately.

PROCEDURE

The basic strategy to eliminate tearing of books involves several simultaneous steps:

- Prevent the child from tearing books.
- Make any necessary environmental changes.
- Reinforce the child for appropriate behavior.
- Ignore the inappropriate behavior.

Definition

Tearing books is defined as any deliberate ripping of the pages of books which happens on a regular basis.

Baseline

Before starting on the program to change this behavior, gather some baseline information. For three days count the number of times the child tears a page of a book. Record each incident by marking it down on paper. For consistency in counting, consider each page ripped as a separate incident. If the child takes a book and systematically tears four pages, record four marks. If, however, two or three pages are torn together in one ripping motion, count this as only one incident. At the end of each day, transfer the total number on to the Record Keeping Graph.

Program

Once you have baseline data, implement the following procedures. It is important that all teachers follow the program consistently.

Prevent the Tearing of Books Whenever Possible. From your informal observation, you should have some clues as to when book-tearing incidents occur and what precedes them. Use these clues to help prevent such behavior. If, for instance, you find that the behavior happens only when the child is playing by himself, and never when he is engaged with a group of children, be more alert to potential book-tearing when he is alone. Stay near the child and keep an eye on any moves toward the book area. Or you might have found that the behavior occurs primarily during cleanup time. In such a case, focus your attention on the child at that time. Utilize cues from your initial observations to help you pinpoint when and how preventive efforts should be used.

Facilitate Prevention of Book-tearing Incidents Through Environmental Changes. The arrangement of the classroom may help teachers prevent incidents of book tearing. The following are some suggestions to help implement such changes:

1. Make the book area more appealing and cozy to encourage reading rather than destructiveness. If necessary, rearrange the entire classroom to find a good spot for the book area. Display only a few books in an attractive manner. Provide one or two simple activities to supplement the books. Set out a few seashells if you have books on shells or oceans. Include a matching game on animals and their homes if you put out books on houses. A warm carpet, pillows, or bean-bag chairs also serve to make this area appealing.
2. Be sure that the book area is visible from most parts of the room. If teachers are to prevent the tearing of books, they should be able to see the area at a glance. The area should retain its coziness and air of seclusion, and at the same time remain visible to teachers from other areas.
3. Another approach might be to incorporate the book area more firmly into the curriculum and activities of the class. For instance, the book and dramatic play areas might be combined to become a library. Children can role play as librarians and customers. Books can be checked out, shelved, and returned. A reading area can be arranged next to the checkout desk. By making the book area a more active part of the room in this way, a teacher can supervise the activity and carry out preventive measures to avert the tearing of books.

Reinforce Appropriate Behaviors. The child needs to know what behaviors are expected as well as what is considered inappropriate. When you begin this program, let the child know what behaviors you appreciate and what you do not like in relation to his handling of classroom materials. Do this at a time when the child has not torn pages of a book, and speak to the child in a friendly and relaxed manner. Say, for instance, "I really appreciate it when you stack the blocks carefully and put the shoes neatly on the shelf. That is the way we should take care of everything in our classroom. I get very upset, though, when you tear books. Other children can't enjoy the books once they have been ruined." Be alert to instances when the child handles materials carefully and frequently give praise for these actions. Reinforce expected behaviors to focus attention on what is appropriate. Eventually the child will find that it is more rewarding to handle classroom materials respectfully rather than to mishandle them. When the frequency of book tearing decreases by about half, start to decrease the frequency of praise for appropriate behaviors. When the child completely stops tearing books, gradually decrease praise. Finally, praise the child as often as you do the other children for taking care of classroom items.

Ignore Book-tearing When It Occurs. If the child does tear a book in spite of your preventive efforts, take the following steps:

1. Go quickly to the child. Take the book away from him and say, "No! You may not tear the book."
2. Move away from the child and give him no further attention for two minutes.
3. If the child is in the midst of other books and you think he may tear another one (based on his behavior during your initial observation), remove him from the area. Take the child by the hand or pick him up if he resists, and move him across the room. Say nothing while you move him and avoid eye contact. Give no attention for the next two minutes.
4. After two minutes, go to the child and try to involve him in another activity. Do not lecture or discuss the incident.

It may be difficult for you to ignore book-tearing incidents because such behavior is destructive and should be dealt with. Remember, however, that your reactions, no matter how negative, still provide attention to the child for the behavior. Ignoring simply removes that attention. These steps should help eliminate book-tearing with time.

Continue Graphing the Behavior. As you implement the program, continue counting the number of book-tearing incidents. Use the Record Keeping Graph. Draw a line after the baseline data and record the total as you did each day during baseline. Keeping the graph helps you see progress and indicates when you have reached your goal.

Maintenance

When the child has stopped deliberately tearing books, maintain this behavior by continuing periodic praise for handling classroom materials with care. Continue assessing the arrangement of the room to be sure that it conveys your respect for books. If the child tears a book again, ignore the incident. At a somewhat later time let the child know that you are very disappointed with such behavior. Do not belabor the point.

RECORD KEEPING GRAPH

CHILD'S NAME _____ AGE _____ DATE _____

GOAL _____

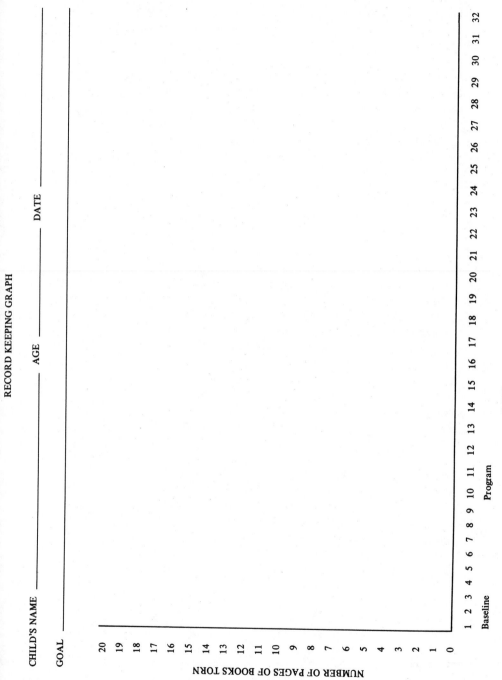

NUMBER OF PAGES OF BOOKS TORN

20
19
18
17
16
15
14
13
12
11
10
9
8
7
6
5
4
3
2
1
0

1 2 3 4 5 6 7 8 9 10 11 12 13 14 15 16 17 18 19 20 21 22 23 24 25 26 27 28 29 30 31 32

Baseline   Program

DAYS

CHAPTER 18

18

Breaking Toys

The class of four-year-olds at the day care center is busy today. Children are involved in a variety of activities. A sudden loud crunching noise is heard above the normal sounds of the room. All three teachers look around simultaneously to see Jenny with her foot on a plastic shape box. Two of the teachers run toward Jenny, who gives the broken box a swift kick and says, "I hate that thing!" One teacher picks up Jenny and moves her, while the other examines the broken toy. "We might as well throw it away," the teacher says in disgust. She searches the floor for broken splinters. Meanwhile, Jenny throws down the oval shape she is holding in her hand and tries to walk away. "Wait a minute, Jenny. You broke another toy. Why did you do that?" Jenny yells, "That dumb piece wouldn't go in. That thing doesn't work anyway. I'm glad it's broken!" The teachers do not know what to do. This is the third toy Jenny has broken this week, and they follow a series of other materials that Jenny has damaged and destroyed.

STATE THE BEHAVIOR

The child deliberately and regularly breaks toys and other materials in the classroom.

OBSERVE THE BEHAVIOR

Spend a few days informally observing the child to gain further insight into the behavior.

A. When does the child usually break toys?
- Unpredictably, at any time of day
- Early in the day

- Late in the day
- During planned activity times
- During free choice activities
- During outdoor play
- Indoors
- During cleanup time
- During transitions
- Around nap time

B. What happens before the child breaks a toy?
- The child is angry
- The child is frustrated with a task
- Another child or a teacher tells her no
- Exclusion from play by another child or by other children
- Prevention from engaging in an activity
- The child is not productively engaged in an activity
- An activity ends

C. What does the child do when she breaks a toy?
- The child looks around to see if an adult is watching
- The child calls a teacher's attention to the broken toy
- The child tries to hide the broken parts
- The child gets upset because the toy is broken
- The child appears unconcerned
- The child walks away from the broken pieces
- The child stays nearby
- The child continues to play with the broken toy
- The child denies breaking it, if asked
- The child admits it
- The child offers an explanation for why the toy broke

D. What kinds of toys are usually broken?
- Any kind
- Large
- Small
- Wooden
- Plastic
- Cardboard
- Metal
- Fabric
- Toys with moving parts
- Items from a particular interest area, such as art or housekeeping

E. How does the child usually break toys?
- The child throws items to the floor with force
- The child tears them

- The child steps on them
- The child rips or pulls apart the toys
- The child forcibly breaks or snaps off parts
- The child pounds the toy with another item
- The child takes out screws or other fasteners

This initial observation should help you gain some idea of when and under what circumstances the child breaks toys.

EXPLORE THE CONSEQUENCES

A child who deliberately breaks toys poses a potential safety hazard to the classroom. Broken or jagged edges on toys, if not removed or repaired immediately, can seriously hurt another child or the child who broke the toy. Furthermore, when toys are damaged, there is cost and time involved in replacement or repair. For these reasons this behavior needs to be eliminated quickly.

It is not always easy to stop a child who engages in such behavior. The child who habitually destroys toys has found a way of gaining immediate attention from adults. Whenever the child breaks a toy, an adult quickly and noticeably responds. Such responses may be verbal (talking, scolding), emotional (show of anger, dismay, frustration), or physical (picking up the broken pieces, throwing them away, repairing them). More than one adult is involved if the teacher who originally responds consults with other teachers or the director of the school. The child gets a great deal of attention when she destroys a toy.

Breaking toys may serve as a way of expressing anger for the child. The typical reactions of adults do not help the child cope with such feelings as anger. The adults' responses provide attention which does not deal with the feelings of anger. This attention does not help eliminate the behavior; it only reinforces it.

CONSIDER ALTERNATIVES

There may be a relatively simple solution to the problem of the child who habitually breaks toys. Consider the following suggestions.

- The child's toy-breaking behavior may not be deliberate. Examine all materials in the classroom to see whether they are as durable as preschool materials should be. It is possible that a number of items in the class are fragile and the child plays rather roughly with them. In this case the breaking of toys may not be deliberate.

- Examine the materials in the classroom for age-appropriateness. If children feel either frustrated or unchallenged by items in the room, they may use them in unacceptable ways. Toys may be broken as a result. If toys in the room are not appropriate for the children, change the materials quickly. This may require exchanging materials with other classes in the school, bringing items out of storage, or gradually buying or making new toys.
- A child may break toys because of curiosity. If a child frequently ruins toys by taking them apart, she may simply be trying to find out what makes the toys work. In such a case talk to the child about the inappropriateness of her behavior. Provide her with items that she can legitimately take apart. These may include old watches, alarm clocks, and other mechanical devices that no longer work. Furnish screw drivers, blunt tweezers, and other tools for tinkering, and supervise such activities to ensure safety.

If none of these suggestions helps to solve the problem of frequently broken toys, then continue with the following program.

STATE THE GOAL

The goal is for the child to stop the deliberate breaking of toys.

PROCEDURE

The basic strategy to eliminate breaking of toys involves four simultaneous steps:

- Prevent toy-breaking incidents whenever possible.
- Praise careful handling of classroom materials.
- Systematically teach the child to control her impulse to break toys.
- Use time-out if the child does break a toy.

Definition

Breaking toys involves any instance where the child deliberately destroys classroom materials or equipment. Do not include unsuccessful attempts to inflict damage.

Baseline

Spend three days to find out how often the child breaks toys. Such information provides a baseline with which to compare later improvement. Mark on paper each time the child breaks a toy. At the end of each day record the total on the Record Keeping Graph. If the behavior is not a daily occurrence, recall how many times per week, over the past three weeks, toys were broken, and make the count on a weekly basis.

Program

After collecting baseline data, begin to implement the following program. It is important that all teachers follow the procedures consistently.

Prevent Toy-breaking Incidents Whenever Possible. Your informal information gathering should provide some clues about when and under what circumstances the child breaks toys. Use this information to help you prevent the behavior as often as possible. If the child consistently engages in this destructive behavior during a particular time of the day, be particularly vigilant at such times. Also, watch for behaviors that tend to precede toy-breaking. If the child usually breaks things when she is playing alone, then stay nearby and help her avoid toy-breaking incidents. If such behavior occurs when the child feels upset because she is unable to complete a task, be alert to signs of frustration. Help her handle the task. The more clues you have as to how and when toy-breaking takes place, the better you will be able to prevent it.

Praise Careful Handling of Classroom Materials. As you work on eliminating a negative behavior, let the child know what behaviors are acceptable in lieu of the inappropriate ones. Look for and reinforce occasions when the child handles classroom materials with care. Praise her for using items correctly, for putting materials back on the shelf when she finishes using them, and for any other signs of respect for classroom equipment. At first, praise such behaviors every time you see them take place. As toy-breaking incidents decrease gradually, also decrease the amount of praise you give. By the time the negative behavior has stopped, reinforcement should be given at about the same rate as it is given to the other children in the class.

Systematically Teach the Child to Control Impulses to Break Toys. Anger or frustration may be the emotion the child feels before breaking a toy. Such a destructive reaction is usually expressed impulsively, before the child thinks through what she is doing. The child needs to learn alternative ways of handling such feelings. She must also learn that it is her reaction, not the emotion itself, that is unacceptable. Set aside a special time each day to talk with the child about feelings. Plan to devote five to ten minutes of undivided attention, though you may need more time if the child is especially responsive. The cooperation of the other teachers will be important for carrying out this time. The following sequence is suggested:

1. Begin by discussing situations that evoke different emotions. For instance, "Yesterday I got a new puppy and I was so excited and happy that I felt like dancing and singing. Boy! I really felt good inside! What makes you feel really happy?" If the child responds, ask for more details. If the child does not respond, name more things that make you happy. Go on to discuss other feelings. "Sometimes I feel just the opposite. I get really sad. I had a very good friend and she had to move away. That made me feel terrible. Do you feel sad sometimes?" Also discuss anger. "You know, sometimes I get really angry. I know you must feel angry about things, too, at times. What makes you angry?" Share some examples of what angers you, and help the child to verbalize situations that anger her. It may take several days to identify situations that evoke various emotions.

2. Once the child acknowledges that she feels differently in response to varied situations, focus your discussion on those feelings. "How does it make you feel inside when you are (happy, angry, sad, lonely)?" Help the child put into words the different inner responses to emotions. Before-hand, think about how to verbalize emotions, because feelings are not easy to describe in words. This way you will be better prepared to help the child discuss them. Be careful, however, that it is the child who talks about the subject with help from you, and not the other way around. This step may require several days.

3. When the child has verbalized how she feels inside when she experiences different emotions, begin to talk about what she does to express such feelings. Do not be critical of what she says. If the child tells you that she punches, hits, bites, or otherwise hurts someone or that she feels like breaking things when she gets upset, accept that for now. Discuss various emotions in relation to how they are expressed in action.

4. The next step is to tell the child that you want to explore some different ways of reacting to emotions. If the child tells you that when she is happy she smiles, ask how else she might express that happiness. Either of you might come up with ideas like clapping hands, jumping up and down, singing, hopping around, and hugging someone. Discuss ways of handling anger and frustration. You might suggest that the child talk to an adult to get help in handling angry feelings, ask for help in finishing a task that seems impossible, or pound on the floor or a table instead of on a toy.

5. Your discussions need not be strictly verbal. Use whatever props you want to help you. Puppets, clay, or blocks might provide a good medium for exploring feelings and emotions.

6. With each discussion step, look for opportunities during the day that illustrate what you and the child have been talking about. At first, focus on the event that has evoked a particular emotion. Switch to how it makes you feel inside. Next, look for examples of how the emotion may be expressed. Finally, encourage the child to verbalize alternative ways of reacting. Be sure to use examples of all kinds of emotions and feelings.

If the Child Does Break A Toy, Use Time-out. Because breaking of toys is a potential safety and health hazard, it needs to be stopped as quickly as possible. Therefore, use time-out whenever this behavior occurs. If the child breaks a toy, do the following:

1. Quickly make sure that the broken toy presents no immediate hazard. If a cleanup is necessary, another teacher should attend to it.
2. Calmly take the child who broke the toy to the time-out area and seat her. Firmly but quietly say, "I cannot allow you to break toys. You will have to sit here until I tell you that you may get up."
3. Note the time and move away from the child. Do not talk with or look at her during the time-out.
4. If another child approaches the time-out area, quietly move this child away. Explain, "Jenny needs to be by herself for a few minutes. You can talk to her when she joins the class again."
5. Promptly, at the end of the time, go to the child and say, "You may get up now." Do not lecture. The child knows the reason for the isolation. To channel the child into constructive behavior, you might suggest that she join an ongoing activity.

Continue Graphing the Behavior. Continue counting the number of toy-breaking incidents and record the total on the Record Keeping Graph. Draw a vertical line after baseline and add the new data each day. The graph shows progress toward the goal and informs you when you have reached it. Your timing of changes in reinforcement for appropriate behaviors depends on accurate record keeping.

Maintenance

When the child no longer breaks toys, continue to let her know what behaviors you value. As she handles classroom materials with care, let her know periodically that you are pleased. Continue to help the child verbalize her feelings.

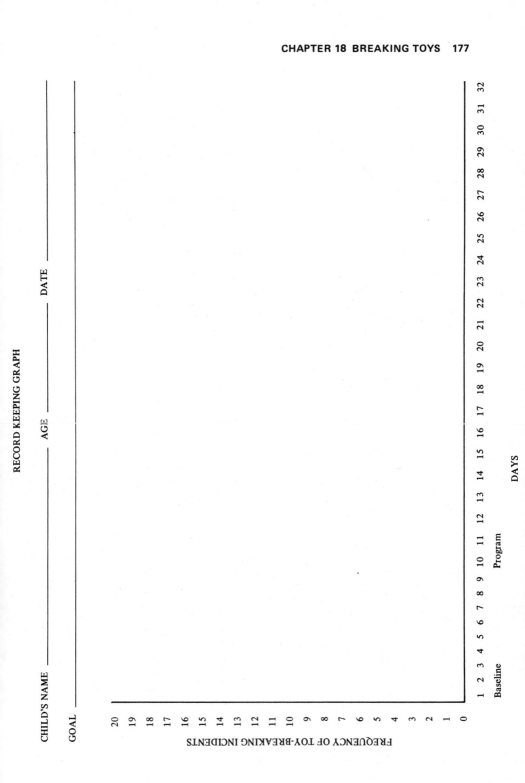

RECORD KEEPING GRAPH

CHILD'S NAME _____ AGE _____ DATE _____

GOAL _____

FREQUENCY OF TOY-BREAKING INCIDENTS

20
19
18
17
16
15
14
13
12
11
10
9
8
7
6
5
4
3
2
1
0

1 2 3 4 5 6 7 8 9 10 11 12 13 14 15 16 17 18 19 20 21 22 23 24 25 26 27 28 29 30 31 32

Baseline   Program

DAYS

CHAPTER 19

19

Flushing Objects Down the Toilet

"Teacher, I'm going potty," says three-year-old Becky, walking past an adult stationed near the swings. "Okay, Becky," she is told. Becky goes inside and is out of sight. Mrs. Connor pushes children on the swings for several minutes. When Becky does not return, Mrs. Connor decides to check on her. She finds Becky flushing an overflowing toilet. A small plastic piece from a Noah's Ark game is circling round and round with the water. Becky turns to Mrs. Connor and exclaims, "It's stuck!" The water reaches the rim and trickles begin to flow over onto the floor. "Becky! What did you put in the toilet?" Becky's eyes open wide innocently, and she shakes her head, saying, "Nothing." "I can see something in there, Becky." With this Mrs. Connor fishes out the toy floating in the water. She hands it to Becky and says, "No one else is in the bathroom. You must have done it. Now, go to the sink and wash this." Becky rinses the plastic carefully, then dries it and her hands. She then goes back to the toilet and watches Mrs. Connor, whose arm is immersed in water as she tries to find a blockage. "There's more water coming out on the floor, teacher," says Becky helpfully. A moment later Mrs. Conner angrily drags out three more plastic animals. Becky watches with interest and willingly helps wash the retrieved toys and wipe water off the floor. Unfortunately, this is not the first time Becky has flushed toys down the toilet. The teachers are upset and baffled by Becky's behavior.

STATE THE BEHAVIOR

The child frequently and regularly throws small objects into the toilet and flushes them down.

OBSERVE THE BEHAVIOR

Observe the child for a few days to gain some more information about this behavior.

A. When does the child flush items down the toilet?
- Unpredictably, at any time of day
- During washup and toileting times
- During free choice activities
- During planned activity times
- During cleanup times
- During transitions
- During outdoor play

B. What does the child do before this behavior occurs?
- The child goes to the toilet
- The child goes to the bathroom to wash her hands
- The child plays with a game that contains small parts
- The child plays in the housekeeping area
- The child engages in activity alone
- The child plays with another child or a few children
- The child does not engage in any activity
- The child does not succeed in gaining a teacher's attention

C. What does the child do when she flushes something down the toilet?
- The child looks to see whether an adult is watching
- The child secretly takes one item or more into the bathroom
- The child openly takes one item or more into the bathroom
- The child plays with the object in the toilet before flushing
- The child calls a teacher's attention to the object in the toilet
- The child calls a teacher's attention after flushing
- The child flushes the toilet more than once
- The child denies flushing objects down the toilet
- The child gets upset when asked if she flushed something down the toilet.
- The child walks away as if nothing has happened
- The child talks about what she has done

D. What objects does the child flush down the toilet?
- Any small object
- Puzzle pieces
- Parts of manipulative materials
- Paper or cardboard items
- Paint brushes
- Toothbrushes
- Soap
- Doll clothes
- Small blocks

These observations should provide you with some idea of when, what, and how the child flushes items down the toilet.

EXPLORE THE CONSEQUENCES

Most likely the child who flushes objects down the toilet has a fascination with water and/or the mechanical operation of a toilet. This absorption is fairly common with very young children. They enjoy and are soothed by the sound, motion, and feel of flowing water. Some enterprising youngsters may take this fascination further to include experimentation. There is, after all, considerable scientific inquiry involved in finding out what floats and sinks, what blocks the toilet, and what disappears or reappears.

When a child flushes an object down the toilet, adults may react strongly. They explain and scold, and try to regain the lost object or unclog the toilet. A plumber may even be called in to help. All this activity reinforces the behavior rather than stops it. The child derives pleasure from flushing objects down the toilet and then receives considerable attention.

CONSIDER ALTERNATIVES

There might be a relatively simple solution to dealing with the child who flushes objects down the toilet. Consider the following suggestions.

- Very young children enjoy and need many activities that provide varied tactile experiences. If such sensory stimulation is not provided in the class program, children may create their own. Water play is an important sensory activity that should be provided frequently in a class for young children. If you do not often allow time for water play and have children who create their own (such as in the toilet), increase water play activities. Provide a water table or plastic bin with plain water, soapy water, or colored water. Add various implements such as funnels, plastic bottles, pieces of hose, sieves, and straws. You may find that as your curriculum satisfies the sensory needs of the children, behaviors like flushing items down the toilet disappear.
- Examine the program provided for the children. It is possible that a child does not find enough activities or materials of interest. Therefore, the child creates her own diversions through activities such as flushing toys or other objects down the toilet. Be sure that what you are providing is age-appropriate. Activities and materials should be

challenging but not frustrating. A child will cease behavior like flushing objects if there are enough stimulating and interesting things to do in the classroom.

- The teacher of two-year-olds should not be surprised by behavior such as flushing toys down the toilet. This behavior is quite normal. If it occurs in a class of very young children, it is best to take a preventive approach. When a child goes into the bathroom, you should follow. In a matter-of-fact manner, stop the child from tossing items into the toilet. Do not make a fuss over the incident. Be sure that you provide many alternative sensory activities, including water play. The child will outgrow this behavior. Until then, simply be extra vigilant and patient.

If none of these suggestions provides a solution to the problem, continue to the following program.

STATE THE GOAL

The goal is for the child to stop throwing toys and other items into the toilet and flushing them down.

PROCEDURE

The basic strategy to stop the child from flushing items down the toilet involves three simultaneous steps:

- Prevent the behavior.
- Provide alternative activities.
- Decrease attention to the behavior when it does occur.

Definition

Flushing objects down the toilet includes any incident in which the child throws an item (other than a reasonable amount of toilet paper) into the toilet and flushes it.

Baseline

It is important to know how often this behavior occurs. For three days count all instances of flushing items down the toilet. Mark on paper each time the child does this. At the end of each day record the total on the Record Keeping Graph. These three days will provide a baseline with which to compare later progress. Because it may not always be evident when the child flushes an object down the toilet, be particularly vigilant to get an accurate estimate.

Program

After gathering baseline data, begin the following program. It is important that all teachers follow it consistently.

As Often as Possible, Prevent the Child From Flushing Objects Down the Toilet. You are in a good position to prevent this behavior because of the limited area that needs to be carefully watched. The access to the bathroom may be observed in conjunction with other duties. A teacher should stay near the door or entry to the bathroom. If necessary, rearrange the classroom so there is an activity center near the bathroom. If the child who flushes toys down the toilet approaches the bathroom door, the adult supervising the activities area should follow.

1. Go immediately to the child before she enters the bathroom and intercept her.
2. Make a fast visual check for obvious or hidden items that can be flushed down the toilet.
3. If the child is not carrying anything, smile and allow her to go on to the bathroom.
4. If you are not sure whether she is concealing an item to flush down the toilet, smile and walk into the bathroom with her. Stay there until she is finished. If she tries to toss something into the toilet, simply take the item away. Say, "No, you may not throw things into the toilet," and then walk out.
5. If the child has a toy with her, take it away and say, "I'll keep this here for you until you are finished in the bathroom." The child may change her mind about going into the bathroom. In this case, you need to make sure she moves elsewhere before you return the toy to her.
6. Whatever course you take, do not make a fuss. The objective is to eliminate as much attention for this behavior as possible.

Provide Alternative Activities to Satisfy the Enjoyment of Water Play. Assume that the child who flushes toys down the toilet simply enjoys playing with water. Therefore, plan to provide water play as an activity option more frequently. If the weather is nice, a water table or bins of water can be set up outdoors. Water play can also be accommodated inside with a sheet of plastic or old newspapers protecting nearby surfaces. If you find the child headed for the bathroom with an object to drop in the toilet, guide her toward the water activity instead. Suggest that the child use the item she is holding at the water table. If the item is inappropriate for water play, provide an alternative object.

Minimize Attention When the Child Does Flush an Object Down the Toilet. Your preventive measures will eliminate most instances of the behavior. If on occasion it does occur, do not overreact. It is important that you say little and show as little reaction as possible. Keep these points in mind:

1. If you notice an item has been dropped in the toilet, say nothing and remove it. Wash the toy and walk away from the child. Do not provide attention for the behavior.
2. If the child comes and tells you she has flushed something down the toilet, say, "Oh, really?" and continue about your business. Later, when the child is not nearby, check the toilet to see if it is clogged. If it is, close it off to further use and make alternative arrangements until it can be repaired. Be particularly vigilant to prevent further incidents from occurring.
3. If another child tells you a toy has been flushed down the toilet, say "Thank you," and check out the situation as unobtrusively as possible. Again, minimize your reactions to the child who flushed down the toy.

Continue Graphing the Behavior. The procedures suggested should work together to eliminate the behavior. Preventive measures should keep such incidents to a minimum. Alternative activities should satisfy the need for enjoyment of water play. Ignoring object-flushing incidents should eliminate the reinforcement that normally follows the behavior. At this point, graph the behavior by counting items thrown into the toilet as well as items taken to the bathroom and there confiscated. Count each item separately. Record the total on the Record Keeping Graph. Draw a vertical line after the baseline data to differentiate before- and after-program counts.

Maintenance

When the child no longer takes items to the bathroom, you can discontinue the close watch you kept on the child. Continue to provide opportunity for water play. It is probable that the child who flushes toys down the toilet is a very young preschooler. By the time you complete this program, she may have outgrown the urge to engage in this behavior.

RECORD KEEPING GRAPH

CHILD'S NAME _____   AGE _____   DATE _____

GOAL _____

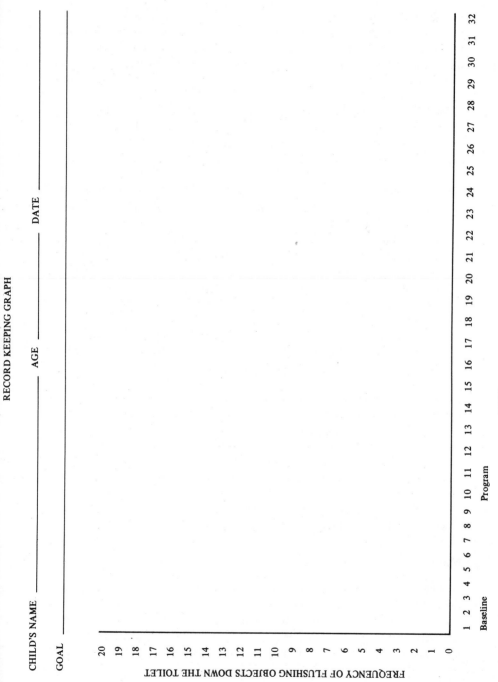

FREQUENCY OF FLUSHING OBJECTS DOWN THE TOILET

20
19
18
17
16
15
14
13
12
11
10
9
8
7
6
5
4
3
2
1
0

1 2 3 4 5 6 7 8 9 10 11 12 13 14 15 16 17 18 19 20 21 22 23 24 25 26 27 28 29 30 31 32

Baseline   Program

DAYS

CHAPTER 20

20

Wasting Paper

Three-year-old Tony washes his hands and pulls out a paper towel to dry them. He wipes the towel over one hand and drops it in the wastebasket. He pulls out another towel, again merely pats a hand, and discards the towel. Tony repeats this procedure seven more times. "Tony!" exclaims a teacher. "You don't need so many towels!" Tony says, "My hands aren't dry yet," and quickly pulls out two more towels. "That's enough now," says the teacher, but Tony yanks out another paper towel. The teacher moves Tony away from the towel dispenser and explains at length why paper towels should not be wasted. Tony fidgets. He has heard this lecture several times before. A little while later Tony is at the easel. He takes a brush saturated with paint and dabs it on the large sheet of paper fastened to the easel. "I'm done," he exclaims. "Can I have more paper, please?" A teacher takes down Tony's creation and secures another sheet of paper. Tony again makes a quick swipe at the paper and exclaims that he is finished. In this way he uses five sheets of paper in as many minutes. "That's enough now, Tony," the teacher tells him. Tony goes to the stack of cut papers, picks up a handful, and drips paint on several before the teacher notices. "Tony, no one else will be able to paint if you use all the paper. That's not fair, is it?" Tony protests that he wants to make more pictures. The teacher talks to him, pleads with him, and finally coaxes him into playing in the block area. The teachers know that soon Tony will again waste paper. He has been doing it for a long time.

STATE THE BEHAVIOR

The child regularly, frequently, and deliberately wastes paper.

OBSERVE THE BEHAVIOR

Informally observe the child for a few days to gain some insight into when, where, how, and why the child wastes paper.

A. When does the child waste paper?
- During art activities
- During free choice times
- During toileting times
- During mealtimes
- During transitions
- Whenever paper is available

B. How does the child waste paper?
- The child flushes it down the toilet
- The child throws it in the trash can
- The child tears it
- The child makes only a line or scribble on the paper when painting or crayoning, and quickly declares the picture finished
- The child deliberately spills liquids and then uses many napkins or paper towels to clean up

C. What happens before the child wastes paper?
- The child engages in an art activity
- The child stays near the art area but does not participate
- The child goes to the bathroom
- The child washes his hands
- The child plays with water
- The child eats lunch or a snack

D. What does the child do when he wastes paper?
- The child announces that he is using a lot of paper
- The child moves away from adults who might be watching
- The child looks to see whether an adult is watching
- The child gets upset when asked to use less paper
- The child shows no concern for requests to use less paper
- The child uses less when an adult is there to monitor

Use this information to help you understand the behavior better so you can deal with it effectively.

EXPLORE THE CONSEQUENCES

Supplies in the preschool classroom are usually abundant so that children can explore and express their creativity. Paper for painting, drawing, cutting, pasting, and folding is usually readily available. To foster self-help skills, children have ready access to toilet paper, paper towels, and napkins. However, with an increasing awareness of ecological concerns and with rising costs of paper, teachers often remind children to use paper products sparingly. A child might realize that the teacher gives extra attention when he pulls out three paper towels instead of one or he paints ten sketchy pictures instead of two or three complete ones. The teacher may talk to the child about not wasting paper, and spend time explaining, reminding, or scolding. If the behavior occurs often enough, the child can gain considerable attention from adults. Efforts to talk the child out of wasting paper will only serve to reinforce the behavior.

CONSIDER ALTERNATIVES

Consider whether any of the following suggestions might help provide a fairly simple resolution to the problem.

- If the child uses a great deal of paper in the art area, be very careful about assuming that the child is deliberately wasting paper. Many young children go through a stage in which they are impressed by the volume of artwork they produce, and thus try to finish as many pictures as they can. Another explanation for abundant artwork may lie in the development of children's graphic art. Children's art evolves in identifiable stages. Scribbles develop into various shapes and eventually into recognizable objects. At any of these stages the child may consider the picture complete though only a small part of the paper is used. The relationship of the picture to the background may be important to the child. A picture may be placed only in the middle, by a side, or in a corner of the paper. You can suggest that the child use other parts of the paper. Do not insist, however, if the child thinks that the picture is complete.
- The child may be handling large amounts of paper because of the sensory experience paper offers. If you suspect this is so, provide a variety of sensory activities for the children. Include a bin of shredded newspaper to run fingers through. Plan papier-mâché projects in which children can handle, tear, soak, and manipulate paper to create shapes.

If these suggestions do not provide an answer to the problem, continue to the following program.

STATE THE GOAL

The goal is for the child to stop deliberately wasting paper.

PROCEDURE

To eliminate wasting paper, the basic strategy involves four simultaneous steps:

- Provide activities in which paper can be handled and used.
- Take preventive measures to avoid the behavior.
- Praise appropriate use of paper.
- Ignore wasting paper if it does occur.

Definition

Wasting paper involves any deliberate overuse of any kind of paper in which the child intends to throw paper away or prevent someone else from using it. All the teachers should discuss and agree on how many papers have to be used to be considered wasteful. For example, using more than two paper towels for drying hands may be considered wasteful.

Baseline

Determine exactly how often the child wastes paper. For three days, gather baseline information by first counting the number of papers wasted, according to your definition. You will need to keep a close watch on the child to gather this information. Each time the child wastes paper, note on a list the number of papers wasted. At the end of each day add up the total number and record it on the first Record Keeping Graph (Number of Papers Wasted) at the end of this chapter. Also note the number of paper-wasting incidents and record them on the second graph (Number of Paper-wasting Incidents). These graphs indicate how much paper is wasted and how often it happens. The numbers on the vertical axes of the graphs vary. The first graph may need to be numbered by fives or tens if large numbers of papers are used.

Program

Once you have gathered baseline data, you are ready to begin the program. It is important that all teachers follow these procedures consistently.

Provide Activities in Which Paper can be Handled and Used. The child's behavior may be prompted by an enjoyment of the feel of paper. In addition to the normal art activities, provide activities that use paper in different ways. Set out paper and scissors for cutting or tearing. Provide papers of various textures to feel, match, and compare. Prepare texture bins with shredded papers of different weights, softness, and textures for the children to run their hands through. Arrange collage activities that use various kinds of paper. Encourage the child who wastes paper to engage in these activities, and convey your approval of his participation in them.

Prevent the Wasting of Paper Whenever Possible. Vigilance on the part of all the teachers will help prevent wasting paper. The areas in the room where there is paper are limited. Therefore, it is easy to watch the areas. Preventive measures depend on where and what kind of paper the child wastes.

1. *Paper towels in the bathroom.* When the child finishes washing his hands, guide his hands on the paper towel holder. Stand in front of the holder after the child has taken one towel. Tell him, "Good! See how nicely you dried your hands with that towel?" Leave the bathroom after the child.

2. *Toilet paper in the bathroom.* When the child is going to the bathroom, allow him to pull a reasonable amount of toilet paper off the roll. (Your definition should tell you how much is not too much.) Put your hand on the roll to stop more paper from being pulled off. Tell the child, "That's just the right amount of paper to use. Good!"

   If the child wants to flush excessive amounts of toilet paper or pull out paper towels for no reason, stop him. Say, "You may not waste paper." Direct him to an ongoing activity, preferably one where paper is used.

3. *Art activities.* If the child is engaged in an art activity, intervene only if you are sure that he is deliberately wasting paper. If this is the case, limit the number of pictures he can make. When the child first enters the art area, let him know you are pleased that he wants to participate, but tell him there is a limit on the number of pictures he can make. This can be worded positively: "You'll be able to paint five pictures today! Here's your first paper. You can help me count when you're ready for more papers." If the child asks for more after five pictures are done, tell him he has used his quota. Help the child count the papers again and suggest that he might want to do some more painting on the five pictures he already made. Point out where there is more room on the papers.

4. *Spills.* If you suspect that the child is spilling liquids so he can use papers to clean up, provide different cleanup props. The child can be given sponges or a mop.

Praise Appropriate Use of Paper. Whenever the child uses paper in a way you expect, praise him. Say, for instance,

"I like the way you used the paint on all parts of the paper." (Don't criticize, however, if the child does not cover the entire paper. Your objective is not to shape his art preferences but to prevent wasting paper.)

"Thank you for using only one paper towel to dry your hands. We have to be sure there is enough for everyone."

"Say, you're really getting good at tearing off just the right amount of toilet paper!"

Give the child attention for engaging in the paper-related activities you have provided. At first, reinforce the child often for using paper appropriately. Later, as wasting paper decreases, decrease the reinforcement also. Once the child no longer wastes paper, you can eliminate such praise. Continue to give attention when he engages in other desired activities, as you do with all the children in the class.

Ignore the Wasting of Paper if it does Occur. You should decrease incidents of wasting paper through preventive steps. If the child does waste paper, however, ignore this behavior as much as possible. Do the following:

1. Go to the child. Take away the paint brush or other materials he is holding.
2. Say, "No! You may not waste paper." Do not explain or go into a lengthy discussion.
3. Move the child away from the area.
4. Turn away from the child and pay no attention. Involve yourself with another child or activity.
5. After about two minutes, go to the child and give reinforcement for any constructive activity or interaction he is engaged in. If the child has not become involved in an activity, help him find one.

Continue Graphing the Behavior. Continue counting and graphing the amount of papers wasted and the number of paper-wasting incidents. Because of your preventive measures, the amount of paper wasted should immediately decrease. If the child shows signs of wasting paper (such as reaching for more towels or art paper) but is prevented from doing so, count these as incidents. The number of papers wasted indicates if your preventive measures are effective. The number of paper-wasting incidents recorded indicates if the entire program to stop this behavior is effective.

Draw a vertical line after the baseline data on both graphs. Record daily counts as you did during baseline.

Maintenance

Continue to intermittently praise appropriate activity . Also, provide sensory activities in the curriculum that involve paper. If the child does waste paper on occasion, give as little reinforcement as possible, as you did when you were working on eliminating this behavior.

RECORD KEEPING GRAPH

CHILD'S NAME _____ AGE _____ DATE _____

GOAL _____

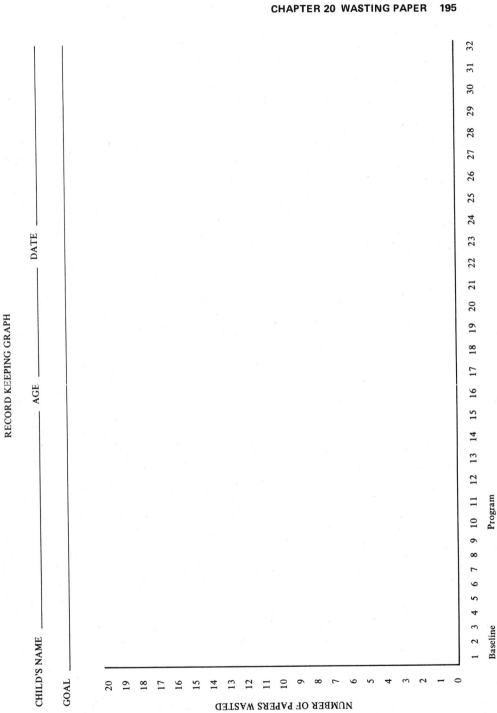

NUMBER OF PAPERS WASTED

20
19
18
17
16
15
14
13
12
11
10
9
8
7
6
5
4
3
2
1
0

1 2 3 4 5 6 7 8 9 10 11 12 13 14 15 16 17 18 19 20 21 22 23 24 25 26 27 28 29 30 31 32

Baseline   Program

DAYS

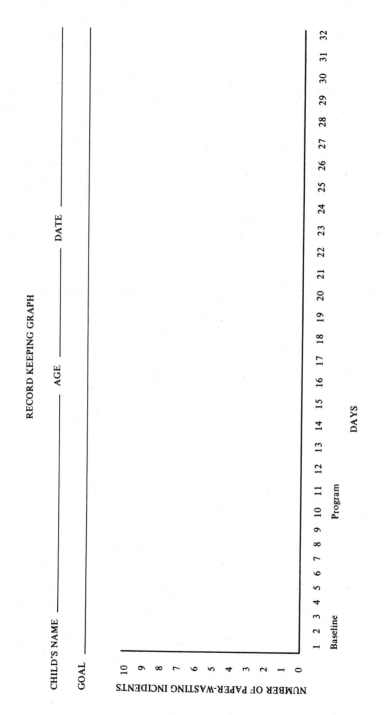

RECORD KEEPING GRAPH

CHILD'S NAME _____ AGE _____ DATE _____

GOAL _____

NUMBER OF PAPER-WASTING INCIDENTS

10 9 8 7 6 5 4 3 2 1 0

1 2 3 4 5 6 7 8 9 10 11 12 13 14 15 16 17 18 19 20 21 22 23 24 25 26 27 28 29 30 31 32

Baseline   Program

DAYS

CHAPTER 21

Destroying the
Work of Others

Arlene has been carefully laying out game cards on the table. Five-year-old Pam walks by and scatters the cards on the floor with a swipe of her hand. Arlene shrieks and a teacher comes to the rescue, saying, "Oh no, Pam! Why did you do that? Arlene has been working so carefully on her game and now you have ruined it. Pick those cards up right now!" Pam stands by without making a move. "Pam, I asked you to pick up the cards you spilled." Pam again makes no move, but then bends down and picks up one card. "That's better," says the teacher, turning to Arlene to soothe her. Pam watches this, then walks away. A little while later, Pam goes to the art area where Chad is putting the finishing touches on a picture. A teacher looks at Chad's work and says "You did a beautiful job, Chad. I really like the way you've made the flowers and trees." Pam goes to the shelf for a piece of paper and crayons and sits down by Chad. She begins making a picture, but suddenly reaches to Chad's paper with her crayon and scribbles several lines through the middle. Chad yells and then punches Pam. The teacher rushes to the scene, tells Chad he should not hit and tries to calm the crying Pam. Later that day Pam knocks down some blocks, tears two paintings, and pulls all the shoes off the dress-up shelf that Susie is arranging. The teachers feel dismayed because Pam is increasingly destroying more of what other children make, and nothing is helping to stop the behavior.

STATE THE BEHAVIOR

The child deliberately destroys the work of other children.

OBSERVE THE BEHAVIOR

Spend a few days observing the behavior to gain further insight into when and under what circumstances it occurs.

A. When does the child destroy other children's work?

- Unpredictably, at any time
- During free choice activities
- During planned activity times
- During cleanup times
- During transitions
- When children are getting ready to go home

B. What is the child doing before she ruins the work of other children?

- The child works by the child whose work she ruins
- The child works elsewhere in the classroom
- The child is not engaged in any activity
- The child plays with a particular child or children
- The child has difficulty completing a task
- The child expresses a dislike for an ongoing activity
- The child is rebuffed by the child whose work she destroys

C. What does the child do when she destroys another child's work?

- The child looks around to see whether an adult is watching
- The child waits for the other child to look away before attacking the other's work
- The child walks away as if nothing happened
- The child gets upset
- The child admits to destroying the other child's work when confronted by a teacher
- The child denies it
- The child apologizes on her own
- The child apologizes when asked to do so by a teacher
- The child offers to make amends

D. Who is usually the victim of the behavior?

- Anyone
- Friends
- Boys
- Girls
- Younger or smaller children
- Older or bigger children
- Children with whom the child has had a conflict
- Children for whom the child has expressed a dislike

E. How does the child destroy work?

- The child knocks over block constructions
- The child knocks over structures made of various construction materials
- The child tears or throws away artwork

- The child crumples artwork or spills water over it
- The child scribbles over artwork with paint, crayons, or other media
- The child knocks props off a table or other surface in the housekeeping area
- The child undresses dolls
- The child messes another child's arrangement
- The child empties puzzle pieces out of the frame
- The child crushes clay sculptures

Use the clues you gain from these informal observations to help you eliminate the problem.

EXPLORE THE CONSEQUENCES

Preschool programs are designed to foster creativity. In almost every area of the preschool class, children have the opportunity to express themselves in their own unique way. Most preschool materials are designed to be used in whatever way each child likes. There is not a right or wrong way to use them. In addition to encouraging creativity, preschool materials also allow for independence and foster good self-concept. Young children are proud of their work. It is, therefore, unfortunate when another child destroys something they have made. The child who deliberately ruins another youngster's work may be doing so out of anger, dislike, frustration, or mischief. Whatever the reason, such destructiveness cannot be tolerated. Teachers are anxious to stop this behavior. They may try reasoning, lecturing, showing anger, expressing disappointment, or insisting on apologies. Their concern is particularly urgent because the children whose work has been ruined also express a variety of reactions. When a child destroys another youngster's work, she is getting doubly reinforced for her actions. On the one hand she has hurt another child, and the child is probably reacting loudly and visibly. On the other hand, a teacher also reacts strongly and spends time letting the child know what she has done wrong. Therefore, a child who repeatedly destroys another child's work gains considerable attention for such behavior. Though this attention is meant to stop the behavior, it only serves to reinforce it.

CONSIDER ALTERNATIVES

Consider whether the following suggestions might provide a relatively simple solution to the problem.

- Examine the classroom to ensure that there are enough materials for all the children who want to use them. A child may be reacting destructively toward others because she is not able to participate in an activity because of a lack of materials. In such a case, provide more materials so everyone who wants to has a chance to take part in any given activity.
- An undue number of destructive incidents may be occurring because of room arrangement. If blocks are frequently getting knocked over, check to see whether the block area is isolated enough. It may be that block structures are being destroyed because the area lies in a major traffic path in the room. Perhaps paintings are being ruined because easels are too close to each other and children inadvertently bump into each other's pictures. Examine the area where problems are occurring and consider whether a different room arrangement might not alleviate the problem.
- Inspect your system of storing children's finished products such as artwork. There needs to be a fairly secluded area where wet paintings or glued products can dry. Each child should have a special place to keep the day's work until it can be taken home. This storage should not be messy or cluttered, since such conditions convey lack of respect for the child's work and leave items vulnerable to damage. How you handle and store creative work lets the child know how much you value it.
- If the child destroys the work of only one particular child, consider separating the two children. The victim may provoke the other's destructiveness. If possible, place one of the children in another class. If you cannot do this, then make an effort to keep the two children separated during periods when destructive acts occur.

If none of these suggestions helps with the problem of the child who destroys the work of others, then move on to the following program.

STATE THE GOAL

The goal is for the child to stop destroying the work of other children.

PROCEDURE

The basic strategy to eliminate this behavior involves four simultaneous steps:

- Encourage the child to engage in creative activities and reinforce such efforts.

- Reinforce appropriate social behaviors.
- Prevent destructive behaviors whenever possible.
- Use time-out if the child does ruin another child's work.

Definition

Destroying the work of others includes any deliberate act to ruin the work of another child. This involves tearing, cutting, spilling on, scribbling over, knocking down, disarranging, or in any other way interfering with the product as the other child created it.

Baseline

For three days, take count of all incidents of destroying the work of others to provide a baseline. Mark on paper each time the behavior occurs. At the end of each day add and record the total on the Record Keeping Graph. This baseline provides a measure with which to compare later progress.

Program

Now that baseline is gathered, begin implementing the following program. It is important that all teachers follow it consistently.

Encourage and Reinforce Creative Activities by the Child. For the child to recognize and respect the value of other children's creative efforts, she first has to be aware of this in relation to her own work. Provide a wide variety of creative activities and encourage the child to participate in these. Give frequent and lavish praise to the child for her own creative work. At first, reinforce the child as often as possible. Later, as destruction of others' work decreases and finally stops, cut back reinforcement gradually until you are giving it about as often as you do to all the children in the class.

Remember also that creative work includes not only art activities, but a much wider range of involvement. Creativity is present with blocks, other construction materials, the housekeeping area, sand and water play, music, dance, and language activities.

Reinforce Appropriate Social Behaviors. While you are conveying to the child your displeasure with destructive behavior, you also have to let her know what behaviors you value. Reinforce the child when she engages in appropriate social behaviors. Convey to her that you and the other children appreciate it when she plays nicely, shares, has fun, and otherwise enjoys positive social interactions. In this way you are letting the child know what you want, not just what you do not want.

Prevent Destructive Behavior Whenever You Can. From your informal observation you should have some idea of what happens when the child acts destructively. Use such clues to help you prevent destructiveness whenever possible. For instance, if you found that the child paints on other children's pictures when she is at the easel, prevent this by turning the easels to different angles and then keeping careful watch. Or, if you found that the child tears other children's pictures once they are finished, find a more inaccessible storage area.

Whatever your clues, use them to anticipate and prevent the behavior. Be especially vigilant during activities in which the child has previously shown destructiveness. If you see clues signaling potential attack on another child's work, block the child by placing yourself between her and the work. Try to redirect her into another activity.

Use Time-out if the Child Does Ruin Another Youngster's Work. If the child destroys the work of another youngster, do the following:

1. Prearrange for another teacher to deal with the child whose work was ruined. This adult should make any repairs possible or help the child reconstruct what was destroyed.
2. Calmly take the child who had destroyed the other child's work to the time-out area. Firmly but quietly say, "I cannot allow you to ruin what other children have made. You will have to sit here until I tell you that you may get up."
3. Note the time and move away from the child. Do not look at or talk with the child during this time-out.
4. If another child approaches the time-out area, quietly move this child away. Explain, "Pam needs to be by herself for a few minutes. You can talk to her when she joins the class again."
5. Promptly, at the end of the time, go to the child and say, "You may get up now." Do not lecture. The child knows the reason for the isolation. To channel the child into constructive behavior, you might suggest that she join an ongoing activity.

Continue Graphing the Behavior. Continue counting the number of times the child destroys the work of others on the Record Keeping Graph. Draw a vertical line after the baseline data and record each day's count of the behavior. This ensures that you are aware of changes in the behavior. The graph helps you know at what pace to decrease the amount of praise you give the child for engaging in creative activities and positive social interaction.

Maintenance

When the child no longer destroys other children's work, you have reached your goal. Continue periodic reinforcement of creative efforts and encourage positive social interaction with other children. If, on occasion, the child does ruin another's work, use time-out.

RECORD KEEPING GRAPH

CHILD'S NAME _____ AGE _____ DATE _____

GOAL _____

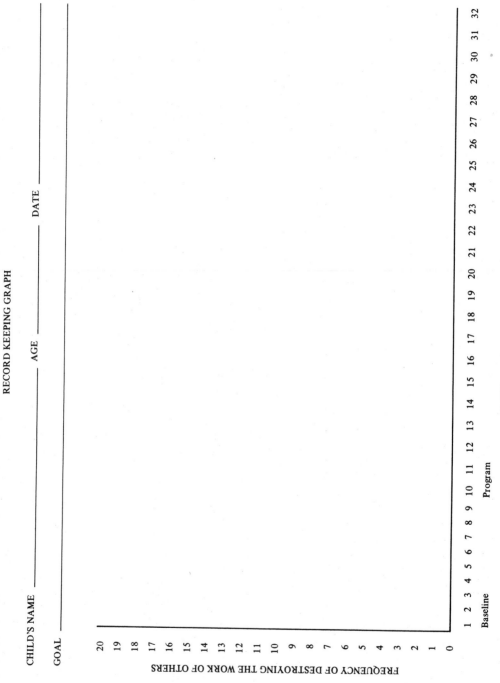

FREQUENCY OF DESTROYING THE WORK OF OTHERS

20
19
18
17
16
15
14
13
12
11
10
9
8
7
6
5
4
3
2
1
0

1 2 3 4 5 6 7 8 9 10 11 12 13 14 15 16 17 18 19 20 21 22 23 24 25 26 27 28 29 30 31 32

Baseline   Program

DAYS

SECTION 4

EMOTIONAL AND DEPENDENT BEHAVIORS

CHAPTER 22

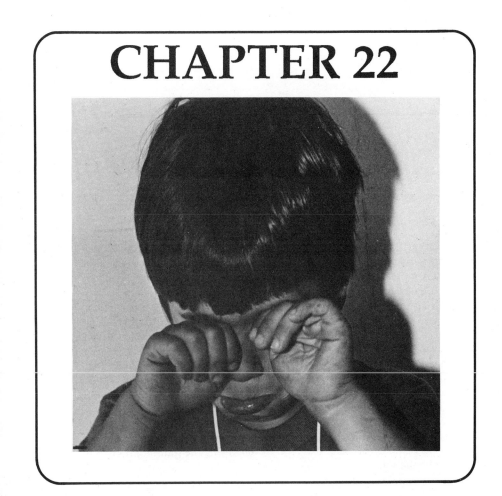

22
Crying

"Teacher!" calls four-year-old Steven. Ms. Courtney turns to Steven, but then is distracted by two children about to topple a block tower behind her. A moment later Steven bursts into tears. After salvaging the tower, Ms. Courtney moves to Steven. She puts an arm about him and asks why he is crying. He continues to cry, and after some coaxing finally gulps, "I need more paper." "That's no problem," says Ms. Courtney, releasing Steven and placing another piece of paper on the easel for him. Steven continues to cry and does not resume painting for several minutes, during which Ms. Courtney continues to comfort and talk to him. Later that morning Steven cried several times: when he was not able to sit next to Rhonda at storytime, when Jimmy called him a cry baby, when all the swings were occupied by the time he got to them, when there were no more blocks for the structure he was building, and when the snack was passed to the right instead of to the left by his right-hand neighbor. The teachers have dried many tears for Steven during the four months he has been in school.

STATE THE BEHAVIOR

The child frequently cries although there is little or no provocation.

OBSERVE THE BEHAVIOR

Spend some time observing the child to gain further insight into the child's crying behavior.

A. When does the child cry?
- Unpredictably, at any time of day
- Early in the day, soon after arriving at school

- Later in the day, when it is time to go home
- Near nap time
- Near mealtimes
- During structured or teacher-directed activities
- During free choice activities
- During outside play
- At cleanup time
- When activities are ending
- During transitions
- At toileting times

B. What happens before the child starts to cry?

- Another child has something the child wants
- Another child takes something away from him
- Another child or several children will not let him join in their play
- The child has a verbal or physical fight with another child
- A teacher does not answer the child
- The child is told no by a teacher
- The child's mother or father has just left
- The child is unable to complete an activity
- The child is not allowed to engage in an activity
- The child does not want to participate in an activity
- The child complains of an injury or other pain
- The child falls or stumbles and hurts himself
- There is no apparent provocation

C. What does the child do when he cries?

- The child stops crying when the problem is remedied (such as getting the toy he wants)
- The child continues crying even after he is given what he wants
- The child stops crying when picked up and comforted by a teacher
- The child stops crying only after a teacher has held him a while
- The child resists the attempts of adults to hold or comfort him
- The child talks about why he is crying (such as, "I want my Mommy!")
- The child says nothing; he only sobs
- The child responds when a teacher talks reasonably to him
- The child does not listen to reason
- The child cries all the harder when someone talks to him

Use these observations to help you find the best way of dealing with the child to eliminate unnecessary crying.

EXPLORE THE CONSEQUENCES

Crying is a way of communication during early life. As a child passes through infancy, he learns to have increasingly more control, and discovers other ways of conveying his needs. Language is the most important substitute for crying that the young child learns. However, crying continues to be a means of communication for most people. In early childhood it is used quite frequently to express hurt, anger, fear, frustration, sadness, and other emotions. Sometimes, however, a child overuses crying. This can develop if the child has been frustrated in getting attention in more acceptable ways. The child finds that crying brings attention from parents and other people. It is easy for a pattern to emerge from such a circumstance. The child wants attention, and tries to get it by talking, but is ignored. The child then cries and gets attention, and is thus reinforced for crying. If this happens often enough, crying may become a primary means of communication. In the preschool setting children often cry. Some children have valid reasons for crying, but others cry because they find it to be an effective attention-getting device. It is important to differentiate between the two reasons for crying. If children cry because they are scared, lonely, hurt, or otherwise upset, it is important to remedy the problem or help them deal with it. If, on the other hand, the child cries for attention, a different approach is needed. If teachers continue to reinforce with attention, crying will continue.

CONSIDER ALTERNATIVES

Because crying is not always used to get attention, it is important to recognize the reason for crying and to deal with the underlying problem. If a child does not cry very often, then there probably is a good reason when he does cry. Even if a child cries quite often, you cannot assume that this behavior is motivated solely by a need for attention. Consider the following situations.

- A child's entry into school may be a traumatic experience. Some children cry for some time after they first begin school. It is important to help the child overcome this distress so he feels comfortable while at school and can gain as much as possible from the experience. One of the parents may stay with the child when he first enters preschool or day care until he gets to know the new environment and teachers a little better. Children who are new to school also need to be reassured that they have not been abandoned and that after school they will return home. Such reassurance may need to be repeated many times.

  A child who cries for part of the day when he first starts school is genuinely distressed. Do not ignore this kind of crying. Soothe and comfort the child by talking to him, attending to him, and holding him. Help the child know that he has not been abandoned. A young child in the process of overcoming his anxiety may form an attachment to you as a substitute for the parent(s) he misses. This attachment may be necessary for a short time, but then should be discouraged once the child feels comfortable with school. In most cases, the need to cling to the teacher decreases as enjoyment of school activities and peer interaction increase.

- If a child's frequent crying is a relatively recent behavior, examine whether some change in his life has caused this. A new baby, a death in the family, a divorce, or any other source of stress might be unsettling. This makes the child more vulnerable to emotional upsets and results in frequent crying. Talk with the parents to see how you can work together to help the child deal with whatever is bothering him. In such an instance, the child needs your support and attention.
- Some children have an excessive number of accidents which result in crying. It is possible that a child has "intentional accidents" for the sake of the attention these bring. Carefully observe the child to help discriminate between real and staged accidents. Be alert to motor or perceptual problems which could cause an undue number of accidents.
- If a child cries frequently because he is hurt in social situations, work to improve his social acceptability rather than work on decreasing crying. Consult Chapter 33, Nonparticipation in Social Play, or one of the chapters related to aggression if the child's nonacceptance results from aggressive behavior. Once you eliminate the cause of the crying, the behavior should decrease.

If none of these situations describes the conditions under which the child cries frequently, and you conclude that the crying is really an attention-seeking ploy, continue to the following program.

STATE THE GOAL

The goal is for the child to decrease crying so that he cries only when the situation warrants it, not as a means of gaining attention.

PROCEDURE

To eliminate attention-seeking crying, use the following steps:

- Ignore the child when he is crying.
- Give attention and reinforcement when the child is not crying.

Definition

Crying is a behavior in which the child weeps, sobs, etc. This behavior is of concern when it is used excessively as a way of getting attention from adults, rather than as a response to pain, anger, frustration, sadness, or other emotion.

Baseline

Spend three days collecting some baseline information. Mark on paper each time the child cries. At the end of each day, total and record that number on the Record Keeping Graph. This will provide you with information with which to measure progress.

Program

Once you have gathered baseline data, you are ready to begin. For the procedure to be effective, all teachers much follow it consistently.

Ignore Crying. Once you determine that crying is one of the child's ways of gaining attention, you can change this behavior by eliminating the attention. Crying continues because it is reinforced through adult attention. A reversal of this pattern is possible if the attention is completely removed. When the child cries, do the following.

1. Take a quick look at the child to make sure that he is not hurt. If you are unsure of the cause of the crying, go to the child for a closer look and ask him what the problem is.
2. If you decide there is a real cause for the crying, take care of the problem and comfort the child. You may find this is not often the case if the child habitually cries for attention.
3. If you conclude that the child is crying for the attention it will bring him, turn away. Ignore the child. Do not look at him or indicate through your facial features or posture that he has gained your attention. Continue ignoring the child for as long as he cries.
4. Crying can be disruptive in the classroom. If the child cries during non-structured, child-selected activities, leave him where he is. If other children seem concerned and remind you that the child is crying, tell them that you are aware of it.
    If crying occurs during storytime, music, or another group activity, you may have to remove the child from the room. If he is disruptive to the point where the other children cannot pay attention to the activity, then prearrange an area to which the child can be removed. Make sure that he is not given attention. When you remove the child from the room, say, "We

cannot hear the story when you are crying like this. I'm going to take you out of the classroom. When you've stopped crying you may come back."

5. Be aware that the child will probably cry longer and louder than usual the first few times his behavior is ignored. This is to be expected since the child continues to try to get your attention by crying. Be persistent. After the first few times of being completely ignored during his crying incidents, the child will quickly decrease the behavior. It is important, however, that he is totally ignored throughout the time he cries. If *any* attention is paid, it reinforces the child's belief that crying is effective for getting attention.

6. Listen to the child, but do not watch him, to be alert to when he stops crying. Go to the child immediately when he stops crying. Give him your full attention at this time. You might say, "There! Now we can see what activity you can do. I'll come and sit with you for a while." Direct the child toward an activity and spend time working with him.

7. The child may begin to cry again when you approach him after he has stopped. Tell him, "I can't talk with you when you're crying." If he stops again, involve him in an activity. If he continues to cry, move away, and ignore him until he stops. (On your daily total, count this as one incident.)

Reinforce the Child When He Does Not Cry. Convey to the child that you will not give him attention when he cries. Let him know what behaviors you expect and value. Be ready to give the child frequent attention when he participates in school routines in expected ways. Tell him often how pleased you are when he engages in activities, joins in constructive play, follows instructions, helps in cleanup, or participates in peer interaction. Give him praise, attention, hugs, or any other appropriate reinforcers. The combination of reinforcing expected behaviors and ignoring crying should result in a fairly rapid change in the child's overall behavior.

Continue Graphing the Behavior. Count the number of instances of crying that occur every day. Continue recording the total for each day on the Record Keeping Graph. Draw a vertical line after the baseline data to differentiate it from the data you gather after the program begins. Remember, the first few days may reflect an increase in total as the child tries harder to get attention by crying. Once the child realizes that he can gain attention in ways other than crying, the total should quickly decrease.

Maintenance

When unnecessary crying stops, continue reinforcing desired behaviors intermittently. Your aim is to let the child know that he should continue in acceptable behaviors and that you will reinforce him for these. If crying for attention occurs again, ignore it as you did during the program. Ignoring the behavior should again eliminate it.

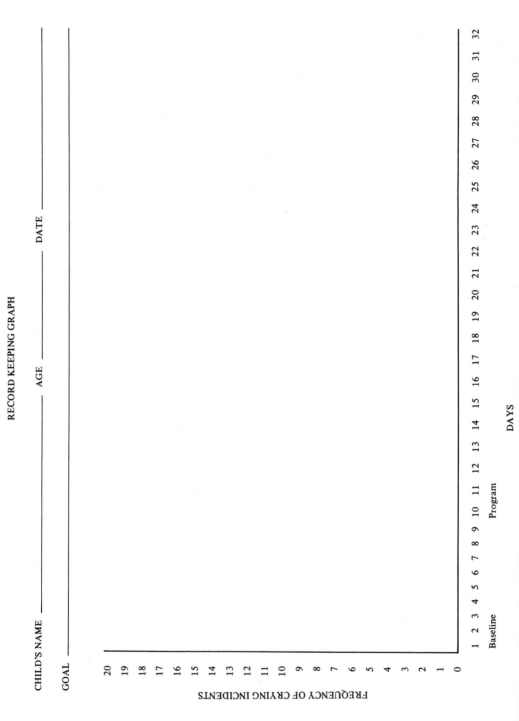

RECORD KEEPING GRAPH

CHILD'S NAME _____ AGE _____ DATE _____

GOAL _____

FREQUENCY OF CRYING INCIDENTS

20
19
18
17
16
15
14
13
12
11
10
9
8
7
6
5
4
3
2
1
0

1 2 3 4 5 6 7 8 9 10 11 12 13 14 15 16 17 18 19 20 21 22 23 24 25 26 27 28 29 30 31 32

Baseline   Program

DAYS

CHAPTER 23

23

Throwing Tantrums

"Caroline, come on! Get up. This is ridiculous. Now get up, please." Three-year-old Caroline continues to lie on the floor kicking, flailing her arms, and crying. The teacher tries to lift Caroline off the floor and only succeeds after he is kicked in the shin. Caroline stiffens her body and resists being held, all the time continuing to scream and to strike out with arms and legs. The teacher loses his grasp and lets Caroline go. The child runs a few feet away. She throws herself on the floor and resumes her tantrum. By this time, several children are watching the performance and another adult has joined in the act. The other teacher says sternly, "Caroline, get up right now. Stop this nonsense!" Caroline continues to wail and kick. Finally, after the two teachers have struggled for several more minutes, Caroline decreases her crying. She eventually sits up and lets herself be consoled. The teachers sigh in relief, but know that the calm is only temporary. Caroline will undoubtedly throw another tantrum soon.

STATE THE BEHAVIOR

The child frequently has tantrums when she does not get what she wants.

OBSERVE THE BEHAVIOR

Spend some time observing the child to see what triggers tantrums and what happens after the child has had a tantrum.

A. When do tantrums occur most often?
- Unpredictably, at any time of day
- During structured times when the children are expected to follow specific guidelines
- During free choice activities

- Outdoors
- During cleanup times
- During transitions
- When it is time to go home
- Early in the day, soon after arriving
- At nap time
- At mealtimes

B. With whom do tantrums occur?

- One particular teacher
- Any adult
- The child's parent(s)
- Certain children

C. What happens to the child just before she throws a tantrum?

- The child does not get something she asks for
- The child is hit by another child
- Something is taken away from her
- The child wants a toy that another child is playing with
- The child is prevented by another child or children from joining in play
- The child is told no by another child or a teacher
- The child does not want to join an activity
- The child does not want to finish an activity at the end of the activity period

D. What does the child do when she throws a tantrum?

- The child looks around to see whether an adult is watching
- The child increases the intensity of noise and/or motion when an adult is nearby
- The child increases the tantrum when an adult tries to talk to her
- The child decreases the tantrum when an adult tries to talk to her
- The child reacts to the presence or comments of other children
- The child stops the tantrum if she is picked up by an adult
- The child increases the tantrum if she is picked up by an adult
- The child hurts herself often while having a tantrum
- The child tries to hurt others, such as by kicking or biting

Use the insight you have gained from these informal observations to help you plan an approach to eliminating tantrums.

EXPLORE THE CONSEQUENCES

The child who throws tantrums has found that such behavior is an effective attention-getting device. Some children, from earliest infancy, show a tendency to be excitable and react strongly to what goes on in their environment. It is such a child, more than the one who was a placid and calm baby, who is likely to throw tantrums as a preschooler. The tendency to react strongly is particularly noticeable during the toddler and early preschool period when the child is striving for autonomy. This is often a time when wills clash, as the child wants to exercise her new-found freedom and adults try to hold her in rein. The young child is still immature and does not understand socially acceptable ways of reacting to something she does not like. She may decide to show how she feels in a very dramatic way. The child may throw herself on the ground, kick her feet, pound with her fists, contort her face, scream, and cry. Such a tantrum is definitely an attention-getter. Adults often react by trying to stop the behavior, but often find that trying to reason with and coax the child to stop the tantrum is ineffective. They may give in to what the child wanted in the first place. The child gets her way and gets considerable attention in the process. Once the child learns that throwing tantrums is effective, she repeats the behavior more often. Adults may continue to try to reason with the child, or they may lose their patience and revert to anger and spanking as a way of dealing with tantrums. Both reactions result in added attention. A child who starts preschool with a history of getting her way through tantrums often tries to use this behavior at school also. Teachers should be aware of this tendency and must be careful to not reinforce it further with their attention.

CONSIDER ALTERNATIVES

The child who resorts to tantrums needs special guidance to overcome this behavior. The following considerations may help you understand and avert unnecessary tantrums.

- Preschool children develop increasing independence and need to be given opportunities to exercise that autonomy. A child is less likely to react with a tantrum when she is given chances to do things by herself and for herself. The classroom and curriculum should be designed to encourage independence as much as possible. For example, classroom arrangement should help children easily reach materials, hang up their coats, and reach the toilets and sinks. The curriculum should allow for choices so that children may learn to make decisions. This is one way of expressing independence.
- Very young preschoolers are the children most likely to have tantrums. Because they are not yet adept at some of the more acceptable ways of expressing their wishes, they often react in physical ways such as tantrums. Recognize the social, emotional, and language abilities and limitations

of two-year-olds and keep these in mind as you deal with their tantrums. It is best to ignore tantrums when they occur and reinforce more acceptable behavior. The main concern with two-year-olds is that having tantrums does not become a habitual behavior. You should discourage the behavior by ignoring it right from the beginning.

STATE THE GOAL

The goal is for the child to stop throwing tantrums and to learn appropriate ways to express wishes.

PROCEDURE

To eliminate tantrums, the basic strategy involves three simultaneous steps:

- Ignore tantrums when they occur.
- Frequently reinforce appropriate behaviors.
- Help the child deal with emotional reactions in acceptable ways.

Definition

Throwing tantrums is a collection of behaviors including the child throwing herself bodily on the floor, kicking, pounding fists, crying, screaming, and other dramatic actions carried out in reaction to an upsetting event.

Baseline

Take three days to collect baseline information against which progress can be measured. Mark on paper each time the child throws a tantrum, and keep a record of how long tantrums last. The child may not, at first, decrease the frequency of tantrums, but may decrease their duration. Have a clock or watch with a second hand available. When the child has a tantrum, time it and write down how long it lasts. At the end of each day, record the total number of tantrums on the first graph (Frequency of Tantrums) at the end of this chapter. Then record the average duration of all tantrums of that day on the second graph (Duration of Tantrums: Number of Minutes). Compute the average duration by totaling the length in time of all the tantrums and dividing by the number of tantrums:

$$\frac{\text{Total Minutes of All Tantrums}}{\text{Total Number of Tantrums}} = \text{Average Duration}$$

Program

Once baseline is completed, continue to the following program. It is very important that all teachers follow these procedures consistently.

Ignore Tantrums When They Occur. When the child throws a tantrum, completely ignore it. In the past, the child was given considerable attention for the inappropriate behavior. The child expects that attention to continue. The duration, the intensity, and the total number of tantrums may increase when you first begin ignoring them. Once the child realizes that she receives no attention, no matter how hard, how long, or how often she throws tantrums, she should quickly decrease and stop this behavior. When the child has a tantrum, do the following:

1. Do not give any reinforcement whatsoever. Ignore all behavior associated with the tantrum. Do not approach the child, talk to her, reason with or explain to her, or even look at her. Act as though she is not in the room. Do not let your facial expression or bodily posture convey that you are in any way concerned with the child's behavior. Even in the midst of a tantrum, a child picks up cues from you that express your concern, your frustration, or your anger with the situation. You must feel, as well as act, your detachment from the child's behavior.

2. Leave the child where she is, if possible. Continue the classroom routine around the tantrum. If the child's tantrum is so disruptive that you cannot continue planned activities, you have one of two choices. You can move the child out of the room to continue her tantrum elsewhere, or you can change the schedule. If you do the former, be sure the child is placed in a spot where an adult can watch her without paying her any attention. It is important that ignoring be carried out wherever the child is. If you decide to change the schedule, be sure you do this only if it is not overly disruptive. For instance, if your plans call for reading a story followed by outside play, simply reverse the order. The child may continue her tantrum where she is while the other children go outside.

3. If another child calls your attention to the tantrum, say that you are aware of it and that you want the other child to stop the tantrum on her own. Convey that you will give the child attention once the tantrum has stopped, but not before.

4. Keep your ear tuned to the child. If you hear that the tantrum has stopped, go to the child. Sit by her if she needs a few moments to calm down, but do not talk about the tantrum. When she is ready, help her select and

join an activity. If the child has been outside the room, tell her she may return.

5. If the child resumes her tantrum after you go to her, walk away. Ignore the behavior until she stops. Do not attend to the child during the tantrum.

Frequently Reinforce Appropriate Behaviors. At the same time you ignore tantrums, let the child know what behaviors you value. Be alert to the child's appropriate behaviors and reinforce them frequently. Look for times when the child is engaged in activities, interacting with other children, helping with clean-up, or in any other way participating as expected. Use your informal observations for clues to what might trigger tantrums. If you see a potential problem situation that the child has handled in an acceptable way, give lavish praise and attention.

Help the Child Find Acceptable Alternatives To Handling Emotional Reactions. The child may react consistently with a tantrum to situations where she feels angry, frustrated, or in some way upset. She must learn to use more acceptable reactions. Carefully watch for situations to which the child might react with a tantrum. If you see a potential tantrum situation, do the following:

1. Go to the child quickly and take any immediate measures that may need to be taken (such as preventing an aggressive act, or preventing a toy from being grabbed from someone).
2. Get down to the level of the child and put your arm around her. Verbally acknowledge the emotion that the situation has aroused. Say, for instance,

> "I know. It really makes you feel angry when you can't have the toy you want."
> "It hurt when Terry and Arnold told you they didn't want to play with you."
> "Boy! When you want to keep working on that wood sculpture but it's time to clean up, it really upsets you."

3. Encourage the child to express her feelings either by agreeing with you, elaborating on your statement, or explaining a different feeling.
4. Now say, "What can we do about it?" Quickly explore a few alternatives for handling the situation with the child.
5. If appropriate, help the child carry out a solution to the problem situation.
6. Provide praise for her handling of the situation. If the child begins to throw a tantrum at any point, move away. Ignore such a tantrum in the way discussed earlier.

Continue Graphing the Behavior. As the program to eliminate tantrums progresses, continue to count and time the tantrums each day. Draw a vertical line after baseline. Record the total number of tantrums and the average time they last on the two graphs. Expect an increase on the duration graph and a possible increase on the frequency graph for the first few days. This increase should soon level off, and then quickly decrease.

Maintenance

Continue to give praise for appropriate behaviors, particularly for acceptable ways of dealing with difficult situations. Give such praise at the same rate as you do for the other children in the class. If the child throws a tantrum again, simply ignore it.

RECORD KEEPING GRAPH

CHILD'S NAME _____ AGE _____ DATE _____

GOAL _____

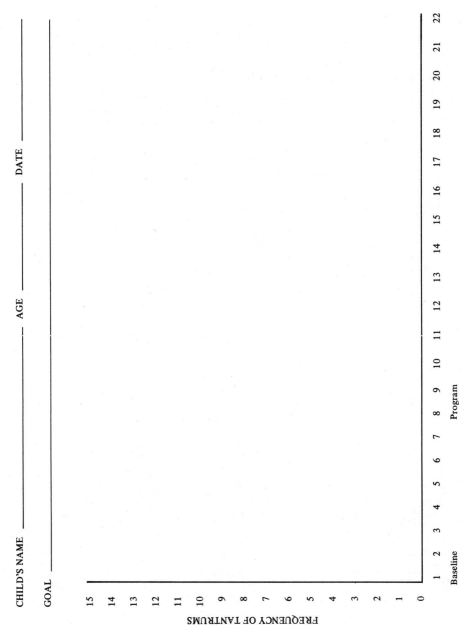

FREQUENCY OF TANTRUMS

15 14 13 12 11 10 9 8 7 6 5 4 3 2 1 0

1 2 3 4 5 6 7 8 9 10 11 12 13 14 15 16 17 18 19 20 21 22

Baseline   Program

DAYS

RECORD KEEPING GRAPH

CHILD'S NAME _____   AGE _____   DATE _____

GOAL _____

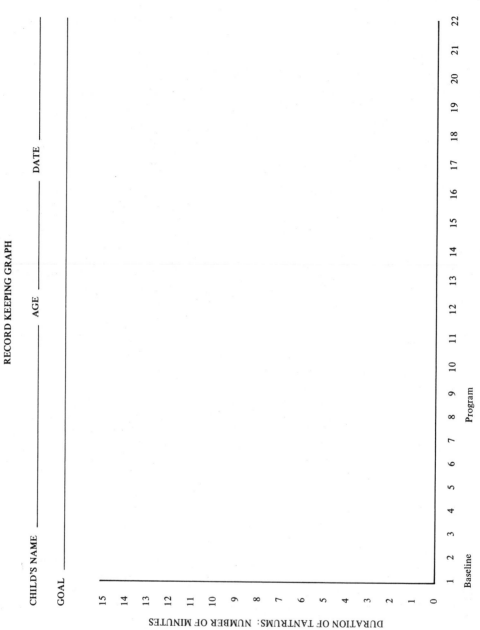

CHAPTER 24

Pouting

"All right, children, it's time to put everything away now. Your parents will be coming to pick you up soon." This statement is made several minutes after the teacher warned that cleanup time was coming. Children start putting away toys and materials. Three-year-old Tessa, however, continues with the matching game she is using. A teacher walks up to her and says, "Come on, Tessa. You have to put things away now. It's almost time to go home." Tessa lays out more cards and ignores the teacher. "Tessa, that's enough now!" says the teacher, beginning to pick up some of the cards. Tessa takes the cards she holds in her hand, slams them on the table, crosses her arms in front of her and pouts. "Come on, Tessa. Help me put these cards back in the box." Tessa mumbles, "I don't want to," and continues to pout. "You know you're supposed to clean up what you use, Tessa." Tessa refuses to help, pouting the whole time. The teacher finally puts the game away, and Tessa is in a foul mood when her mother arrives to take her home. The teachers are concerned because Tessa frequently refuses to do what is expected of her and shows her displeasure by pouting.

STATE THE BEHAVIOR

The child pouts frequently to express displeasure.

OBSERVE THE BEHAVIOR

Take several days to observe the child's behavior closely. Such observation should give you some clues about when and under what circumstances the child pouts.

A. When does the child seem to pout most?
- Any time of day
- Early in the day

- Late in the day
- Around nap time
- Around mealtimes
- During free choice activities
- During structured activities
- At cleanup times
- During transitions
- During outdoor play periods
- When an adult is nearby
- When other children are nearby

B. What seems to trigger the pouting?
  - The child is told no by a teacher or another child
  - The child is prevented from doing something
  - The child does not want to do something she is asked to do
  - The child is prevented from joining in play by other children

C. What happens when the child pouts?
  - An adult tells her to stop pouting
  - The child gets what she wants as a result of pouting
  - The pouting changes to crying
  - The child verbally expresses what is bothering her
  - The child does not talk about what is bothering her

Use these observations to help you determine how to prevent and then stop the child's pouting behavior.

EXPLORE THE CONSEQUENCES

When a child pouts, she uses a nonverbal means of expressing her displeasure. Her face screws up, her mouth and forehead pucker, and her body may stiffen with the arms crossed in front. Pouting often signals that the child is going to stand firm to what she wants. It underlines the child's struggle for power with an adult. The child is conveying that she does not want to do what someone has asked her to do or that she is upset because someone will not let her do what she wants to do. Often in this kind of situation, the adult continues to insist and the child continues to refuse. At some point the child learned that she could get her own way by standing firm against the adult's wishes and pouting. Later, pouting and stubbornness become standard behaviors for the child. When such a child enters preschool, she expects to continue getting her way. She uses pouting to convey that she wants to do something other than what has been asked of her and to display her feelings if she is not allowed to do what she wants. If teachers give attention to the child when she pouts, they reinforce the behavior.

CONSIDER ALTERNATIVES

Consider if one of the following suggestions will help you deal with the child who pouts.

- The child may have noticed another youngster pouting and may be imitating this child. Children learn by assuming different roles. A child may simply be trying out an expression she has seen on another child or even an adult. Unless the pouting is accompanied by marked stubbornness, ignore it and do not worry about it.
- Be careful to avoid situations which put you in direct confrontation with the child. Provide many choices in the program. The child should have a chance to select what she wants to do. Take care to word requests so they do not result in a stubborn reaction. For instance, say, "Let's get these beads back in the box. I'll start picking up the red ones. Which color do you want to pick up first?" rather than, "You're going to have to pick up all these beads you dumped out." The opportunity to make choices and some tactful wording by teachers may help avert stubbornness and pouting.

If neither of these suggestions provides help for the child who pouts, move on to the following program.

STATE THE GOAL

The goal is for the child to stop pouting by discontinuing the stubborn clashes of wills with adults.

PROCEDURE

The basic strategy involves three simultaneous steps:

- Avoid situations that might result in pouting and stubbornness.
- Reinforce compliance.
- Ignore pouting when it does occur.

Definition

Pouting involves a child's physical reactions, such as puckering the mouth and forehead, which reflect the child's unwillingness to comply with what she is asked to do or not to do.

Baseline

Before continuing, spend three days gathering baseline information. Every time the child pouts, mark it down on paper. At the end of each day, total the marks and transfer the total to the Record Keeping Graph. These three days provide you with information with which you can compare later progress.

Program

Follow this program once you have collected baseline data. It is important that all teachers follow it consistently.

Avoid Situations That Might Result In Pouting and Stubbornness. Examine the information from your informal observation for clues as to what triggers pouting and when it is most likely to occur. Avoid potential pouting situations as often as possible, as they result in the child having negative feelings about herself. If she gets her own way, she is still aware of the adult's displeasure or anger with her. If she does not get her way, she gets neither satisfaction nor the adult's approval. It is important, therefore, to avoid potential problem situations to protect the child's sense of self-worth. Following are some suggestions that will serve as preventive measures:

1. Avoid giving direct orders to the child. Word requests to the child in a way that reflects your respect for her as a person. Children are much more likely to comply if you say, "I would appreciate it if you would..." than if you say, "You have to...." Children deserve consideration and courtesy as much as adults do.

2. Give the child choices. There is less likely to be a clash of wills if you ask a child, "Would you like to put the napkins on the table, or would you rather pour the juice?" than if you say, "You have to put the napkins on the table." The child who is given a choice by the teacher does not feel trapped in a black and white situation of "do it and please me" or "don't do it and risk displeasing me."

3. Give the child the chance to say no if a choice is really hers to make. If you say, "Would you like to work at the woodworking table?" and the child answers "no," there should be no negative reactions from you. In such a case simply say, "Fine. You might want to paint at the easel or build in the block area." If you ask the child a question to which she can answer yes or no, be sure to accept either answer.

4. If there is a task about which the child has no choice, be careful with the wording you use. You might make a game of such a situation. Rather than say, "You have to go to the rug and sit down for storytime now," try, "Let's pretend we're bunnies and we're hopping over to the rug for storytime."

5. If the child wants to do something which you cannot allow, stop the child in an understanding way. Let her know that you understand there is something she would really like to do. Explain why you cannot let her do it. Provide an alternative if you possibly can. For instance, say, "I know you really want to paint right now, but we have to put the paints away and get ready for lunch. After nap time I'll bring out the paints again and then you can have a chance to paint if you'd like. Is there a special color of paint you'd like me to prepare?"

Reinforce Compliance. When you ask the child to do something and she complies with your request, praise her. Let the child know you are pleased with such behavior and that you value it. You might say, "Thank you! I really appreciate it when you help with cleanup when I ask you!" or "What a lovely smile! That's the way I like to see my helpers!" The child will feel good from such a response and will also realize that you feel good. Given time, the child will recognize that there is nothing to be gained from resisting and pouting, but that there is reward for positive reaction.

If the child wants to do something that you cannot allow and she stops when asked, praise her. Help her find an alternative activity.

Ignore Pouting When It Occurs. Pouting is a habit the child has acquired over a period of time. When you make a request and the child reacts by pouting, do the following:

1. Immediately stop what you are saying when the child starts to pout. Pause for a few seconds, and look at the child.
2. Say to her, "I cannot talk to you when you are pouting."
3. Wait a few more moments. If the child continues to pout, walk away. "I'll talk to you when you stop pouting."
4. If the child makes an effort to stop pouting when you ask her to, praise her and continue talking to her.
5. If you have asked the child to do something that she refuses to do, do not make an issue of the matter. You are only reinforcing her pouting if you insist or argue with her. Simply walk away. Do not engage in a clash of wills.
6. If the child wants to do something that you cannot allow, walk away. If the child persists in the activity, particularly if it poses a safety hazard or is disruptive, remove her from it. Take the child to a chair in a quiet corner of the room or outside the class and ask her to stay there for a few minutes. Then move away and pay the child no attention. After about three minutes, tell her she may return. Remember that your aim is to minimize attention for pouting. Place the child in a chair or remove her from the room only as a last resort.

With time, these steps should help the child realize that there are more effective ways of reacting to requests than pouting.

Continue Graphing the Behavior. Each day of the program, count the number of times the child pouts. Record the total on the Record Keeping Graph. Draw a vertical line after the baseline data to differentiate it from the data you collect during the program. Progress will probably be slow because you are trying to eliminate a habitual response. You should see a steady decline on the graph over a period of time. Be persistent until you reach your goal.

Maintenance

When the child has stopped pouting, remember that part of the change is due to your change in response as well. Therefore, continue communicating with the child in ways that reflect your concern for her interests, your understanding, and your respect. Give appropriate choices whenever possible. Also, continue giving reinforcement for desired behaviors. If the child occasionally responds by pouting, ignore it as you did when you were implementing the program.

RECORD KEEPING GRAPH

CHILD'S NAME _____ AGE _____ DATE _____

GOAL _____

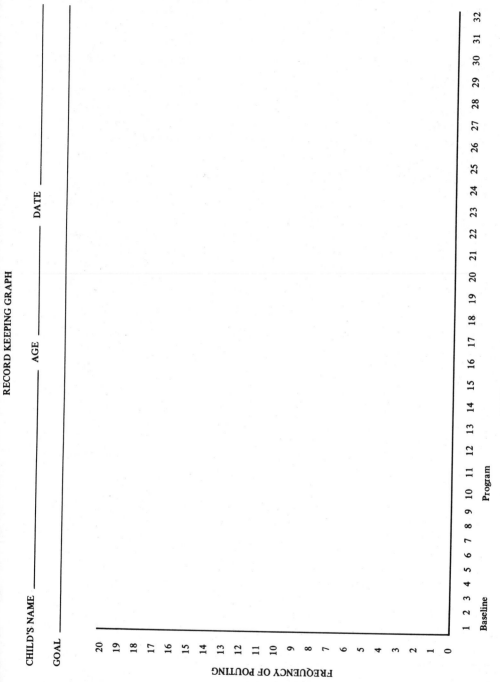

FREQUENCY OF POUTING

20
19
18
17
16
15
14
13
12
11
10
9
8
7
6
5
4
3
2
1
0

1 2 3 4 5 6 7 8 9 10 11 12 13 14 15 16 17 18 19 20 21 22 23 24 25 26 27 28 29 30 31 32

Baseline   Program

DAYS

CHAPTER 25

Baby Talk

"Baby want cwacker." "Arnold! What do you want?" "Cwacker," answered four-year-old Arnold. "Come on, Arnold, stop the baby talk. What do you need?" The teacher begins to feel exasperated and her voice reflects this. "Me want cwacker. Me want eat cwacker," responds Arnold. "Oh! You want a cracker. Well, we'll be having snack in a few minutes." Arnold smiles, and as the teacher walks away, says, "Goo-goo!" Later that day Arnold engages in a similar conversation with another teacher when he wants to swing. "Baby wanna swing." After several minutes of tolerant explanations about all the swings being occupied (which Arnold knows), a swing becomes vacant and Arnold gets into it. Arnold sits with his thumb in his mouth until a teacher asks, "Why aren't you swinging, Arnold?" Arnold pulls his thumb from his mouth long enough to say, "Baby no know how swing." The teacher sighs and pushes Arnold several times. She knows he is quite capable of pumping himself. Throughout the rest of the day, Arnold continues using baby talk and acting like a baby — much to the concern of the teachers. His use of appropriate speech for his age is becoming more and more rare.

STATE THE BEHAVIOR

The child uses "baby talk," speaking in a manner not characteristic of his age.

OBSERVE THE BEHAVIOR

Take some time to observe the child informally so you can gain some insight into this behavior.

A. When is the child most likely to use baby talk?
- Early in the day, soon after arriving
- Late in the day

- Near nap or rest time
- Around mealtimes
- During teacher-directed activities
- During group activities
- During child-selected activities
- At toileting times
- During transitions
- At cleanup times

B. What is the child doing when he uses baby talk?

- The child is talking with an adult
- The child is asking a question
- The child is requesting a toy or material
- The child is seeking the teacher's attention
- The child is playing alone
- The child is playing with other children
- The child is upset
- The child has been asked not to do something
- The child has hurt himself
- The child has been hurt by another child
- The child is not engaged in any activity
- The child is asking for help in carrying out an activity
- The child is playing in the housekeeping area
- The child often assumes the role of the baby in the housekeeping area
- The child often engages in activities such as crawling or sucking his thumb

C. What happens when the child uses baby talk?

- Teachers usually pay attention
- Teachers ignore such talk
- Teachers ask the child not to talk like a baby
- Other children take note of the child
- Other children laugh
- Other children pay no attention
- Other children fall into play with the child, assuming he will take on the role of baby

D. What does the child talk about when he uses baby talk?

Use the insight you gain from these observations to eliminate baby talk.

EXPLORE THE CONSEQUENCES

The child who uses baby talk deliberately, not because of a speech impediment, is probably doing so because this behavior brings him attention. It is

possible that as the child was growing up he found that the use of appropriate speech did not gain the attention he desired and needed. Somehow, he discovered the use of baby talk as a way of getting attention. He may have made some statements in a style recognizably below his ability and age level and found that adults listened, laughed, and commented as a result. The child may also revert to baby talk if his status changes from only child to older brother. A child may try to regain the singular position he enjoyed before the new baby came by imitating that baby in the hope that his parents will attend to him more and treat him like that baby. Once the child finds that baby talk gains him attention, whether indulgent or critical, he may decide to continue to use it.

When a child in preschool uses baby talk to a considerable extent, the teachers may unintentionally reinforce the behavior. Reactions like, "Aren't you a cute baby!" or "Stop it, now. You're too old to talk like that!" only serve to reinforce the behavior. A more systematic approach is necessary to eliminate baby talk.

CONSIDER ALTERNATIVES

Consider whether one of the following suggestions might help you deal with the problem of the child who uses baby talk.

- A child's immature speech may be due to a speech defect of some kind. A hearing problem or developmental delay could cause the child to use language that is inappropriate for his age. If the child constantly uses baby talk and you note other signs of immaturity or poor hearing, recommend to the parents that medical testing be done.
- The child who uses baby talk may be doing this for a relatively short period after a new brother or sister has entered his life. Such a reaction is fairly common and can be handled in a way that will prevent the problem from becoming bigger. The child who talks like a baby is expressing some confusion and concern about his new status. As a teacher, you can help the child deal with the situation by being understanding, clarifying his feelings, and answering questions. Follow the program outlined in this chapter to discourage baby talk. At the same time, spend time with the child talking about his new brother or sister and what has happened to him as a result.
- Children enjoy role playing and engage in this activity frequently. Most children prefer taking on the role of adults rather than of younger children when they have this choice. Some children, either by their own choice or by peers, are cast into the role of the baby during dramatic play, and enter such a role wholeheartedly. Do not confuse the child's assumption

of the baby role during role playing with baby talk as defined in this chapter. It is only when talking like a baby is inappropriate (at the wrong time, wrong place, or wrong occasion) that it may present a problem.

- Be sure that your expectations of the child are appropriate. There is a wide range in the abilities and development of young children. Some two-year-old children have large vocabularies and are very expressive in their use of language. Others are barely beginning to talk, using single words or two-word combinations to communicate. Both are common among two-year-olds and should not give cause for concern. By age three, however, children should have a fairly good command of the language. If a child is not talking in sentences and has a very limited vocabulary, then developmental, speech, or hearing tests may be needed to pinpoint the cause of the language delay.

If none of the previous suggestions serve to answer the problem, continue on to the following program.

STATE THE GOAL

The goal is for the child to stop using baby talk when this is inappropriate and to speak in a manner characteristic of his age.

PROCEDURE

The basic approach to eliminating baby talk involves ignoring it when it occurs and reinforcing appropriate use of language.

Definition

Baby talk means that the child speaks in a way that reflects less than his ability. It may include use of incomplete sentences, single words, gurgles and coos, mispronunciation of words, or elimination of certain consonants.

Baseline

Spend three days collecting baseline information. Carefully listen to the child and record each time he uses baby talk by making a mark on the paper. Consider each incident in which the child uses only baby talk as one count; this may include just a word or two or it may involve an entire conversation of several minutes. If the flow of baby talk is broken by normal speech and then resumed, count this as two incidents. At the end of each day, add all the marks and record the total on the Record Keeping Graph.

Program

After gathering baseline data, you are ready to begin. It is important that all teachers follow the procedures at all times.

Ignore Baby Talk When It Occurs. Baby talk is easy to reinforce if you give it attention. Whether your reaction is tolerant and amused or whether it conveys that you're displeased with the baby talk, the fact that you are reacting is reinforcing this behavior. It is important, therefore, to ignore baby talk whenever it occurs.

1. If you hear the child using baby talk, do not turn toward him, look at him, speak to him, or otherwise convey that you are paying attention to this behavior. Your actions should say that you're not even aware of it.
2. If you are talking to the child and he uses baby talk, stop what you intended to say and tell him instead, "I cannot talk to you when you use baby talk." Wait a few seconds. If the child talks normally, resume your conversation. If he continues to use baby talk, turn you back to him and walk away. It is important when you do this to give him attention for appropriate speech as soon thereafter as possible.
3. The child may want physical attention (to be hugged, to sit on your lap, to be picked up) and may convey this through baby talk. He may connect affectionate responses with being babylike. Let him know that show of affection is not reserved for babies. Tell him, "I'll be glad to pick you up when you tell me in *your* voice." If the child drops the baby talk, give him the response he asked for. If he continues the baby talk, walk away. As soon thereafter as possible, however, give him a hug or a squeeze when he uses appropriate speech.
4. If the child uses baby talk during a group activity, ignore it as well. When you call on the child to answer a question or make a comment, if he answers in baby talk, first look away from him. Then say, "Can someone else tell me_____?" Call on another child then. Do not comment on the baby talk or in any way call attention to it. Your reaction should not be punitive, merely neutral. Do not let your facial expression show displeasure or annoyance. Such a reaction would only convey that the child did annoy you by using baby talk.
5. If another child calls your attention to the fact that the child is using baby talk, simply say, "I know." Try to redirect this child's interest into an activity. It will be helpful to decrease peer attention as well as your own reaction as much as possible.

Reinforce Appropriate Use Of Language. As you ignore the undesirable behavior, let the child know what behavior you expect and value by reinforcing it when it occurs. Be alert to the use of appropriate language by the child. Pay attention to him when he speaks properly. You can reinforce proper speech by being attentive and responsive when he uses it. Periodically tell him, "I really like the way you are talking," or "It's great to hear you talk so nicely!" If the child uses baby talk a great deal, it is especially important to reinforce him when he speaks properly. Listen for appropriate language and praise it or attend to it immediately. Once the rate of baby talk decreases considerably, you can reinforce less often. Be sure you still reinforce appropriate speech, or the child may revert to baby talk.

Continue Graphing the Behavior. Each day, continue to keep a record of the number of incidents of baby talk in the same way as you did during baseline. Draw a line after the baseline data; record the total each day. A decline in incidents of baby talk tells you when to cut back on frequency of reinforcement given for appropriate language use.

Maintenance

After baby talk has been eliminated, continue to attend to appropriate speech. If the child talks to you normally, give him your attention and the courtesy he deserves. If he occasionally uses baby talk, simply ignore it.

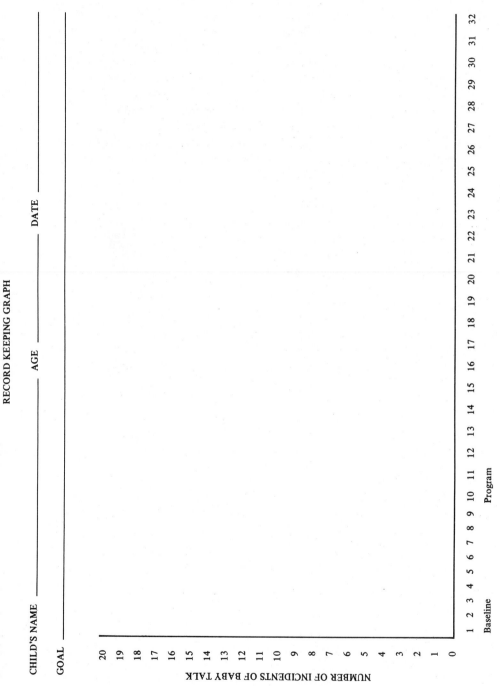

RECORD KEEPING GRAPH

CHILD'S NAME —————— AGE —————— DATE ——————

GOAL ——————

NUMBER OF INCIDENTS OF BABY TALK

20
19
18
17
16
15
14
13
12
11
10
9
8
7
6
5
4
3
2
1
0

1 2 3 4 5 6 7 8 9 10 11 12 13 14 15 16 17 18 19 20 21 22 23 24 25 26 27 28 29 30 31 32

Baseline   Program

DAYS

CHAPTER 26

Thumb Sucking

Corey has been in the day care center for two years, since he was two years old. As a two-year-old, his thumb sucking was tolerated because it was not unusual for his age. Now that he is four, his teachers worry because Corey spends so much time with his thumb in his mouth, doing nothing else. They have tried pulling his thumb from his mouth, coaxing him to remove it, and telling him that he is too old to suck his thumb. Corey is happier when he has his thumb in his mouth. The teachers feel frustrated but are resigned to his behavior. They wish they could get Corey more actively involved in classroom activities. They feel he is missing too much.

STATE THE BEHAVIOR

The child frequently keeps a thumb (or fingers) in his mouth.

OBSERVE THE BEHAVIOR

Observe the child for a few days to gain some insight into his behavior.

A. When is the child most likely to suck his thumb?
- Throughout the day
- Early in the day
- Toward the end of the day
- Near nap time
- Around mealtimes
- During group times
- When children are required to listen
- During self-selected activities
- During transitions

B. What is the child doing just before he puts his thumb in his mouth?

- The child is not engaged in an activity
- The child takes a brief break while participating in an activity to suck his thumb
- The child plays alone
- The child plays with other children
- The child engages in an activity that does not require him to use both hands
- The child sits by a teacher
- The child sits alone
- The child talks to an adult or another child
- The child seems tired
- The child is unable to complete a task
- The child becomes upset
- The child holds a favorite blanket or other security object

C. Does the child engage in activities while he sucks his thumb?

D. What happens when the child stops sucking his thumb?

E. How long does the child usually suck his thumb?

EXPLORE THE CONSEQUENCES

Thumb sucking is usually a long-standing habit which starts in early infancy. In fact, some babies suck their thumbs even before they are born, *in utero*. For some children, thumb sucking partly satisfies the need for sucking which all infants have. It assumes the function of providing security as the child gets older. When a preschooler frequently sucks his thumb, he does so not only because it is a long-standing habit but also because it has become a way of reacting to unknown or even everyday events. By the time the child reaches the preschool years, it may be difficult to eliminate thumb sucking. Usually some form of social pressure makes the child change this habit, often at the cost of his feelings of self-worth. Such a child is frequently told that what he is doing is "baby stuff." He may be ridiculed, laughed at, and even punished. Parents are usually quite concerned about thumb sucking. This behavior can affect tooth development, which may result in costly orthodonture later. Also, it seems inappropriate for a child no longer in infancy. Parents and teachers should help the child stop sucking his thumb. This is a long-range goal that must be achieved in such a way that it does not compromise the child's self-esteem and self-confidence.

CONSIDER ALTERNATIVES

If a child habitually sucks his thumb, this behavior is easy to identify. Usually children who suck their thumbs do so more often under conditions of stress. This section explores some causes of thumb sucking and possible ways of reducing the behavior.

- Examine the activities and curriculum provided for the children. These must be appropriate for the children enrolled. They should not be above their level, causing frustration, nor below their ability, causing boredom. Children may react to a program that does not really meet their needs by inappropriate behavior such as thumb sucking. Change activities as needed if you decide that the children's needs are not being met. When children are involved in and enjoy what they are doing, they are less likely to feel the need for thumb sucking.
- Thumb sucking may provide sensory stimulation. Consider children's indirectly expressed need for activities that provide such stimuli. Include these in your program. Plan more water play, sand play, mud play, bins with a variety of textures, cooking projects, and smell and taste discrimination activities. Provide a variety of activities to help satisfy the enjoyment of sensory stimulation.
- Examine the interaction between teachers and the child. A child may react with thumb sucking if he perceives the adults as overly directive, overpowering, or domineering. Such a child responds more openly to gentle and quiet guidance. Observe adult-child interactions in the classroom. If one or more of the teachers seem to upset the child, consider making some changes. Discuss the problem with all of the teachers in a group meeting. Look for ways to make interaction with adults less stressful for the child.
- A child whose hands are busy with activities will not be able to put a thumb in his mouth. Provide a well-balanced schedule of activities and options so the child has numerous opportunities to use his hands and does not find himself with nothing to do.

Consider these suggestions and incorporate any that are appropriate into the following program.

STATE THE GOAL

The goal is for the child to decrease thumb sucking while at school. It is probably unrealistic to expect the child to completely stop this behavior. A decrease will help the child to eventually eliminate it.

PROCEDURE

The basic strategy for eliminating thumb sucking involves three simultaneous steps:

- Provide a chart for the child to keep track of his progress.
- Provide activities that are alternatives to thumb sucking.
- Frequently reinforce the child for not sucking his thumb.

Definition

Thumb sucking is a behavior in which the child keeps a thumb or other fingers in his mouth and often does not participate in activities while he is doing so.

Baseline

Spend three days gathering baseline information. About every fifteen minutes throughout the day, look at the child. Do not include nap time. If the child has his thumb in his mouth, make a mark on paper. At the end of the day, transfer the total number to the Record Keeping Graph. The maximum number of marks will be determined by the length of the program. If the child is enrolled for three hours, then the maximum possible number of marks is twelve. (One mark every fifteen minutes equals four marks per hour, times three hours, equals twelve.) If the child is enrolled for ten hours per day, then the maximum number of marks may be thirty-two or thirty-four. (Exclude one and one-half to two hours for a nap.) Set up the following chart for collecting the daily counts:

Date	9:00	9:15	9:30	9:45	10:00	10:15	10:30	10:45

This kind of information gathering tells you not only how often the child sucks his thumb, but also when the behavior is most likely to occur. A pattern may emerge to help you focus your program on times when the behavior happens most often.

Program

After gathering the baseline data, start on the following program. It will be best if one teacher consistently implements the first step (charting) of the program. The other two steps should be carried out by all the teachers.

Make the Child Aware of Your Goal and Keep Track With Him On A Chart.
Thumb sucking is not maintained by adult attention and reinforcement. The
child receives intrinsic satisfaction when he does it. Ignoring the behavior will
not eliminate it. Tell the child the goal and your reasons for it. Actively involve
the child in reaching that goal.

1. Before you begin, have a talk with the child about thumb sucking. Tell
   him that you realize he enjoys sucking his thumb; do not deny the pleasure and reassurance he derives from it. However, convey to the child that
   the behavior concerns you. Tell the child that you really would like him
   to take part in and enjoy all activities but that you know he cannot do
   so when his thumb is in his mouth. If you think the child can understand,
   talk to him about the long-range effects thumb sucking can have on his
   teeth.
2. Tell the child that you want to work with him to decrease some of the
   thumb sucking. Say, "Let's see if the two of us together can cut down your
   thumb sucking. We'll make it a game that we can play. I'll put up this
   chart [described later], and you'll get to put a special star on it every time
   you don't suck your thumb for ten minutes [shorter if the child sucks his
   thumb constantly]." Speak enthusiastically and let the child know that
   you fully expect him to succeed.
3. Purchase a box of gummed stars and make the chart on which the child will
   keep track. This is not the same as your data collection chart. Use the
   child's chart for about one hour per day. Select an hour during which various activity choices are available to the child. The chart can be decorated
   to make it more appealing, but basically it should look as shown here. Each
   horizontal row represents one day.

CHILD'S NAME							
Date	10:00	10:10	10:20	10:30	10:40	10:50	11:00

4. At the beginning of the hour during which you will be checking the behavior, tell the child that it is time to begin the game. Tell him, "Remember,
   you'll get a star for your chart if you don't suck your thumb for ten minutes. I'll watch you, and you watch yourself. Ready? Begin!"
5. Encourage the child frequently. Tell him how well he is doing and how
   proud you are of him. Do not wait until the end of the ten minutes to give
   praise.

6. If the child finishes the ten minutes without sucking his thumb, be lavish and enthusiastic in your verbal praise. Give the child a star and let him paste it in the appropriate space on the chart. Tell the other teachers that the child earned a star so they can also reinforce him.

7. If the child does not go the full ten minutes, do not make a fuss. Simply say, "Let's try again." If the child consistently cannot last ten minutes without putting a thumb in his mouth, decrease the time interval to five or even fewer minutes. Arrange the situation so that the child can experience success.

8. At the end of the hour tell the child that the "game" is over for today, but he can play it again tomorrow. Remind him not to suck his thumb during the rest of the day.

9. Share the chart with the child's parents at the end of the day. Do this when the child is present.

Provide Many Activities That Offer Alternatives To Thumb Sucking. As indicated before, when the child's hands are busy, he is less likely to suck his thumb. As you plan the curriculum, keep the following considerations in mind:

1. Be sure most activities involve action by the children. During storytime the children may pantomime parts of the story with their hands and arms. There should be no activities in which the children are required to merely watch an adult do something. Young children learn by doing, not by passive watching.

2. Provide activity choices. There should be times of the school day when children can select what they want to do. If a given activity does not interest a child, there should be other activities from which to choose. Not only does this provide for varied interests within the group, but it also encourages conscious decision making by the children.

3. There should be a variety of sensory activities planned into the curriculum. Children respond well to media that provide different types of tactile and other sensory stimulation. Water, sand, mud, clay, finger paint, glue, rice, beans, styrofoam, corn starch, and liquid soap all have unique textures. Each helps to satisfy the need for varied sensory stimulation.

4. If the activities begin to seem stale because you have done them so often, plan some changes to rekindle the children's interest. A child may suck his thumb because he is bored. Plan changes through new activities, new interest centers in the classroom, and rearrangement of the daily schedule. Look for activity ideas in some of the many preschool activity books that are on the market. Add new interest centers such as a music area, a science table, or a beauty shop. Rearrange the classroom to accommodate a new center. Change the schedule to add new types of activities, eliminate old ones, rearrange the order of daily events, or adjust some time blocks. Periodic novelty revitalizes the children's interest and yours in the program.

Frequently Reinforce the Child for Not Sucking His Thumb. At all times of the day, look for occasions when the child does not have his thumb in his mouth. Reinforce what he is doing by your presence, or by praise, a pat, or a hug. Periodically tell the child you are proud of him because he is sucking his thumb less and less. Let him know that you are aware of the effort he is making to change his behavior and that you appreciate it.

Continue Graphing the Behavior. Throughout each day of the program, continue to check the child about every fifteen minutes and mark whether he is sucking his thumb. Record the total each day on the Record Keeping Graph. Draw a vertical line after baseline to differentiate it from the program information. Because thumb sucking is a long-standing habit, progress may be slow. Expect the program to take some time; you will see a gradual decline on the graph.

Maintenance

Discontinue the chart when the child loses interest or reaches the goal. Continue to provide a well-rounded program. Give the child periodic reinforcement for participation, as you do with all the children. The child may again suck his thumb at times when he is tired, does not feel well, or feels stressed. This is to be expected and should be accepted by adults.

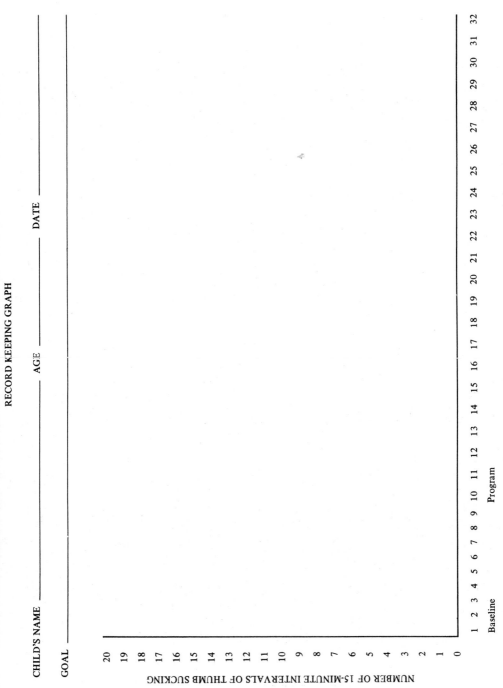

RECORD KEEPING GRAPH

CHILD'S NAME _____   AGE _____   DATE _____

GOAL _____

NUMBER OF 15-MINUTE INTERVALS OF THUMB SUCKING

20
19
18
17
16
15
14
13
12
11
10
9
8
7
6
5
4
3
2
1
0

1 2 3 4 5 6 7 8 9 10 11 12 13 14 15 16 17 18 19 20 21 22 23 24 25 26 27 28 29 30 31 32

Baseline   Program

DAYS

CHAPTER 27

Pant Wetting

This is the beginning of Cheryl's second year in the Head Start Center. Since she began in the program, the teachers have watched her blossom from a shy and reluctant child into one who eagerly engages in school activities and enjoys the friendship of other children. During her first year at the center, the teachers spent much time and effort getting Cheryl to be a fully participating member of the group. Now Cheryl is one of the veterans.

About a month after this school year began, Cheryl came up to one of the teachers and whispered, "Mrs. Ritter, I went potty in my pants." Mrs. Ritter took Cheryl to the bathroom, took off her wet clothes, and found some dry things for her to change into. About a week later the incident was repeated. It happened twice more that same week. For the last three weeks, Cheryl has had two to three accidents every day. The teachers are concerned since this behavior never happened last year. They have tried to shame Cheryl into stopping by telling her, "Big girls don't do that."

STATE THE BEHAVIOR

The child frequently wets her pants.

OBSERVE THE BEHAVIOR

It is very important to get as many clues as possible about the child who wets her pants. Your informal observation will be helpful.

A. When does the child usually wet her pants?
- Unpredictable; there seems to be no pattern
- Within an hour of meals and snacks
- During nap

- During outside play
- Indoors
- Soon after arriving at school

B. What usually precedes pant wetting?
- The child is in the bathroom
- The child sees another child urinate
- The child undresses to go to the bathroom
- The child has gotten up from the toilet
- The child washes her hands
- The child is engaged in water play
- The child drinks water or juice
- The child sits on a teacher's lap
- The child is unable to complete a task
- The child is told no by a teacher or another child
- The child is tired
- The child is engrossed in an activity

C. What does the child do after she wets her pants?
- The child announces the accident to anyone nearby
- The child quietly tells one teacher
- The child tells no one
- The child prefers to remain in the wet clothes
- The child wants to undress and put on fresh clothes by herself
- The child asks the teacher to change her

This preliminary observation should give you some ideas about what might trigger pant wetting, when it occurs, and how the child feels about it. Such information is very useful in trying to end this behavior.

EXPLORE THE CONSEQUENCES

It is important for the preschool teacher to keep in mind the relatively short time the young child has been toilet trained. Many young preschoolers have accidents because they are not yet completely trained. The excitement of the moment can easily become more important than the urge to urinate. Suddenly the child can wait no longer and wets her pants. It takes time and practice for the young child to master the timing and to recognize the bodily cues that accompany toileting. Preschoolers three years old and younger can be expected to have occasional accidents. If the child has already mastered toilet training but still has frequent accidents, it may be a bid for attention. If the teacher reacts by providing this attention through lecturing, changing the child's pants, or punishment, the child's notion that pant wetting is a way to get attention is reinforced. At the same time, the child is given the message that what she has done is not fitting for a child her age. This causes the child to feel shame and question her self-worth.

CONSIDER ALTERNATIVES

There are many factors besides behavioral ones that can cause a child to wet her pants. Carefully consider whether one of the following might be the root of the problem.

- Young children are susceptible to urinary tract and kidney infections. A medical problem may cause pant wetting. Be alert to complaints or indications of pain, burning, or itching by the child. Even if you do not notice such cues, discuss the behavior with the parents. You may recommend they take the child to a doctor for a checkup.
- A child's level of maturity is also an important factor in dealing with pant wetting. It should be expected that young preschoolers will have accidents. When accidents occur, they should be handled in a matter-of-fact way. Children should be praised when they urinate in the toilet. At the same time, teachers of two- and three-year-olds should build frequent toileting times into the program and should be alert to cues such as a child holding herself. With young children, toileting is still a learning process rather than an accomplished skill, and should be treated as such.
- Sometimes children have accidents because they cannot undo their clothing quickly enough. Overalls, small buttons, belts with complicated buckles, tight snaps, and other gadgets can prove to be obstacles to getting undressed. Look at the children's clothes and watch how the youngsters handle them in the bathroom. If clothing is the problem, talk with the parents and suggest some alternatives or simple alterations.
- An unusual occurrence or stress in the child's life may also cause her to start to wet her pants. If something is amiss, take time to talk with the child and reassure her as much as possible. Understanding the unknown may relieve the problem, if the child is worried about something that no one has explained.
- Accidents can also be averted by careful scheduling. Teachers should give a reminder and provide time for going to the bathroom before nap, before going outside, and before leaving on a field trip. This is especially important if the children are going to be spending some time in a place where a bathroom is not readily available.

If one of these suggestions does not solve pant wetting, study the more detailed approach that follows.

STATE THE GOAL

The goal is for the child to stop wetting her pants.

PROCEDURE

This program is intended for an older preschooler who has been thoroughly toilet trained for at least half a year, but who unexpectedly begins having regular toileting accidents. A medical cause for the problem must be ruled out before proceeding. The basic strategy includes these procedures:

- Frequent reminders to go to the bathroom.
- Withdrawal of attention when accidents occur.

Definition

Pant wetting is any time when the child does not urinate into the toilet but instead urinates in her clothes. This is considered a problem if it happens frequently and regularly.

Baseline

Before starting any changes, keep track for three days of how often pant wetting occurs. Jot down the time of each accident. Mark on paper each time the child has an accident. At the end of each day, record the total number on the Record Keeping Graph. This information provides a baseline against which you can measure success once you implement the program.

Program

After gathering baseline information, begin the following procedure. All adults should use the procedure consistently.

Frequently Remind the Child to go to the Bathroom. Your baseline data should give you an idea of how often toileting accidents occur. Compute an average time and use it as a guide for timing reminders. For instance, if accidents occur every hour on the average, remind the child to go to the bathroom every 30 minutes.

1. Tell the child it is time to go to the bathroom. Take the child by the hand and lead her to the bathroom.
2. Ask the child to pull down her pants to urinate. If she objects, tell her she must try. Be firm.
3. If she urinates in the toilet, praise the child.
4. If the child is unable to urinate after two minutes, let her leave the bathroom.

If after three to five days the child is urinating regularly in the toilet and if the number of accidents has decreased, begin to lengthen the time between reminders. Gradually eliminate the reminders when the child's pant wetting decreases substantially.

Praise the Child For Going to the Bathroom By Herself. If the child goes to the bathroom without a reminder or if she tells you she has to go to the bathroom and then does so, praise her. Let her know how much you appreciate her behavior when she does not wet her pants. If the child is not embarrassed about her accidents, let other teachers and children know in her presence that she went to the bathroom without a reminder and that you are proud of her. *Do not* do this if it embarrasses the child.

When An Accident Does Occur, Ignore It. If the child comes to you and tells you she had an accident do the following:

1. Do not comment on it. In an unconcerned manner say, "I guess you'll have to change clothes."
2. Be prepared ahead of time. Keep a change of clothes and a plastic bag for the wet clothes to give to the child. Do not spend time with the child hunting for a change of clothes because this gives the child attention.
3. As soon as you give the child the clothes, leave. Do not stay nearby. Go elsewhere and let the child take as long as she needs to change. Withdraw the attention that usually follows an accident.
4. When the child has changed, let her put away the wet clothes and rejoin the group. Make no comments about the accident. If she tries to talk about it, do not respond.

Continue Graphing the Behavior. At the end of each day of the program, record the number of pant wetting incidents on the Record Keeping Graph. This record shows the progress and indicates when to decrease the number of reminders to go to the bathroom.

Maintenance

When pant wetting has ceased to occur for several days, you can assume the behavior has been changed. Discontinue reminders to go to the bathroom, and gradually discontinue praise for going to the bathroom without a reminder. Remember, however, that the child began the behavior in an effort to gain attention. Continue to give her praise and reinforcement for appropriate behaviors just as you do with the other children in the class.

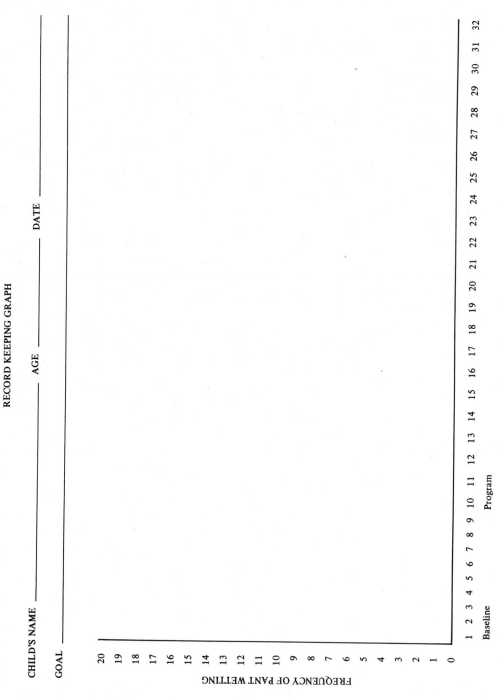

RECORD KEEPING GRAPH

CHILD'S NAME _____ AGE _____ DATE _____

GOAL _____

FREQUENCY OF PANT WETTING

20
19
18
17
16
15
14
13
12
11
10
9
8
7
6
5
4
3
2
1
0

1 2 3 4 5 6 7 8 9 10 11 12 13 14 15 16 17 18 19 20 21 22 23 24 25 26 27 28 29 30 31 32

Baseline   Program

DAYS

CHAPTER 28

28
Clinging

Mrs. Estes returns to the classroom after a break. Rusty rushes toward her and flings his arms around her legs. Three-year-old Rusty had been standing near the door, neither participating in activities nor talking to anyone, since Mrs. Estes left ten minutes earlier. Mrs. Estes smiles and ruffles Rusty's hair, then moves across the room. Rusty releases his hold on her legs, but hangs onto her skirt and follows her around the room. Mrs. Estes often talks to, smiles at, and touches Rusty. "Rusty, I need to get some more red paint," Mrs. Estes tells him. She tries to release the child's hold on her skirt. Rusty, however, hangs on. "Well, all right. Why don't you come with me and help me?" Rusty happily leaves the class with Mrs. Estes. An hour later, Rusty is still hanging onto her. Mrs. Estes and the other teachers are concerned. Her mobility is hampered, and she is not able to give as much attention to the other children as she would like. Rusty has been clinging to Mrs. Estes since school began almost three months ago. Lately, however, this behavior is more pronounced.

STATE THE BEHAVIOR

The child clings to the teacher. The child does not engage in appropriate class activities, and the teacher's time is tied up in dealing with the child.

OBSERVE THE BEHAVIOR

Gain further insight into this behavior by informally observing the child for a few days.

A. When does the child usually cling to a teacher?
- Throughout the day
- Soon after he arrives at school

- Toward the end of the school day
- Around rest or nap times
- At mealtimes
- During outdoor play
- During free choice activities
- During group times
- During teacher-planned activities
- During structured activity times
- During transitions
- At cleanup times
- When the child is required to use self-help skills (putting on a coat or undressing for the bathroom)

B. How does the child cling to a teacher?

- The child physically holds onto a part of the teacher or the teacher's clothing
- The child frequently asks to be picked up
- The child climbs onto the teacher's lap whenever the teacher is seated
- The child puts his arms around the teacher
- The child stays close to, but does not necessarily touch, the teacher

C. To whom does the child cling?

- Any adult
- One specific teacher
- Whichever teacher first greets him in the morning

D. What does the child do when the teacher to whom he clings is not available (out of the room, absent for the day, or busy elsewhere)?

- The child cries
- The child finds another teacher to cling to
- The child does not participate in activities
- The child joins classroom activities more than when the teacher is present

E. What are the child's relations to other people?

- The child clings to his parents
- The child parts from his parents with difficulty when brought to school
- The child leaves school with difficulty when picked up at the end of the day
- The child interacts with teachers other than the one to whom he clings (if he clings to only one teacher)
- The child interacts with the children at school

These informal observations should provide you with some information about the behavior to use as you work on eliminating it.

EXPLORE THE CONSEQUENCES

The child who persistently clings to a teacher probably began this behavior in response to a need for assurance and security. A child may feel such needs when he first starts school, when his usual routine is changed, or when a traumatic event disrupts his life. At such times the child needs to be given whatever reassurance he seeks to deal with the situation that has caused the insecurity. Once the child feels comfortable with his life, clinging should decrease and stop. Clinging is stopped by the child himself, through subtle withdrawal by the teacher, or through a combination of the child's and teacher's actions. Sometimes, however, such dependent behavior continues beyond the child's need for special reassurance. The child learns that when he clings to the teacher, he gets considerable attention.

It is also likely that if clinging persists over an extended time, the teacher begins reacting negatively to it. The teacher may be paying attention to the child, but the attention is paid in a way that reflects the teacher's annoyance, exasperation, or even anger. The child's message is, "I'll take attention in whatever way I can get it." The teacher's message is, "If you force me to pay attention to you, I'll let you know indirectly how annoyed you make me feel." As a result, the child feels that he is not worth positive attention from the teacher. He feels insecure because his relations with the teacher result in negative reaction. Therefore, the child clings all the more because he wants assurance that he is worthwhile. Clinging can lead to a self-defeating cycle in which neither child nor teacher is happy but which neither is able to break.

CONSIDER ALTERNATIVES

Consider the following suggestions for a solution to the problem of the child who clings to the teacher.

- Carefully examine possible reasons for the child's behavior. There may be a real need which causes the child to feel insecure. If clinging began recently, check with the parents to determine whether something unusual is upsetting the child. Talk with the child to ask what is bothering him. If you can pinpoint the reason for the behavior, you can help the child understand the situation better and find appropriate ways to deal with it.
- If the child clings to only one adult but is a functioning member of the class when that adult is absent, you may find the cause of the problem outside the child. This teacher may behave in a way that invites clinging by the child. When this is the case, the teacher should examine such behavior and how it affects the way the child acts. The effect this teacher

causes should be discussed in a helpful and nonthreatening manner. It would be helpful if such a discussion is based on objective observations made by another teacher or the director of the school.

To record such observations, an adult should write down as clearly as possible everything that was verbally and nonverbally conveyed at a time when the child was clinging to the teacher. (Direct quotes, gestures, and facial expressions should be noted.) The observations should contain no interpretations by the writer but should be based on what visibly happened. Objective observations can be recorded in ten or fifteen minutes. You need only a few of these for valuable information on what actually happens to cause the child's clinging behavior. By pinpointing the cause, the behavior can be more easily changed.

- The child may cling because he feels uncomfortable in the class. Perhaps the child has been placed in a class where the children are older and larger than he is or are beyond his developmental level. He may feel justifiably insecure in this setting and therefore clings to the teacher. If this is the case, move the child to a more appropriate class if possible.

If none of these suggestions helps deal with the problem, then continue to the following program.

STATE THE GOAL

The goal is for the child to not cling to a teacher but to engage constructively in the ongoing activities of the class.

PROCEDURE

The basic strategy to stop clinging behavior involves four steps:

- Tell the child what is expected of him.
- Move away from the child when he starts to cling.
- Give reinforcement when the child engages in desired activities.
- Set aside time for special attention, depending on if the child does not cling.

Definition

Clinging behavior involves all actions that keep the child close to the teacher, such as following, hugging, grabbing, or holding on to clothing. The teachers, as a group, should list all behaviors they consider to be clinging so they agree on a definition.

Baseline

Establish a baseline before continuing. For three days establish what percentage of time the child spends clinging to the teacher. Decide on one particular hour during which you expect considerable clinging to occur. Time how much of that hour the child clings to the teacher. The total number of minutes the child clings can then be converted into a percentage.

$$\frac{\text{Number of Minutes of Clinging}}{60 \text{ Minutes}} \times 100 = \% \text{ of clinging}$$

For instance, if the child clings 45 minutes out of the hour, compute as follows.

$$\frac{45}{60} = 0.75 \text{ or } 75\%$$

Transfer this percentage to the Record Keeping Graph. These three days of baseline provide a basis for comparing later progress.

Program

After establishing baseline, begin the following program. It is important that it be followed consistently by those to whom the child clings, and supported by all other adults in the classroom.

Let the Child Know Your Expectations. Tell the child what behaviors you expect from him in place of clinging. Tell him that you do not appreciate his clinging because it prevents him from participating in planned classroom activities, prevents you from doing your job, and deprives other children of your attention. Explaining these reasons will help you convey that you often feel annoyed when he clings. Be sure to express your feelings honestly. Be careful to assure the child that it is his behavior, and not him, that upsets you.

Emphasize the behaviors that you appreciate and will reinforce. Tell the child that from now on you will ignore clinging but will pay attention to him when he behaves in appropriate ways. Explain how he can earn special attention from you by not clinging.

Move Away From the Child When He Starts to Cling. Whenever the child starts clinging to you, move away. If you are seated, stand up. If you are standing, walk elsewhere. If you are not busy, find something to do. You may have to remove the child physically by gently undoing the grasp he has on you. The main point of moving away from the child is to give as little attention as possible when he clings. Say nothing. Do not show concern, exasperation, amusement, or any other emotion related to the clinging by facial or bodily expressions. Remember that any reaction is reinforcement because you convey to the child that he is affecting you. It may be difficult to carry out this step, but be persistent. The sooner you convince the child, by ignoring him, that clinging will get him no attention, the sooner the behavior will stop.

Reinforce Appropriate Behaviors As Often As Possible. While you ignore clinging, take every opportunity to praise the child for appropriate behaviors. Any participation in activities, interaction with peers, or other desired behavior should be well reinforced. If the child participates in a limited way in classroom activities, reinforce his efforts, even if these are only approximations of what you want. As time passes, you can expect more of the child before you give praise.

At first, be constantly on the lookout for things to praise. Once clinging begins to decrease, you can gradually decrease the amount of reinforcement you give. By the time clinging has been eliminated, praise the child as often as you do other children.

Consider what kind of reinforcement is most meaningful to the child. Since the child seems to seek physical contact through clinging, reinforce with hugs and pats as well as with verbal praise.

Provide A Time for Special Attention, Depending On if the Child Does Not Cling. Set aside a "special time" of five minutes per day to spend on a one-to-one basis with the child. This time will provide the child with positive, undivided attention. After the first day, provide this time if the child decreases the clinging behavior.

During the special time make sure the child has your undivided attention. To do this, you will need to have the cooperation of all the teachers. Let the child decide how the five minutes will be spent. Tell him, "I have five minutes to spend just with you." On a clock or watch, show the child when the time will be over. Tell the child that you and he will do whatever he wants. Be prepared with some suggestions, such as taking a walk, reading a book, or playing a game, in case he is unsure of how he would like to spend the time.

Do not expand the time. At the end, tell the child that the special time will be held again the next day.

1. On the first day, have the special time as soon as the child arrives at school. Make whatever arrangements you need to provide the five minutes. At the end of the first session tell the child that the special time will be held a little later the next day.

2. On the second day, tell the child as soon as he arrives at school that the special time will be held in a few minutes *if* he does not cling to you but instead gets involved in an activity. Wait no longer than ten minutes. Hold the special time if the child did not engage in clinging behavior. Start out the special time by praising him for expected behaviors. Do not wait the full ten minutes to give other reinforcement.

    If the child is unable to refrain from clinging, do not hold the special time. Tell him that he will have another chance the next day and explain why you will not hold it this day. Shorten the waiting time a bit the next day.

3. When the child has three successive days of special time, lengthen the waiting time to fifteen minutes. Continue holding the special time somewhat later every few days. The child should be able to spend increasingly longer periods being constructively engaged in activities and not clinging. If he is not, then slow down the rate of increasing the waiting period to the special time. Pace the timing to ensure success for the child.

4. When there is a marked decrease in the overall rate of clinging, begin having the special time every other day. Tell the child what you are doing and why. Cut back special times even further as behavior changes. Be sure to continue giving the child attention for appropriate behavior and general positive interaction.

Continue Graphing the Behavior. Continue measuring behavior to be aware of improvement. Use the same hour of the day to time the clinging behavior as you used for baseline. Compute the percentage of time the child clings to the same way, as during baseline. Draw a vertical line after the baseline data and record each day's percentage on the Record Keeping Graph.

Maintenance

Once the child has stopped clinging, continue to reinforce appropriate behaviors periodically. Let the child know what behaviors you value by praising these. If the child tries to cling, ignore it. Be sensitive to the child's need for assurance, but do not offer it by allowing him to cling.

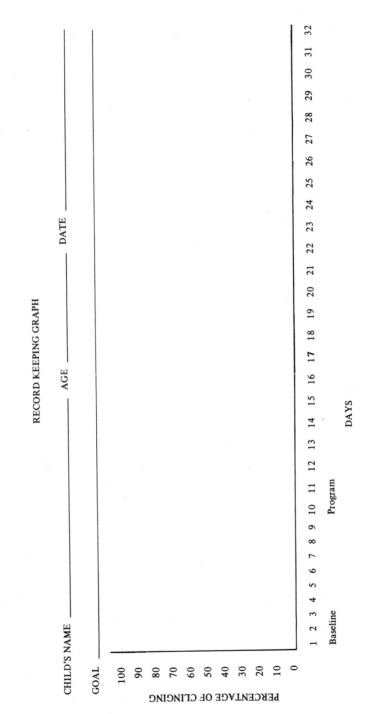

RECORD KEEPING GRAPH

CHILD'S NAME _____ AGE _____ DATE _____

GOAL _____

PERCENTAGE OF CLINGING

100
90
80
70
60
50
40
30
20
10
0

1 2 3 4 5 6 7 8 9 10 11 12 13 14 15 16 17 18 19 20 21 22 23 24 25 26 27 28 29 30 31 32

Baseline   Program

DAYS

CHAPTER 29

Seeking Attention

The day usually begins for Lisa in the day care center at 7:00 a.m. She immediately heads for Mrs. Mason, one of the teachers. At three and a half, Lisa is a very precocious and verbal child. She loves to talk to the three teachers in the classroom and converses with any other adult who walks into the room. Throughout the day, Lisa follows a teacher around, asking questions or talking incessantly. She expects attention and responses from the adults. At first, Lisa's chatter was enjoyable to the teachers. They found her bright and amusing. Recently the teachers have become aware that they spend an inordinate amount of time with Lisa at the expense of time spent with the other children. Lisa spends little time with her peers, apparently preferring the company of adults. When she is with other children, she seems to be quite able to interact. The teachers have begun to tell Lisa that they do not have time to talk with her, but such statements leave her undaunted. She usually returns within half a minute with another question or statement. Mrs. Mason notices that none of the teachers approach Lisa. She always seems to approach them. Also, the teachers rarely call on Lisa during group discussion times.

STATE THE BEHAVIOR

The child requires the attention of the teachers more often than is necessary. The teachers find themselves giving time to this child more than to the other children. The requests for attention are usually unnecessary and not related to a specific need, other than for attention.

OBSERVE THE BEHAVIOR

Spend some time observing to gather information that can give you a clue to the behavior.

A. When do bids for attention usually come?
- At any time of day
- During specific activity times

- During structured activities
- When children have free choice
- During meals
- During nap
- At toileting times
- Indoors
- Outdoors
- When it is time to go home
- When other children require a teacher's help

B. From whom does the child request attention?

- Any adult
- A familiar teacher
- A specific teacher

C. How is attention requested?

- The child asks questions of the teacher
- The child talks to the teacher about herself
- The child talks repeatedly about the same subject
- The child hints at a concern or problem
- The child asks for help in getting materials
- The child asks for help when engaged in activities or projects
- The child interrupts when the teacher is talking with someone else
- The child asks for physical attention such as hugs, being picked up, and help in dressing or undressing
- The child sticks close to the teacher's side
- The child calls for attention from other parts of the room

D. What else might be relevant?

- Interaction with other children (often such a child does not have satisfactory interaction skills with peers)
- Participation in activities (the child may not get involved in activities because her energies are directed elsewhere, namely toward the teachers)

This informal observation will help you approach the behavior systematically. It will be helpful to know when to implement your plan and who can best implement it.

EXPLORE THE CONSEQUENCES

It is important to be aware of how the teacher is affected by the child's behavior. All children need attention. When a child requests an undue amount of attention, it is easy for the teacher to get exasperated and then give attention in negative ways. If tired of the constant requests, the teacher may respond crossly. The child is thus reinforced negatively for seeking attention.

The teacher may begin to avoid the child because she already requests such a large share of time. The teacher may rarely attend to this child except when the child is asking for attention. The child thus does not get reinforced for any appropriate behaviors that occur during the times when she is not seeking attention. The child also learns that the only way to get attention is to pester the teacher. The child does this more because she wants the attention. As a result, the child feels negatively about herself as a person, since the teacher's attention is neither spontaneous nor positive.

CONSIDER ALTERNATIVES

There might be a fairly simple solution to the problem, particularly if a change in the environment can remedy the situation. Consider the following possibilities.

- There may be an unusual event in the child's life, such as a new baby or a death in the family. Perhaps the child is seeking reassurance. Take the time to help the child understand what is happening in her life.
- There may not be enough materials and activities in the classroom to interest the child. She might be seeking your attention because of boredom. In such a case, be sure to provide the age-appropriate resources to keep the child constructively occupied.
- Materials in the classroom should be easily accessible to the child. Requests for help may be based on a genuine need for assistance. Rearrange the room and storage for materials so that children can be as independent as possible at school.
- From your informal observation you might have found that the child interacts very little with peers. The cause of seeking excessive attention may be basically poor peer interaction skills. Help the child learn how to interact appropriately with her peers. As she spends more time with peers, she will seek less attention from adults.

If the solution to the problem does not lie in one of these suggestions, it is time to use a more detailed approach.

STATE THE GOAL

The goal is for the child to seek attention from the teacher in a positive manner and no more frequently than the other children in the class.

PROCEDURE

The basic strategy is to refuse attention to the child when such attention is demanded unnecessarily. At the same time, give attention on occasions when the child engages in desirable behavior.

Definition

Seeking attention is any overly frequent and unnecessary verbal or nonverbal demand for a teacher's attention.

Baseline

Before implementing changes, keep track of how often the child requests attention. Decide on a one-hour time block each day to keep a record, and mark on paper each bid for attention. The time period should be a time when the child usually asks for attention frequently and the teachers are free to participate. At the end of each day count up the number of marks and record them on the Record Keeping Graph. Keep track for three consecutive days. This provides your baseline.

Program

After you have baseline data, begin the following program. The program must be followed consistently by all teachers.

Ignore All Unnecessary Bids for Attention. When the child approaches you, involve yourself in an activity. Briefly tell the child, "I am sorry, but I must do this now." Physically turn away or walk to another area of the room.

Give the Child Attention At Other Times. When the child engages in a desired activity, let her know that you are pleased with her behavior. If the child responds to verbal praise, say, with a smile,

"I like how you are working!"
"Thank you for helping us pick up."
"Wow! You're doing that really well!"

If the child enjoys physical contact, give her a hug or a pat.

Plan A "Special Time" Each Day. A special time of five minutes per day may be spent on a one-to-one basis with the child. It provides undivided, positive attention to let the child know that she is special and that attention from the teacher can be a positive experience for both. After the first day, whether you provide this special time depends on the child's behavior. You must be able to do your work, and she does her work until the special time.

During the special time, make sure the child has your undivided attention. You need the cooperation of all the teachers to accomplish this. Let the child determine how the five minutes are to be spent. Say, "I have five minutes to spend with you." Show her on a clock or watch when the time will be over. "We can do whatever you'd like." If the child is unsure of what she would like to do, you might suggest talking, playing a game, taking a walk, reading a book, or another favorite activity of the child.

Do not extend the time past five minutes. At the end, tell the child that tomorrow you will do this again.

The timing for this special time is important.

1. On the first day, the special time should occur as soon as the child arrives at school. At the end of the first session, tell the child that tomorrow the special time will be held a little later in the morning.

2. On the second day, tell the child immediately that the special time will be held in a few minutes *if* she lets you do your work and she does her work until then. Be specific in telling the child what your expectations are.

   The timing of the special time depends on the information in your baseline data. Determine the average time of attention seeking for the three days. If the child sought attention three times in one hour, the average is twenty minutes. If the behavior was recorded twelve times an hour, the average is five minutes.

   Let the number of minutes of the average time pass after the arrival of the child and then hold the special time. Continue the special time on that schedule for three days.

   If the child is not able to refrain from unnecessary attention bids during the waiting time, do not hold the special time. Explain to the child why you did not have special time, and assure her that she will have a chance the next day. Shorten the waiting time a bit the next day.

3. When the child has had three successive days of special time, begin to lengthen the waiting time by a few minutes. As the child's behavior changes, extend the waiting time every few days. The child should be able to go for increasingly longer periods of time being constructively engaged in activities and not asking for undue attention. If she is not, then slow down the rate of increasing the waiting time. Arrange the timing to ensure success for the child.

4. When you see a marked decrease in the overall rate of attention seeking, have special times every other day. Be sure to tell the child what you are doing. Cut back the special times even further as behavior changes. Of course, general interaction should continue.

Continue Graphing the Behavior. Throughout this time, keep track of behavior on the Record Keeping Graph. Draw a vertical line after the baseline data.

Continue recording the number of attempts to seek attention for one hour a day. This should be the same time of day used during baseline.

Maintenance

Continue giving the child attention for expected behaviors as you do with all the children. If there is an occasional slip, ignore it. Let the child know that she is special and that you appreciate appropriate behavior. Remember, too, that as the child seeks less attention from adults, she receives reinforcement from other sources, including peers.

RECORD KEEPING GRAPH

CHILD'S NAME _____ AGE _____ DATE _____

GOAL _____

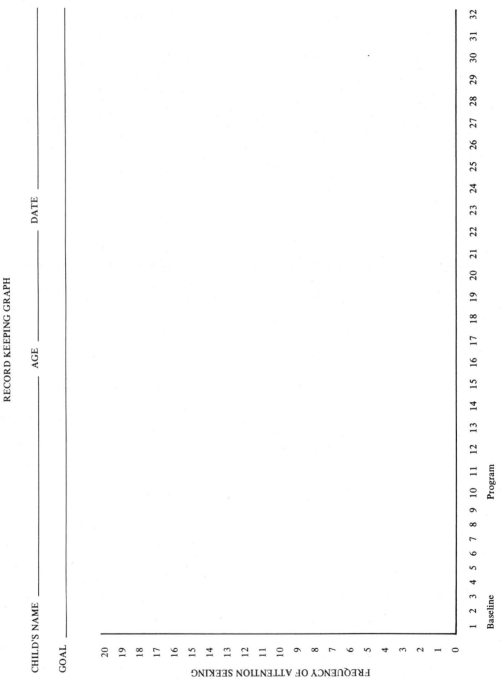

FREQUENCY OF ATTENTION SEEKING

20
19
18
17
16
15
14
13
12
11
10
9
8
7
6
5
4
3
2
1
0

1 2 3 4 5 6 7 8 9 10 11 12 13 14 15 16 17 18 19 20 21 22 23 24 25 26 27 28 29 30 31 32

Baseline   Program

DAYS

CHAPTER 30

30

30
Whining

At teacher conferences, five-year-old Eric is a frequent topic of conversation. The teachers feel very frustrated with Eric's constant whining at preschool. Eric rarely talks without a whine and often complains. Common statements include, "Teacher, they won't let me play." "Teacher, there's not enough paint for me." "Teacher, I hurt my finger." "Teacher, I want to go outside now." "Teacher, I can't get my belt unbuckled." "Teacher, I can't find my jacket." On closer examination, teachers usually find that there is enough paint, that the finger shows no signs of injury, or that the jacket is exactly where it usually is. The teachers have been answering Eric in increasingly more impatient and exasperated ways. Often they turn the other way when they see him coming. They rarely approach Eric to talk to him.

STATE THE BEHAVIOR

The child frequently whines when talking to adults.

OBSERVE THE BEHAVIOR

Spend some time observing and gathering information to gain insight into the child's behavior.

A. When does whining usually occur?
- At all times of the day
- At particular times, such as early or late in the day
- At mealtimes
- At nap time
- During group activities
- During free choice activities

B. What message is usually accompanied by whining?
- The child requests help from the teacher
- The child complains about another child
- The child wants the teacher's attention
- The child asks to be held or picked up
- The child does not want to do something
- The child wants attention for an injury, real or imagined
- The child wants a toy that another child is using
- The child conveys any and all messages to adults

C. To whom does the child whine?
- All adults
- A specific teacher
- Children as well as adults
- The parents

From this informal observation you should have some idea of when and under what circumstances whining usually occurs. This helps you to implement a systematic approach, because you are able to anticipate whining and thus deal with it more effectively. It also indicates which adult or adults should implement the plan. If the child whines mainly to one teacher, that teacher should confront the behavior. If the child whines to all adults, all teachers need to be involved in the implementation.

EXPLORE THE CONSEQUENCES

Whining is a learned behavior. At some point in early life a child may learn that by whining he gets attention. Perhaps the adults in the child's life do not attend to him consistently when he speaks in a normal tone of voice. He tries alternatives to get attention and discovers that talking in a whining voice usually gets someone to listen. A pattern is established over a period of time. The child wants attention and finds that adults give it more often when he whines. The adults pay attention to the child when he whines because they find the whining annoying and feel a need to get rid of the annoyance. This attention is given in a negative manner, in exasperation or even anger. The child finds that adults usually listen to him when he whines, but that their reaction is usually unresponsive and unfriendly. A teacher may attend briefly when the child whines, to get rid of the whining, but otherwise ignores him for fear that he might whine again. The behavior pattern is strengthened as the child gets the attention he needs by whining. The price of getting that attention, however, is that the attention is basically negative. As whining becomes more and more a part of everyday communication, the child feels less and less secure about his self-worth because of the reactions of others.

CONSIDER ALTERNATIVES

From your informal observation there might be some clues to help you deal with the whiner. Consider the following.

- The child may whine primarily with one teacher. This teacher's behavior may encourage whining in the child. The adult may, for example, ignore the child when he talks in a normal tone of voice. A careful self-examination by this teacher, with the help of other staff members, might disclose the problem. The teacher can then change the behavior as needed and help the child to stop whining before it becomes a habit. In addition, the staff should consider the following program and use it to deal with whining. It may be directed toward one teacher, as appropriate.
- If the child does not whine with his parents but only in the school setting, there is probably some factor in the school environment that elicits such behavior. A careful examination of the child's actions at school might uncover the problem.
- Some children whine when they get tired. Your observations should tell you if this is the case. If so, plan an earlier rest or nap time or channel the child into quiet activities when whining begins.

In most cases, whining is a long-established habit that is exhibited both at home and at school. For habitual whiners, the following procedure should be used.

STATE THE GOAL

The goal is for the child to communicate with adults without whining.

PROCEDURE

Basically, the strategy involves refusal to listen to whining and systematic shaping of nonwhining behavior.

Definition

Whining is any verbal communication in which the child does not speak in a normal voice but instead uses a complaining, usually nasal, tone.

Baseline

For three days, before implementing any changes, keep track of how much whining occurs each day. You will want to know not just how often the child whines but what proportion of verbal communications are made in a whining voice. Select an hour of the day when you expect a considerable amount of whining. This same hour should be used whenever you count incidents of whining. Each teacher should have a conveniently located pencil and paper with a line drawn through the middle of the sheet. Each time the child talks to a teacher without whining, it should be recorded in one column. Each time the child whines should be recorded on the other side. At the end of the time, combine the counts from all the teachers. Compute the percentage of time the child whines:

$$\frac{\text{Whines}}{\text{Whines + Nonwhines}} \times 100 = \% \text{ of whining}$$

If there are no Nonwhines, the the child whined 100 percent of the time. If the child whined 10 times and did not whine 10 times, then he whined 50 percent of the time.

$$\frac{10}{10 + 10} = \frac{10}{20} = 0.5 \text{ or } 50\%$$

A percentage score gives an accurate idea of how much whining there actually is in relation to all communication. Record this percentage score on the Record Keeping Graph for three days to provide a baseline.

Program

Once you have the baseline, begin the following program. All teachers to whom the child usually whines must use this program consistently.

For the First Week, Whenever the Child Whines, Tell Him Your Expectations. Follow these steps:

1. Get to the child's eye level and say to him, "I cannot understand you when you whine. Please tell me again without whining."
2. If the child restates his comment without whining, say, "Good! Now I can understand you!" Answer his question, or comment on his statement, as appropriate. This attention is very important.
3. If the child repeats his statement with a whine, repeat that you cannot understand him. Praise him if he talks without a whine after your second try.

4. If the third repetition is still a whine, say, "I'll be glad to listen to you when you can tell me without whining." At this point, model for the child what you expect. State in a clear and uncomplaining manner a sentence conveying what the child wants and ask him to repeat it after you.
5. If, after your modeling, the child still whines, get up and move elsewhere. Any immediate repeats of whining should be ignored. Nonwhining should be well praised.
6. Handle each incident of whining in this manner.
7. At the same time, take every possible opportunity to praise and reinforce appropriate behaviors.

In the Second Week, Give the Child Fewer Cues. After one full week of being directly told that you cannot understand him when he whines, the child should understand that you expect him to talk without whining.

1. If the child spontaneously talks without whining, tell him each time that you like the way he is talking.
2. If the child tells you something in a whine, do not say anything, but look directly at him. Your silence and expectant look should serve as a cue to repeat without a whine.
3. If the child now repeats his statement in a normal tone of voice, let him know you are pleased.
4. If the child again whines, tell him, "I'm sorry, but I cannot understand you," and turn away. If he approaches you after this without a whine deal with his question and praise him.

In the Third Week, Withdraw All Cues. If after two weeks the child has stopped most whining, he is indicating that he understands your expectations.

1. Praise the child for nonwhining behavior less frequently. Gradually cut back reinforcement. Reinforce every other time for a few days, then less and less frequently.
2. Give the child praise and attention for other behaviors, as you do with the other children in the class. Continue to be responsive when he talks with you. Remember, the child's habit of whining began when he did not receive adequate attention from adults for talking in a normal tone of voice.
3. If occasionally the child whines, ignore it. Do not respond. He will probably repeat his statement without whining. Then be sure to pay close attention to let him know that you are pleased with his behavior.

Continue Graphing the Behavior. Throughout this time, continue recording the percentage of whining on the Record Keeping Graph. Draw a vertical line after the baseline days; then compute and enter each day of the program. Count original communications only. If the child whines and then repeats himself without whining after the teacher's response, the corrected nonwhining behavior is not counted. By the end of the second week, the percentage of whining should be below 25 percent. If it is not, continue the second week's program until it is.

Maintenance

If whining occurs at home, this would be a good time to share your success with the child's parents. Encourage and help them to try this program at home. At school, continue to give full attention to the child when he communicates with you. If he whines, ignore it.

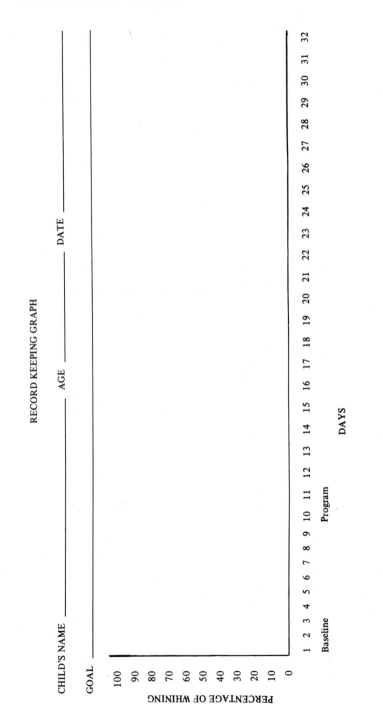

RECORD KEEPING GRAPH

CHILD'S NAME _____ AGE _____ DATE _____

GOAL _____

PERCENTAGE OF WHINING

100
90
80
70
60
50
40
30
20
10
0

1 2 3 4 5 6 7 8 9 10 11 12 13 14 15 16 17 18 19 20 21 22 23 24 25 26 27 28 29 30 31 32

Baseline   Program

DAYS

CHAPTER 31

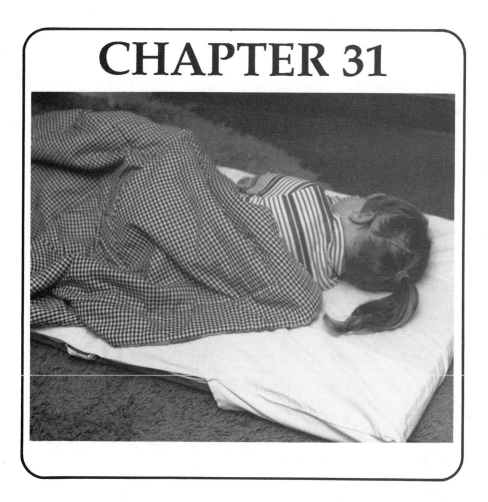

Self-Stimulation

It is group time, and Allysa, age four, listens to the story the teacher is reading. After a couple of minutes her eyes wander away from the page and scan the room. She rubs her right knee with her left hand, then starts scratching up her thigh. With her other hand, she pulls up her dress and continues to scratch at the top of her leg. Her fingers move inside her panties and she starts to rub herself. She stares over the teacher's head, continuing to rub herself for the remaining twelve minutes of the story and song. At the end of group time, Allysa gets up with the other children and moves on to the next activity. Later, during nap, she again self-stimulates, putting herself to sleep. The teachers are uncomfortable with Allysa's behavior but have not said anything to her, and the parent of another child has commented on it to the director.

STATE THE BEHAVIOR

The child regularly self-stimulates.

OBSERVE THE BEHAVIOR

Observe the child for a few days to gain some insights into the behavior.

A. When is the child most likely to self-stimulate?

- Unpredictably, any time of the day
- Throughout the day
- During nap time
- Early in the day
- Toward the end of the day
- During self-selected activity periods

- When children sit quietly to listen
- During transitions

B. What usually precedes self-stimulation?

- The child is not engaged in an activity
- The child plays alone
- The child seems upset
- The child seems tired
- The child expresses disinterest in ongoing activities

C. Where is the child when she self-stimulates?

- Indoors
- Outside
- On a nap cot or mat
- In the bathroom
- In the housekeeping or dramatic play area

D. What happens when the child self-stimulates?

- She is told to stop
- She is told that what she is doing is "wrong" or "bad" or something "nice children don't do"
- She looks around to see if anyone is watching her

E. How long does the child usually self-stimulate?

- Very briefly
- For a few minutes at a time
- For long periods of time
- Until she is asleep
- Continues even after she falls asleep

F. Does the child talk about her self-stimulation?

- In negative terms
- In guilty terms
- In a way that calls attention to the self-stimulation
- In a matter-of-fact way

EXPLORE THE CONSEQUENCES

Self-stimulation is a fairly common act among young children. Body exploration starts in infancy, and the child soon discovers pleasurable sensation in playing with the genital area. But such body play is disconcerting to many adults. They may subtly, or not so subtly, convey negative messages to the child by consistently removing the child's hands, slapping, or saying "No!" or "Bad!" Such messages can set up conflicting feelings in the child. On the one hand, the child is made to feel guilty about the genital play, while, on the other hand, such stimulation feels pleasurable and soothing. The guilt and shame set up by these negative messages can have a long-lasting impact, affecting adolescent and adult sexuality as well as identity. The self-stimulation of young children should be considered normal; however, what should be addressed with preschoolers is the issue of privacy and what kinds of behaviors are appropriate in public and private settings. Self-stimulation can be accepted as a private behavior that the child may engage in in a private place.

CONSIDER ALTERNATIVES

It is important to give careful thought to why a child might be self-stimulating and to the reactions and attitudes of the adults around her, both parents and school staff. This topic needs to be handled sensitively.

- A child who has been sexually abused may self-stimulate because she has been stimulated in the abusive situation by an adult. This is *not* a normal reason for self-stimulation by a child. A child who has been abused may give verbal or behavioral clues, talking about or acting out sexual acts that are beyond the normal knowledge or experience of preschoolers. If the teacher suspects that the child is or has been the victim of sexual abuse, she has legal and ethical obligations to report her suspicions after discussion with the director.
- It is important to talk with parents about a child's self-stimulation if the child does not seem to distinguish between private and public settings for the behavior. If the parents tell you that they are not particularly concerned and consider the behavior normal, then discuss a common strategy to help the child confine the behavior to an appropriate setting with which both you and the parents are comfortable. If the parents are upset about the child's self stimulation, you should discuss their concerns and feelings in an accepting and matter-of-fact manner. It is important, however, that you feel comfortable about discussing this topic; if you are not, you may want to have another adult

handle this discussion with the parents. You can offer reading material to the parents to reassure them that the behavior is normal and to reinforce what you are telling them.

- Be sure that the genital play is not a sign of a bladder or vaginal infection. The child may actually be rubbing herself because she hurts.
- Children react differently to anxiety, and some may respond by self-stimulation to make themselves feel better. If you see a variety of signs of anxious behavior in a child, take time to talk to her and try to find out what is bothering her.

These suggestions alone may help you resolve your concerns about the child who self-stimulates. Continue on to the next section if the child frequently and openly engages in this behavior; if this behavior concerns the parents; and if others in the school setting, both adults and children, notice and comment on the behavior.

STATE THE GOAL

The goal is for the child to avoid self-stimulation in places designated as inappropriate.

PROCEDURE

To have the child not engage in self-stimulation in places designated as inappropriate, the basic strategy involves the following procedures:

- Discuss the self-stimulation with all staff who are involved with the child.
- Discuss the self-stimulation with the child's parents.
- Discuss privacy and social acceptability of self-stimulation with the child.
- Remind the child gently if she self-stimulates in an inappropriate situation or place.

Definition

Self-stimulation involves the child's using her hands to play with, rub, or fondle the genital area. In this case, self-stimulation in public places is considered reason for changing the behavior.

Baseline

Before attempting to change the child's behavior, discuss the matter with other staff. Keep in mind that the behavior you want to change is self-stimulation in a public, inappropriate setting. The child's home, for instance, may be the appropriate place. Decide what is acceptable before starting baseline.

Spend three to five days recording how often, for how long, and in what public circumstances the child self-stimulates. Each time the behavior occurs, clock and write on a piece of paper how long and in what circumstances the child self-stimulated. Use this list to determine when and where the child self-stimulates. At the end of each day, record the frequency or total number of incidents of self-stimulation on Record Keeping Graph 1. On Record Keeping Graph 2, record the average duration for all the day's occurrences. Add up the total number of minutes for all incidents, then divide by the number of incidents to determine average duration:

$$\frac{\text{Total minutes of all self-stimulation}}{\text{Total number of incidents}} = \text{Average duration}$$

These graphs will help you measure progress.

Program

While you are collecting baseline, you can begin the first two steps of this program, discussion with staff and parents. The last two steps, discussion with the child and reminders if the child does engage in the behavior inappropriately, should not be implemented until after the baseline period.

Discuss Self-Stimulation with the Staff. Our reactions to sexually related matters differ greatly, depending on our own upbringing, experiences, and information. Attitudes toward self-stimulation can vary among the staff from acceptance of the behavior as normal, to conviction that the behavior is bad and should be stopped before it does irreparable harm. All staff who work with the child, as well as the director, should be included in this discussion. It might be helpful to invite a professional who is knowledgeable about the topic to join the discussion. At this meeting, the discussion should focus on each person's attitudes about self-stimulation and their observations of the child relating to self-stimulation. The outcome of this meeting should be a common agreement about what is and what is not acceptable, as follows:

- Agreement by the staff on situations where self-stimulation is not socially acceptable. Such agreement will depend on the staff's attitudes and opinions, and may conclude that general classroom activity is not an acceptable circumstance in which the child can self-stimulate.

Discuss Self-Stimulation with the Parents.   Just as teachers may have strong opinions about self-stimulation, so may parents react in different ways. Some may accept the behavior as normal and not be concerned, while others will carry a variety of opinions, ideas, and possible misconceptions about the topic. You need to be prepared for a meeting with parents and have information about the topic. Written material by a credible authority, which you can recommend for them to read, might also be helpful. Depending on the feelings of the parents, the opinions of the staff, and the circumstances in which self-stimulation occurs, you have different avenues to take:

- If the parents are not concerned about self-stimulation and the child's behavior occurs in private circumstances, you need not pursue any course of action.
- If the parents are not concerned about self-stimulation but the child's behavior occurs frequently and in public circumstances, you should discuss this with the parents. Children eventually learn that some behaviors are not socially acceptable in public and that these behaviors should be carried out in privacy. You and the parents can work together to help the child learn this distinction without making the child feel guilty or ashamed.
- If the parents are concerned about the self-stimulation but the staff is not, a discussion may resolve the problem. Parents may be reassured to hear you say that the behavior is common. If the parents continue to be concerned, you may want to state the school's position that self-stimulation is not a "bad" behavior and that the teachers will only respond if it occurs in inappropriate circumstances.
- If both you and the parents are concerned about the self-stimulation because it occurs frequently in public circumstances, then you should come to an agreement about how you both can deal with it. It is helpful to the child if a similar approach is taken at home and at school.

Discuss the Self-Stimulation with the Child.   Once the staff and parents have had the opportunity to share information, concerns, and feelings about the child's self-stimulation, and once baseline has been taken, you should spend some private time with the child to discuss self-stimulation. Listen to what the child has to tell you on this topic and also convey that:

- Self-stimulation is a common behavior among children.
- Self-stimulation is a private behavior.
- Self-stimulation should not be done in public but in places designated as acceptable.

Your discussion with the child is intended to be reassuring and not in any way punitive or negative; thus, an accepting approach is vital. Children are very sensitive to underlying feelings, and if what you say is not congruent with what you feel, you may still convey a negative message to the child. If you feel negative or ambivalent about the normalcy of self-stimulation by young children, then it may be better if another staff member talks with the child about this.

Remind the Child if Self-Stimulation Occurs in an Inappropriate Circumstance. The child may continue to self-stimulate occasionally in inappropriate places even after you have had a discussion with her. If this occurs, give her a gentle reminder of your discussion. Be sure that this is done in a discrete way that does not embarrass the child. Remind her that you agreed on circumstances that are acceptable for self-stimulation and that where she is doing this is not one of those places. You may want to redirect the child into an activity if that is appropriate at the time.

Continue Graphing the Behavior. Continue to count frequency and duration of self-stimulation after you have started the program. Draw a vertical line after the baseline data to designate the point where you begin to record data after the program starts. It is quite likely that you will see a quick drop in inappropriate circumstances where the child self-stimulates. When the graph shows no self-stimulation in inappropriate circumstances for a period of two weeks, you have achieved your goal and do not need to continue recording data.

Maintenance

Once the child internalizes the messages you have conveyed, she will probably discontinue self-stimulating in inappropriate circumstances. In case there is an occasional lapse, a gentle reminder should resolve the situation.

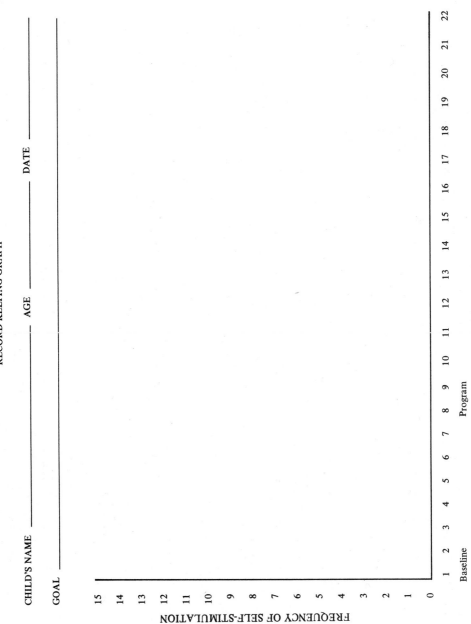

RECORD KEEPING GRAPH

CHILD'S NAME _____ AGE _____ DATE _____

GOAL _____

FREQUENCY OF SELF-STIMULATION

15
14
13
12
11
10
9
8
7
6
5
4
3
2
1
0

1 2 3 4 5 6 7 8 9 10 11 12 13 14 15 16 17 18 19 20 21 22

Baseline   Program

DAYS

RECORD KEEPING GRAPH

CHILD'S NAME _____ AGE _____ DATE _____

GOAL _____

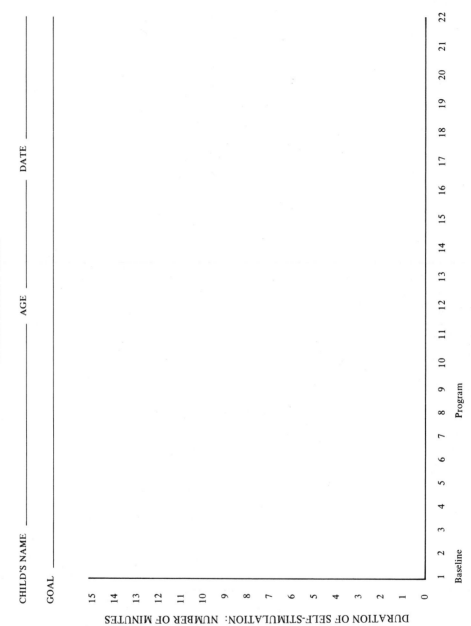

DURATION OF SELF-STIMULATION: NUMBER OF MINUTES

DAYS

SECTION 5

PARTICIPATION IN SOCIAL AND SCHOOL ACTIVITIES

CHAPTER 32

Nonparticipation
in Activities

Throughout the class, children are busy with various activities. Four-year-old Sarah stands near the door, uninvolved and seemingly uninterested. A teacher walks by her and smiles. "Come on, Sarah, help me get out the paint." Sarah stands still and the teacher moves on to complete his errand. A few minutes later he returns and kneels down to Sarah's eye level. He pulls Sarah toward him, puts an arm around her, and talks to her for several minutes, trying to interest her in an activity. Sarah, however, stands firm in her refusal to participate. She does not resist physically. In fact, she lets herself be led around the room to the various activities. When she is brought to an activity, she simply makes no effort to become involved. Since Sarah entered the preschool six weeks ago, she has not actively participated in any activities. The teachers have all spent considerable time with her, gently trying to interest her in what is going on. Nothing has helped. Sarah continues to be passive.

STATE THE BEHAVIOR

The child rarely or never participates in either planned or spontaneous school activities.

OBSERVE THE BEHAVIOR

Spend some time observing the child to gain further insight into this behavior.

A. If the child occasionally participates in activities, what are these?
- No one particular activity
- Activities where each child works alone
- Group activities

- Listening to stories
- Looking at books
- Music
- Art
- Dramatic play
- Blocks
- Woodworking
- Outdoor play
- Sand or water play
- Sensory activities
- Manipulative materials

B. What does the child do while not participating?

- The child watches other children engage in activities
- The child looks out the window
- The child stays near the door
- The child cries
- The child holds or plays with a personal possession like a sweater or blanket
- The child talks to no one
- The child follows an adult or particular child around

C. What does the child do when asked to join an ongoing activity?

- If coaxed, the child joins in
- The child verbally refuses to participate
- The child refuses nonverbally
- The child turns away
- The child begins to cry
- The child pouts
- The child goes to where the activity is being held but does not join in

Use the information from your observations to find a way to help the child who does not participate in school activities.

EXPLORE THE CONSEQUENCES

A very shy child may find it difficult to join into school activities, especially if the school experience is new to her. This initial hesitation usually disappears after the child has a chance to become familiar with the school routine and develops a relationship with the teachers. In some cases, a child may discover that nonparticipation in activities results in considerable attention from adults. These adults are anxious that all the children benefit as much as possible from the preschool experience. Concerned teachers may spend time talking to the child. They may coax the child, provide special incentives and privileges, and otherwise try to encourage her to join in. When this is the case, the attention gained by not participating becomes more attractive than the activities. The teachers' attempts to involve the child in school activities only serve to reinforce noninvolvement because of the attention they give the child.

CONSIDER ALTERNATIVES

Before assuming that the child's behavior needs to be changed, consider whether one of the following suggestions might remedy the situation.

- The child's reluctance to participate in school activities might be based on a genuine anxiety or fear about school or something related to school. In this case help the child overcome such feelings. Give whatever attention and encouragement is needed to increase the child's security and trust at school. The program outlined in this chapter is intended for a child who does not participate in activities because of the attention such behavior brings. Be very careful in deciding whether the child's motive is attention rather than anxiety or fear. The child who seeks attention usually gives clues to this underlying motivation. She looks for adult reaction, responds positively to adult attention, and subtly maintains adult response once it is given. The child who acts out of fear withdraws from such attention. If the underlying motive is not attention, then you can work on allaying fears and building a trusting relationship.
- Examine the classroom to be sure that materials and activities provided are suitable for the children. It is possible that the child is reluctant to participate because what is offered in the classroom does not interest her. If this is the case, move the child to a class that is better suited to her interests or provide more appropriate materials and equipment.
- Check the child's sensory perception skills. A child may be reluctant to engage in activities because of a hearing or sight defect that makes her reluctant to try. If the child seems to be overly clumsy or if she fails to respond to sounds and noises about her, discuss your concerns with the parents and recommend a physical examination.
- If the child refuses to participate in only one type of activity, it is possible that she has some kind of misconception about it. Ask the child why she does not want to join the activity. A child may, for instance, not want to finger paint because she was told to stay clean, or she may resist playing with blocks because someone told her that blocks are

only for boys. Once you understand the child's reason for refusing to participate in certain activities, then you can try to remedy her misconceptions.

- It should be noted that children cannot and should not be expected to participate in classroom activities constantly. Children, like adults, need time to reflect, observe, think, and rest without being perpetually busy. Some children are more active than others. Some take more time to reflect quietly on what goes on around them than others. Do not mistake a naturally reflective child for an inactive one. A child may participate in activities at times, and sit by quietly to watch at other times.
- Be careful not to confuse age-appropriate behavior with nonparticipation in play. At all stages in play development, a child participates in some form of play. She may be by herself giving little attention to others, or she may be totally involved with others. When a child begins to become aware of her peers, she may spend some time observing others rather than participating. Rather than being nonparticipation, this is the normal development of play.

If none of these suggestions provides a solution, continue on to the following program.

STATE THE GOAL

The goal is for the child to become actively involved in classroom activities on a regular basis.

PROCEDURE

The basic strategy to deal with the child who does not participate in school activities involves two steps:

- Reinforce the child for engaging in activities by using the technique of successive approximations.
- Ignore nonparticipation in activities.

Definition

Nonparticipation in activities involves all instances when the child is not constructively and actively participating in school activities, whether these are teacher planned or self-initiated. Nonparticipation includes standing around, not handling classroom materials, remaining apart from the class during group activities, and refusing to participate when asked. The teachers, as a group, should discuss and add to the definition any other behaviors they consider as nonparticipation. It is important that all adults share the same definition.

Baseline

It is important to collect some baseline data with which to compare later changes. Observe the child for a selected hour each day, for three days. This hour should be one in which various activity options are available. During the hour use a time-sampling technique to gather information. A watch or clock and a pencil and paper are necessary to collect this data. Once every five minutes observe the child for fifteen seconds. If the child meets the definition for nonparticipation, make no mark on the paper. If the child is engaged in an activity, make a mark. At the end of the hour you will have between zero and twelve marks. Record each day's total on Record Keeping Graph E of the graphs at the end of this chapter.

Program

Once baseline is established, start the program. All teachers should follow these procedures consistently to ensure success.

Use the Technique of Successive Approximations to Reinforce the Child for Engaging in School Activities. The aim of this program is to convey to the child that she will be given attention when she takes part in school activities and ignored when she does not. Since the child at this point engages in few activities, there may be few opportunities to give reinforcement. Therefore, the technique of successive approximations provides a way to give reinforcement more often. In the technique of *successive approximations,* the child is reinforced for behaviors that come nearer and nearer to the desired behavior. Participation in school activities is broken down into steps or components. Each step is closer to the desired behavior. At first the child is reinforced for the first step, which is only an approximation of the desired behavior. When the behavior is consistently achieved, she is only reinforced for the second step, which is a closer approximation of the desired behavior. This continues until the child reaches the desired behavior through successive steps, or approximations. Follow these steps one at a time.

Step 1. Reinforce only those occasions when the child watches other children involved in activities. Do not react in any way if the child is not observing her peers. Ignore her at such times. When the child watches other children at play and work, reinforce her with a smile, a pat, or a comment like, "It's fun to watch, isn't it?" Do not try to coax the child into joining the activity. Your verbal comments should convey approval for what she is doing. Do not insinuate that it is less than what you want.

Continue to use the time-sampling technique of recording, as in baseline. When the child consistently watches other children, you are ready to move on to the next step. The child should achieve a count of eight for two consecutive days on Record Keeping Graph A before proceeding to the next step.

Step 2. Reinforce only on occasions when the child is within five feet of an ongoing activity that she is watching. Again, do not pay any attention to her when she is removed from areas of activity, when she does not watch a nearby activity, or when she observes an activity from across the room. If she watches an activity close by, reinforce her with a hug, a glance, a smile, or a few words to say you like what she is doing. Your actions should encourage this behavior.

Continue to record progress. When Graph B shows a count of at least eight for two consecutive days, move on to the next step.

Step 3. Reinforce the child only when she is directly at the activity, though not necessarily participating. For example, the child sits with the group at circle time, sits at a table where manipulative games or art projects are provided, or stands directly in the midst of the house-keeping or block area. An activity should be within easy reach. If the child is not in such a position, ignore her. When she is within easy reach of an activity, reinforce her as you did in the previous two steps.

Record your daily count on Graph C. When the count is at least eight for two consecutive days, begin the next step.

Step 4. Expect the child to show some involvement in the activity beyond observation. This does not necessarily imply full involvement. The child may hold a toy or material, poke at a piece of clay, or stroke a doll. Reinforce her only when she shows partial involvement and ignore her at other times. If you reinforce verbally, do not imply that she is doing less than you expect. Make comments such as, "That clay feels soft, doesn't it?" or "You're holding a piece of the kitten puzzle!"

Move on to the next step when the child shows consistent partial involvement, and Graph D reads at least eight for two consecutive days.

Step 5. This step requires full involvement in the activity. The child should participate in activities as often as do the other youngsters in the class. Provide reinforcement for involvement in school activities every time you notice it.

Step 6. Once the child is fully involved, begin gradual decrease of reinforcement. Every few days, cut back the amount of praise you give. Finally, you should provide reinforcement at the same rate as for the other children in the group.

It should be mentioned that if the child "skips over" steps, reinforce the behavior that is closest to what is desired. It is possible, for instance, that after the first step, in which you reinforce observation of activity, the child suddenly participates partially in what is going on in the class. In this case, move directly from Step 1 to Step 4.

You may find that once you give reinforcement selectively, the child quickly picks up your unspoken cues and does what is expected. Remember, her behavior is motivated by a desire for attention. Provide attention in a way that requires compliance.

Ignore Nonparticipation in Activities. The process of successive approximations tells you exactly which behaviors to ignore. When you ignore a behavior, be sure you do it fully. Show neither approval nor disapproval for what the child does. React neutrally. If the child's behavior does not meet your expectations, do not speak to her, smile at her, respond to her, or look at her directly. Try not to stay too close to her. If you have to be nearby, make it clear by your manner that you are attending to someone or something else. Watch the child so that you know when to reinforce, but do not let her know that she is the object of your interest or attention.

Continue Graphing the Behavior. Use the graphs at the end of this chapter to record the progress for each step of the program. Be sure to observe and record for the same hour of the day that you used for baseline.

Maintenance

When the child is fully involved in classroom activities, you have reached your goal. Continue periodic reinforcement of her involvement. If you find the child not involved on occasion, suggest an activity for her. Do not give undue attention to nonparticipation. If the behavior recurs, simply ignore it.

RECORD KEEPING GRAPH A

CHILD'S NAME _____ AGE _____ DATE _____

GOAL _____

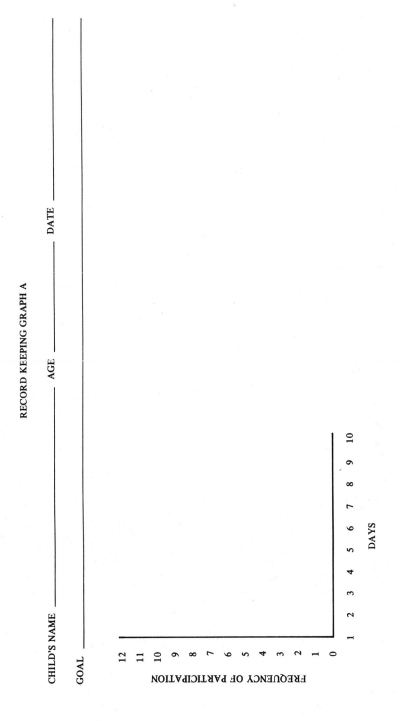

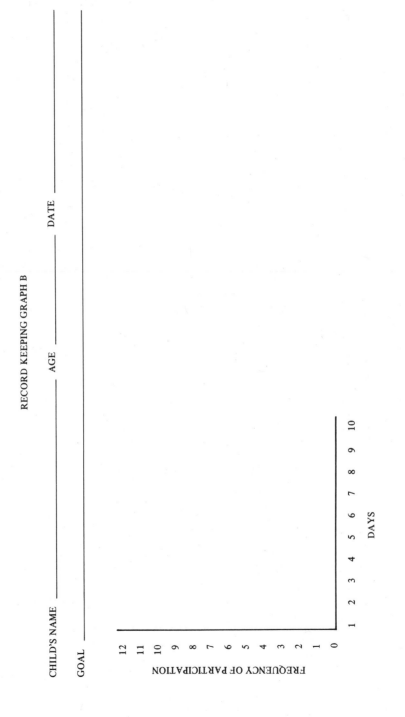

RECORD KEEPING GRAPH B

CHILD'S NAME _____ AGE _____ DATE _____

GOAL _____

FREQUENCY OF PARTICIPATION

12
11
10
9
8
7
6
5
4
3
2
1
0

1 2 3 4 5 6 7 8 9 10

DAYS

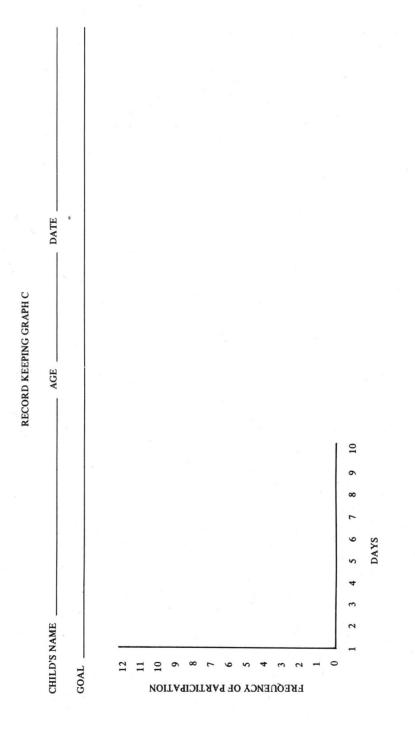

RECORD KEEPING GRAPH C

CHILD'S NAME _____ AGE _____ DATE _____

GOAL _____

FREQUENCY OF PARTICIPATION

12
11
10
9
8
7
6
5
4
3
2
1
0

1 2 3 4 5 6 7 8 9 10

DAYS

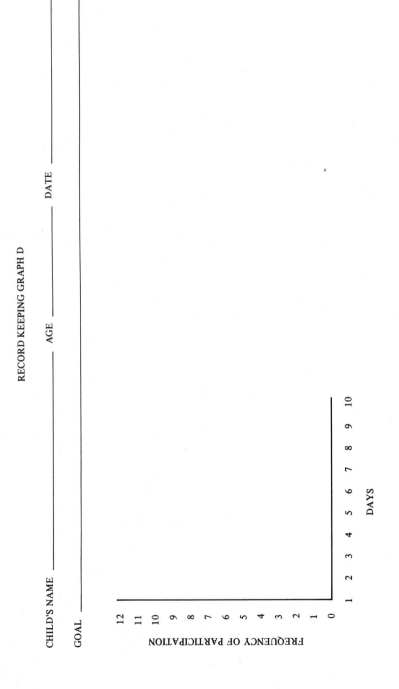

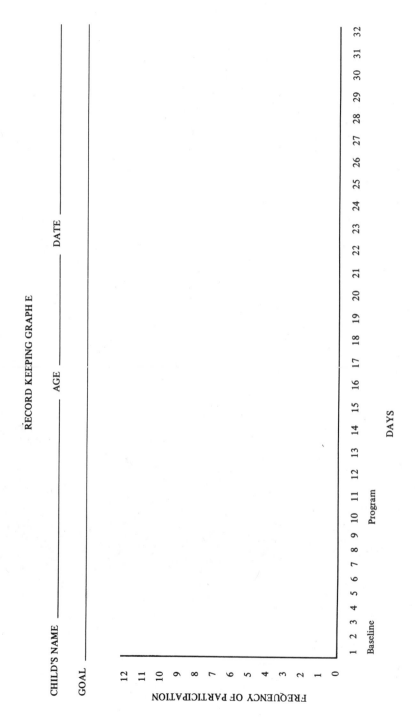

RECORD KEEPING GRAPH E

CHILD'S NAME _____ AGE _____ DATE _____

GOAL _____

FREQUENCY OF PARTICIPATION

12
11
10
9
8
7
6
5
4
3
2
1
0

1 2 3 4 5 6 7 8 9 10 11 12 13 14 15 16 17 18 19 20 21 22 23 24 25 26 27 28 29 30 31 32

Baseline   Program

DAYS

CHAPTER 33

Nonparticipation in Social Play

The children at the preschool engage in a variety of activities. Some activities require the cooperation of several children. Five-year-old Aaron works with projects he can do by himself. He works with puzzles, matching cards, building games, and other materials. He never ventures into activities where other youngsters are working and playing together. Aaron is a quiet child. He never seeks out other children and is rarely sought out by them. The teachers are concerned about Aaron, who is an only child, because he seems to avoid social contact with peers. Teachers usually seek him out when he is alone, and he seems responsive to adults when they talk to him. Often, when Aaron is working by himself, a teacher will stop and sit by him, talk, or work with him on the activity. The teachers hoped that with time Aaron would begin to join his peers. However, he has been in the preschool more than four months and still avoids social interactions.

STATE THE BEHAVIOR

The child rarely or never interacts with other children or participates in social play.

OBSERVE THE BEHAVIOR

Take a few days to observe the child informally to gain insight into the behavior.

A. What does the child do instead of participating in social play or interaction?
- The child uses only toys and materials that he can play with alone
- The child follows adults around
- The child follows one specific teacher around
- The child stands or sits in one place, doing nothing observable

B. What does the child do when another child or children initiate interaction?

- The child ignores the other youngsters
- The child responds briefly
- The child turns away
- The child moves elsewhere
- The child seems uncomfortable (shows facial distress or fidgets)
- The child appears relaxed
- The child becomes aggressive
- The child offers to share what he is playing with
- The child accepts a toy or material another child offers him
- The child calls a teacher to step in

C. If the child occasionally interacts with other children, who are they?

- One specific child
- A few children
- Any child in the group who approaches him first
- A youngster he knows outside of school (such as a neighbor or relative)
- Shy children
- Younger or small children
- Bigger or older children
- Boys
- Girls

Utilize the information from these observations to help the child who does not interact with other children.

EXPLORE THE CONSEQUENCES

Between infancy and the time when children enter elementary school, they begin to learn how to get along with other people. This ability comes through repeated practice and through positive experiences in dealing with others. Young children move increasingly out of the realm of egocentric concerns, where they can think only of themselves, into a world where other people exist and must be considered. Preschool facilitates this process. One of the main goals of early childhood education is to help preschool-aged children learn social skills. They learn through many opportunities for peer interaction.

Generally, this process of socialization is a natural one. Occasionally a child has difficulty learning how to interact with other children. In this case, the teachers must examine the situation. The child may lack some of the social skills that help him interact. Perhaps he does not interact because he prefers adult attention. If the child lacks social skills and is not given some help in learning these, he continues on to elementary school deficient in social development. The child may avoid other children because adults then pay more attention to him by trying to coax him into interaction. The child, then, will continue this avoidance as long as he gets the attention he wants. Helping the child increase peer interaction requires a careful assessment of the situation. Otherwise, the teachers' attempts to help are not effective.

CONSIDER ALTERNATIVES

Consider whether some of the following suggestions might provide a relatively simple solution to the situation.

- Consider the developmental level of the child. Very young preschoolers are not yet very social, preferring instead isolate or parallel play. For the most part, two-year-olds and many young three-year-olds are not yet interested in or ready for social play. If the child you are concerned about is very young, examine your own expectations rather than the child's behavior. Given time and appropriate guidance, this child should soon emerge from his preference for solitary play into a more social world.
- The child's avoidance of interaction with peers might be a result of the classroom in which he has been placed. The child might be the youngest and smallest in the group. He might feel overpowered and intimidated by his classmates. In such an instance, move the child to a more appropriate class if possible.
- A child who is new to your school or to group experience in general may not interact with other children because he does not yet feel comfortable in the new setting. Time, patience, and gentle guidance will help the child become integrated into the group.

If none of these suggestions provides a solution to the problem, continue on to the following program.

STATE THE GOAL

The goal is for the child to interact with other children and participate in social play at school. The child should spend at least one-third of his time during free-choice activities engaged in social play or interaction with peers.

PROCEDURE

The program for the child who does not participate in social play includes four steps:

1. Reinforce social interaction with other children.
2. Reinforce other children for interacting with the child.
3. Systematically teach social skills to the child.
4. Ignore the child when he does not interact with peers.

The approach used for a particular child depends on the teacher's assessment of the cause of the behavior. If the child does not interact because of a lack of social skills, use Steps 1, 2, and 3. If the child's behavior is motivated by a desire for attention from teachers, then use Steps 1, 2, and 4. If his behavior is caused by a lack of skills as well as a bid for attention, follow all four steps of the program.

Definition

Nonparticipation in social play includes any behaviors that are not involved with other children, such as playing alone, sitting or standing alone, seeking out adults, or talking solely to adults. Social play includes playing the same game or with the same materials as another child, talking to peers, sharing, and otherwise interacting with peers in verbal and nonverbal ways. The teachers should discuss and list the behaviors they consider as nonparticipation in social play so they agree on the definition.

Baseline

Spend three days gathering baseline data with which to compare later progress. Select one hour during the day when children are free to select activities and can engage freely in social play. Use this same hour consistently during baseline and later during the program. Use a time-sampling method to measure how much time the child is spending in interaction with peers. You need a watch or a nearby clock and a pencil and paper to keep track. Every five minutes in the hour, observe the child for fifteen seconds. If the child is participating in social play, make a mark on the paper. You may record a maximum of twelve marks during the hour. At the end of the observation period, record the total number on the Record Keeping Graph.

Program

After establishing a baseline, continue to the following program.

Reinforce the Child's Social Interaction with Other Children. Whenever you try to increase a particular behavior in a child, frequently reinforce the child to let him know that you value that behavior. Take every opportunity possible to praise the child for engaging in social play. If the child does not participate because such behavior gets him teacher attention, remove that attention. Giving your attention elsewhere quickly changes his behavior. Therefore, there should be ample opportunities for reinforcement, whatever the child's underlying motivation may be.

Carefully choose the type of reinforcement you give. If the child avoids social play because he gets teacher attention, it may be somewhat tricky to give attention when he does interact. You run the risk of the child abandoning the social play situation because he thinks you will now attend to him. How you praise will depend on how the child reacts. Try various methods of reinforcement to see which works best. Nonverbal reinforcers such as a smile, a pat, or just your presence nearby for a few seconds may be effective. Verbal praise, if carefully worded, may also work. Say, for instance, "You two are baking such a nice cake together," or "Would you like these little stones to put on top of the cake you two are making?" Your praise should include both children and imply that you are not staying with them for more than a brief time.

Reinforce Other Children for Interacting with the Child. Since interaction is an activity requiring at least two people, other children should be reinforced for interacting with the child. Give other children reinforcement through a smile, a hug, a thank you, or a few words. This should encourage others to seek out the company of the child more often which, in turn, should help him feel more comfortable in social situations.

Systematically Help the Child Learn Social Skills. Before moving on with this step, confirm your feelings that the child is lacking in social skills by talking with the parents. If they indicate that the child has had little experience with other children his age or that he is shy around other youngsters, you are probably correct in assuming that he needs help in social development. You can help him acquire interactive skills through a step-by-step process:

1. For the first three or four days, help the child observe the social activities of other children. Take him by the hand (if he does not object) and go from area to area in the classroom. Verbally point out what the children are doing. Focus on social aspects. Say, for instance,

   "See, Mitch is the grocery store owner and Charlotte is shopping. She wants to buy eggs and he is getting them for her."

   "Carmen and Larry are painting next to each other. Larry gave Carmen his red paint because she didn't have any."

"Look! Patrick is putting a block on top of the tall tower he is building with Marsha and Pete. It must be pretty funny from the way they're all laughing!"

Do this several times a day. It should only take a few minutes each time. Encourage the child to talk about what he sees as well.

2. Once the child feels comfortable in the observer role, try to get him a little closer to the activities. Scan the room to find one or two children who you think will be cooperative and not reject the child. Do not always choose the same children, however. Take the child to where the other youngsters are working. Watch for a minute or so. Sit down nearby with the child. Begin to join in the play and then encourage the child to do so also. Verbally describe what each child is doing to contribute to the play. Emphasize the shy child's role. Physically guide him if necessary. For instance, place a block in his hand and help him add it to the block structure.

Do this several times a day. Spend several minutes with the child at the activity. Let him know you are moving on when you are ready to leave. Continue with this step until the child begins to take initiative in joining in the play. This may take some time, but remember that the child is just learning these social skills.

When the child begins to show some pleasure in playing with other children, move on to the next step.

3. Take the child to another youngster or group. Watch with him for a few moments. Then ask, "Would you like to play with them?" If he does, encourage him to join in the play. This time, do not take an active role beyond helping the child become part of the social group. It might be helpful to provide a prop for the child to contribute to the group's play. For instance, give him a piece of rope to serve as a fire hose. Say to the other child, "See, here is the firefighter with a hose to help you put out that fire." Step back and let the child join the play. Provide reinforcement through comments about the play, praise, or a smile.

Do this several times a day. Continue with this step as long as the child seems to need this support from you. As the child joins in social activities on his own more often, withdraw your help in initiating social play.

4. When the child joins other children in play on his own, provide intermittent reinforcement. At first, try to give some form of reinforcement whenever you notice the child engaged in social play. Smile at the child and give verbal comments. As the child interacts more, he derives more and more pleasure and satisfaction from social encounters with his peers. Reinforcement comes from the situation itself.

Gradually decrease the frequency of reinforcement. When the child interacts normally with other children, you need not reinforce him any more often than you do the other children.

If the Child Avoids Social Play Because He Gets Adult Attention, Withdraw That Attention. When you see the child avoiding social interaction, ignore him. It is natural to go to a child who is isolated from the rest and try to get him involved by talking and attending to him. When the attention you pay him in this way becomes more important than the social interaction he is missing, your reactions are counterproductive. Instead of reinforcing the child when he is alone, ignore him. Do not talk to him, smile at him, or even look his way. Whenever he does interact, be lavish in your praise and attention. In this way the child knows which behaviors you expect and value.

Continue Graphing the Behavior. Using the same hour of day as during baseline, continue counting behaviors. Use the Record Keeping Graph. Observe the child for fifteen seconds once every five minutes. If he is engaged in social play, mark it down. Do not record during times when you are systematically helping the child learn social skills. Record spontaneous interactions and social play. Draw a vertical line after the baseline data. Record the total count for each day. When the graph shows that the child interacts socially at least one-third of the time, you have reached the stated goal.

Maintenance

Positive peer interactions are in themselves rewarding and should help maintain the behavior once the goal has been reached. Continue giving periodic reinforcement to all the children for engaging in interactive play.

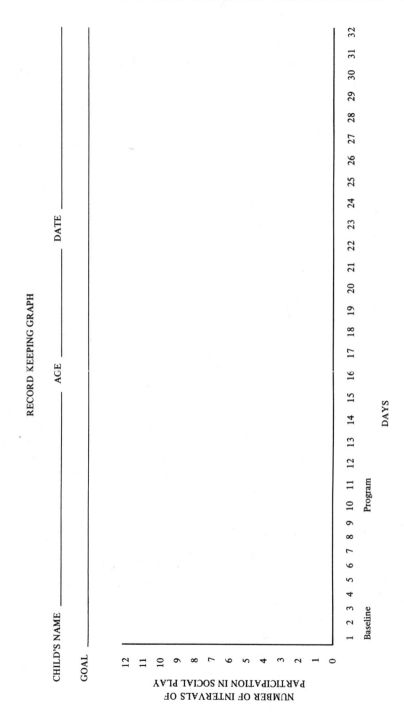

RECORD KEEPING GRAPH

CHILD'S NAME

AGE

DATE

GOAL

NUMBER OF INTERVALS OF
PARTICIPATION IN SOCIAL PLAY

12
11
10
9
8
7
6
5
4
3
2
1
0

1 2 3 4 5 6 7 8 9 10 11 12 13 14 15 16 17 18 19 20 21 22 23 24 25 26 27 28 29 30 31 32

Baseline   Program

DAYS

CHAPTER 34

Shyness at Group Time

With the exception of Todd, the entire class is singing a song. The four-year-old sits quietly with his eyes cast down, his hands folded in his lap, and his face expressionless. The song ends and the lead teacher demonstrates a new fingerplay. A few children follow her hand movements and repeat parts of words. She repeats the fingerplay and most of the children follow along. By the third time, all of the children, except Todd, participate. The teacher promises to include the new fingerplay the next day. She suggests that the group join in on another fingerplay before she reads the story. All the children participate, except Todd. Another teacher notices his passivity and moves next to him. She takes his hands during the last fingerplay and guides them in the appropriate motions. Todd makes his arms and hands limp, so the result is ineffective. Now the lead teacher picks up the book she has selected for the day. The children listen attentively as she tells the story, and raise their hands eagerly when she asks a question. At one point she directly asks a question of Todd, but he continues to sit quietly. He makes no move to answer or even indicate that he has heard. After a few moments, another child answers the question. Later, at a staff meeting, the teachers wonder what they can do to help Todd participate in group activities.

STATE THE BEHAVIOR

The child does not participate during group activities. The child does not speak when called on, sing, join in fingerplays, or otherwise contribute to the group.

OBSERVE THE BEHAVIOR

Observe the child carefully during group times for a couple of days to gain insight into his shyness.

A. What does the child do during group participation activities such as songs and fingerplays?

- The child sits quietly, not speaking, singing, or moving
- The child does not participate, but shows enjoyment by smiling
- The child seems distressed during group participation activities
- The child watches the lead teacher and/or the children
- The child looks away from the others in the group
- The child tries to move away from the group

B. What happens if the child is asked a question or called on in some way by the lead teacher?

- The child says nothing
- The child whispers an answer
- The child tries to answer but only manages a few words
- The child answers only with a yes or no
- The child answers nonverbally, such as with a nod
- The child gets upset
- The child hides his face
- The child whimpers or cries
- The child leaves the group
- The child seeks reassurance from another adult

Use the information from your observations to help the child overcome shyness during group activities.

EXPLORE THE CONSEQUENCES

People are born with different temperaments and dispositions. Some children are outgoing and meet new experiences with anticipation. Others are withdrawn and anxious about what is unknown. Adults cannot and should not try to change innate characteristics. However, they can help children understand themselves better and put their personalities and characteristics to best use. The child who is reluctant to participate in school group activities is probably a naturally quiet and shy child. If the teacher tries to force the child to participate, he may withdraw further because he is intimidated by such an approach. Through a patient and systematic approach, however, the child can be helped to participate and to enjoy that participation.

CONSIDER ALTERNATIVES

Consider whether a relatively simple solution might not help with the problem.

- Examine the activities you provide at group times. Perhaps the child is reluctant to participate because the activities are too simple, too difficult, or boring. Make sure you provide age-appropriate activities. They should be varied enough to avoid boring the child.
- The child should be in the appropriate class. He may be unwilling to participate because he feels intimidated by older or bigger youngsters. If possible, move the child to a class that is better geared to his developmental level.
- Poor hearing may cause the behavior. If a child cannot hear well, he may react with silence. He may not sing because he does not understand the words. He may not answer questions because he does not hear them. If you suspect a hearing problem, use a simple test to verify your concerns. Make a variety of sounds and noises behind the child and look for reactions from him. If this procedure confirms your suspicions, talk with the parents. Ask that they have his hearing further tested.

If none of these suggestions provides a solution to the problem, move on to the following program.

STATE THE GOAL

The goal is for the child to participate in group activities fully and with enjoyment.

PROCEDURE

The basic approach to help the child participate more fully in group activities involves two simultaneous steps:

- Systematically help the child increase involvement in group activities.
- Reinforce involvement in group activities.

Definition

Shyness at group time involves nonparticipation in group activities. Participation includes singing, dancing, playing games, discussing and answering questions, and other behaviors. The teachers should discuss and list desired behaviors they consider as participation so they agree on the definition.

Baseline

Take two days to gather baseline data with which to compare later progress. During group times when children have some opportunity to actively participate, measure the child's participation. Since opportunity for participation varies, count chances for involvement as well as actual involvement. Compute a percentage score.

Total the chances for involvement by counting every opportunity for children to be involved through use of voice, hands, feet, or total body. For example, count each song as one, each fingerplay (and every repetition) as one, and each question to be answered as one. Keep track of the number of activities in which the child actually does participate or demonstrates a willingness to participate, such as by raising his hand.

When you have these two counts, you can compute a percentage. For example, if during a group time you play "Duck, Duck, Goose" (1), sing one song (1), do two fingerplays and repeat one of them (3), and read a story in which the lead teacher asks five questions (5), the total chance for involvement is 10. If the child participates in none, the percentage of participation is zero. If he participates in one fingerplay (1) and puts up his hand to answer one question (1), the participation is 20 percent. Someone other than the lead teacher must keep count. At the end of each group time, record the percentage on the Record Keeping Graph.

Program

Once baseline has been established, you are ready to proceed. One teacher should be chosen to sit with the child during group times and carry out the program.

Systematically Help the Child Increase Involvement in Group Activities. If the child feels uncomfortable in participating in group activities, help him cope with his feelings by structuring situations that are not as stressful as dealing with the total group.

1. At least once a day sit with the child for a few minutes and read a story to him. Ask many questions as you read.

"What is he doing in that picture?"

"How many animals do you see there?"

"Do you remember what the man said he would do if the rabbit came back?"

Encourage the child to answer and to expand on his answers. Praise answers, whether correct or not. If the child is incorrect, you might say, "Good! Let's count them together this time." Remember, your aim is to get the child to verbalize, not just to read a story.

Continue with this step until the child talks freely and shows enjoyment for this one-to-one situation. You may wish to substitute other activities such as storytelling, songs, card games, or looking at pictures or posters.

2. Invite another child to join the activity. Choose a child who will talk freely but not monopolize the conversation. Use different children in the class on different occasions. Encourage both children to answer questions and make comments. Praise their answers. If the child you are concerned about tends to answer less freely and less frequently when another child is present, encourage and praise him all the more. Involve the other child in this process, too. For instance, say, "Let's let him have a chance to answer now," or "Wasn't he smart to see the butterfly that was hidden in the picture?" When the child seems comfortable talking with another child present, move on to the next step.

3. Gradually add more children to your small group. At first, involve two children other than the one you are concerned about. As the shy child is able to deal with this situation, add one child or two more children each time. Add participants only as the child is able to handle larger groups. By now your small groups should engage in a variety of activities besides story reading. When the child freely converses in a group of six or seven, you are ready for the next step.

4. Continue the daily small group activities. Make more effort to involve the child during total group times. There are several ways to do this:

- Sit by the child and smile or whisper your encouragement.
- Ask the child a question he already answered during small group times. Remind him of how well he answered earlier if he hesitates.
- During discussion, ask the child to share something he told you earlier.
- Encourage the child to bring a prop to the group for discussion. This might be a colorful fall leaf, a rock, a pine cone, or some other object he can share.
- If the child raises his hand to answer a question, call on him immediately.

When the child seems to participate as well as the other youngsters in group activity, you can gradually decrease and then stop the small group activities.

Reinforce Involvement in Group Activities. As you work on getting the child to feel more comfortable in small groups, encourage and reinforce involvement in total group activities. Sit with the child at group times. Do not push him into talking unless you think he is ready. Use his reactions during the small group activities to judge his readiness. Praise any involvement that he initiates. If he follows a fingerplay with his hands, reinforce him. If he sings even one line of a song, reinforce him. Give him verbal reinforcement or a smile, a pat on the knee, or a squeeze. As he opens up more in small groups, you can expect more of him in the larger groups. Encourage and lavishly praise involvement.

Once the child takes part in group activities at the same rate as the other children in the class, gradually decrease and discontinue this individual attention. Continue reinforcing involvement in the same way that you do with the other children.

Continue Graphing the Behavior. During each group time, count chances for involvement and actual involvement or willingness to be involved, as during baseline. Compute the percentage. Record it on the graph, and draw a vertical line after the baseline data. You have achieved your goal when the child consistently participates between fifty and one hundred percent of the time.

Maintenance

When the child is involved in group activities to the same extent as the other children, continue to provide reinforcement. Praise appropriate answers or comments. Periodically praise the group for involvement in such activities as fingerplays, songs, dances, and games. There is no need to continue the small group activities on a regular basis. You may want to plan these for the curriculum at other times.

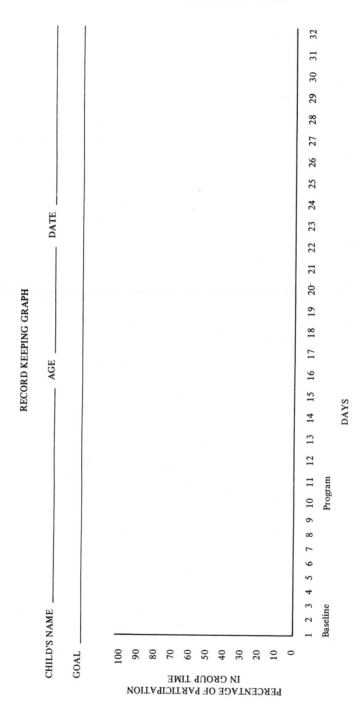

RECORD KEEPING GRAPH

CHILD'S NAME

AGE

DATE

GOAL

CHAPTER 35

Playing with Only One Toy

"Suzanne, come and try the finger paint. We have green and red paint today because those are Christmas colors." Three-year-old Suzanne briefly looks at the paint, but then picks up the doll she has tucked into the cradle and hugs it. "I don't want to," she tells Mr. Chan. Mr. Chan stays with Suzanne a few minutes. He helps her dress the doll, occasionally asking her if she would like to try another activity. Later, after storytime, Suzanne again heads for her favorite doll. Other children cut and glue Christmas ornaments, paint, build with blocks, look at books, blow bubbles at the water table, put together puzzles, and hammer or saw at the woodworking table. Each of the teachers spends time with Suzanne. They try to coax her to another activity, or they play with her with the doll. Suzanne is uninterested in their offers of other activities, but enjoys their presence and chats happily while they are with her. Since September Suzanne has shown little interest in other materials in the classroom. She focuses her attention on her favorite doll and the props for playing with it. The teachers try to expand her interests, but so far their efforts have failed.

STATE THE BEHAVIOR

The child spends most of her time playing with one toy or type of toy to the exclusion of other materials in the classroom.

OBSERVE THE BEHAVIOR

Spend a few days observing the child to gain some insight into the behavior.

A. What type of toy does the child usually play with?
- It lends itself to isolated play
- It lends itself to social play

- It requires muscle involvement
- It is quiet
- It requires imagination and creativity
- It is fairly structured
- It requires frequent teacher help
- It produces a tangible end product

B. What does the child do if her favorite activity is not available?

- The child finds something else to do
- The child refuses to get involved in an activity
- The child asks why her favorite activity is not available
- The child finds an activity that is similar to the one she usually does
- The child wanders aimlessly about the room
- The child whines
- The child complains
- The child gets angry

C. When does the child play with her favorite toy?

- As soon as she arrives at school
- Every opportunity during the day
- During free play
- During activity times
- During group times
- During nap time
- Outside

Use your informal observations to help the child expand her interests.

EXPLORE THE CONSEQUENCES

The preschool classroom and its contents are designed to facilitate young children's social, emotional, physical, and cognitive development. A large variety of materials, equipment, and activities are provided. These are designed and selected to meet a variety of developmental needs. During their preschool years, young children use and interact with most of the materials and activities available to them. They are naturally active, curious, and eager for new experiences. Occasionally, however, a child does not want to try a variety of activities, preferring to stick with the same toy day after day. When this happens, the teachers feel concerned. The child does not gain as wide a range of experiences as she should. The teachers may attend to the child when she is busy with her one toy and try to interest her in something else by talking about it and coaxing. The child may soon find that she not only gets to continue what she likes doing, but that she also gets considerable adult attention in the process. Therefore, a systematic strategy is needed to expand the child's interest so she will use a greater variety of classroom materials.

CONSIDER ALTERNATIVES

Your informal observations may provide clues to a simple solution to this behavior. Consider the following suggestions.

- Examine the materials and activities provided in the classroom. Are they truly appropriate for the developmental level and interest of the children? A child may focus on one toy or type of toy because the other items in the class are too simple or difficult. If this is the case, provide more appropriate materials for the child.
- Check to see if there are enough materials for all the youngsters in the class. The child may limit herself to one toy because little else is available. Other items may be either too scarce or less appealing, leaving few alternatives. If this is the case, provide more materials.
- Examine the classroom to see if there is enough variety. You may unconsciously limit what the child can use by providing few alternatives. There must be a wide range of materials and activities which help to enhance social, emotional, physical and cognitive development. If necessary, provide more variety.
- Consider whether the child is in the right class. If the child is younger or older than the others in the class, and classroom materials are geared to the majority, the child may find only a few items that are appealing. In this case, move the child to a more suitable class if at all possible.
- Sometimes children use one particular toy over and over again for a period of time because they are trying to master it. Do not mistake such behavior with the problem described in this chapter. Children often repeat an activity many times because they are working on understanding and accomplishing the task. A child may do the same puzzle over and over until she can do it quickly and independently. Once she has mastered the puzzle, she loses interest in it, since it no longer challenges her. It is typical that a child who repeats an activity to gain mastery stops doing it once she has accomplished her goal.

If none of these suggestions serves as a solution to the problem, continue on to the following program.

STATE THE GOAL

The goal is for the child to use a wider variety of materials, spending time with at least five different categories of materials each day.

PROCEDURE

Basically, your approach to the problem involves three steps:

- Systematically introduce the child to different activities.
- Reinforce involvement in various activities.
- Ignore involvement in the old, favored activity.

Definition

Playing with only one toy is defined as limited involvement in classroom activities. The desired behavior is involvement in a minimum of five types of activities during the school day.

Baseline

Take three days to collect baseline data with which to compare later progress. At the end of this chapter is a chart listing ten activity areas, and a graph for recording a number of different areas in which the child is involved each day. The graph reflects how diversified the child's play is. The following lists the ten activity areas and examples of activities included in each:

- GRAPHIC ART – painting, drawing, crayoning, chalk drawing
- MODELING ART – clay, collage
- DRAMATIC PLAY – housekeeping, other spontaneous role playing
- MANIPULATIVES – puzzles, nesting toys, beads
- BLOCKS – all types
- LARGE-MUSCLE ACTIVITIES – outdoor and indoor climbing, sliding, swinging, riding equipment, woodworking
- SENSORY ACTIVITIES – water, sand, mud, finger or foot painting, cooking, smell, feel, taste, and sound discrimination
- COGNITIVE ACTIVITIES – math, classification and seriation activities, discrimination tasks, matching games
- LANGUAGE ACTIVITIES – books, storytelling, flannel board, story records, tape recorder
- MUSIC – dancing, singing, listening to music, playing rhythm instruments

Each day, during nonstructured activities (free choice or child-selected rather than teacher-directed activities), mark down on the chart the activity areas in which the child participates. To ensure that the activities are not ones that the child is flitting in and out of, mark only those where she spends at least three continuous minutes. At the end of each day, record the total number of areas in which the child was involved on the Record Keeping Graph.

Program

After gathering baseline data, start the program. All teachers should participate so they can plan appropriately and help the child's activities become more diversified.

Systematically Introduce the Child to Activities in the Ten Activity Areas. Each day ensure that there is at least one activity available to the children in a minimum of eight activity areas. At the beginning of each child-selected activity period, before children have a chance to become involved, go to the child and do the following:

1. Have an activity in mind. At first, choose one that is fairly similar to the activity in which the child has been engaged. Use baseline and observation data to help you determine what activity to select. For instance, if the child has been working only with blocks, try toy building materials. Use this type of toy for about a week.

   During the next week, select a type of toy that is somewhat less similar. Do not, however, aim for the most dissimilar activity. Continue introducing the child to new activities. Choose those that are increasingly different from what she has been doing. Take cues from the child if she indicates an interest in a new activity. Select activities and structure them to ensure success. The child enjoys an activity more if she feels a sense of accomplishment in what she does.

2. Tell the child you have a special activity you would like to do with her. Take her by the hand to the selected activity, and stay for three to five minutes. Help the child get started, and then encourage, praise and talk with her as appropriate. Interact with the other children in the area also, but concentrate on the child you are concerned about.

3. Reinforce the child for finished products in new activity areas, such as paintings and completed puzzles. Also reinforce sustained interest beyond the time in which you are paying special interest. Your objective is to convey to the child that you approve of what she is doing.

4. If the child does not want to try a new activity but wants to go to her old, familiar toy, let her do so the first time. However, before you let her go, explain to her that you want her to try other activities also. Tell

her she can derive enjoyment and satisfaction from these as well as from her favorite activity, and that you want to spend time with her each day in new activities. Tell the child that she will be able to play with her old toy only after she has spent some time in a new activity.

If possible, remove her favorite activity or close the activity area in which she usually spends her time until she has spent a minimum of three minutes constructively engaged in another area. Give ample attention to her activity in other areas. After this, allow her to go to her old toy if she so wishes. Do not reinforce such activity, however.

5. Continue leading the child to different activities at the beginning of each activity time. Pay special attention to her for the first few minutes and continue intermittent reinforcement. Once the Record Keeping Graph indicates that the child is spending more time throughout the day in other areas of the class, begin to gradually decrease this special attention. Decrease attention to every other time, then to approximately every third time, and so on. Eventually, you should no longer need to lead the child to diverse activities because she should participate on her own.

6. During this systematic approach to expanding the child's interests, keep watch on the data shown in the activity area chart. This reveals interest areas in which the child spends time as well as areas in which she spends little or no time. After several weeks of the program, when she begins to expand her involvement, introduce the child more often to the areas in which she does not show an interest.

Reinforce Involvement in Various Activities. At times other than the systematic introduction to various interest areas just described, be alert to the child's activities. Whenever you notice the child involved in an activity other than the one she has been engaged in, praise her. Let the child know you like what she is doing. Reinforce as soon as you see the child involved. There is no need to wait three minutes, although this is the time you use to determine whether involvement in this activity is noted on the chart.

Once the chart shows that the child has begun to expand her activities, cut back on the amount of reinforcement you give. Before you do this, however, the child should consistently be engaged in at least five different activities each day. Decrease reinforcement gradually until you give it at about the same frequency as you do to other children in the class.

Ignore Involvement in the Favored Activity. Whenever the child goes back to her old activity, do not reinforce her in any way. Do not speak to her, look at her, or in other ways pay attention to her. Children enjoy and need adult approval and attention. Withhold these when the child engages in the old activity, and give attention freely when she is involved in other activities. This lets her know what behaviors you expect and value. Once the child diversifies her involvement in all school activity areas, you can go back to giving periodic reinforcement.

Continue Graphing the Behavior. Each day, keep track of the number and type of activities the child engages in for a minimum of three minutes. This data should be for the total day, not just for individual activity periods. Each day record the number of activity involvements in each activity area on the chart. Count the total number of marks for the day and record this on the Record Keeping Graph. This information tells you how to pace reinforcement and the systematic program to increase involvement.

Maintenance

Continue intermittent reinforcement of involvement in many activities. Once the child is interested in a variety of activities, involvement in these should become self-rewarding. If the child diversifies play on her own, she undoubtedly finds pleasure in what she is doing. There may be times in the future when the child spends an entire day or even several days in one activity. This may reflect total involvement or a striving for mastery of the activity. As long as she does not do this day after day, week after week, the child is involved in school activities as she should be.

INVOLVEMENT IN ACTIVITY AREAS

ACTIVITY AREA   DATE

Baseline   Program

ACTIVITY AREA																									
1. GRAPHIC ARTS																									
2. MODELING ARTS																									
3. DRAMATIC PLAY																									
4. MANIPULATIVES																									
5. BLOCKS																									
6. LARGE-MUSCLE ACTIVITIES																									
7. SENSORY ACTIVITIES																									
8. COGNITIVE ACTIVITIES																									
9. LANGUAGE ACTIVITIES																									
10. MUSIC																									

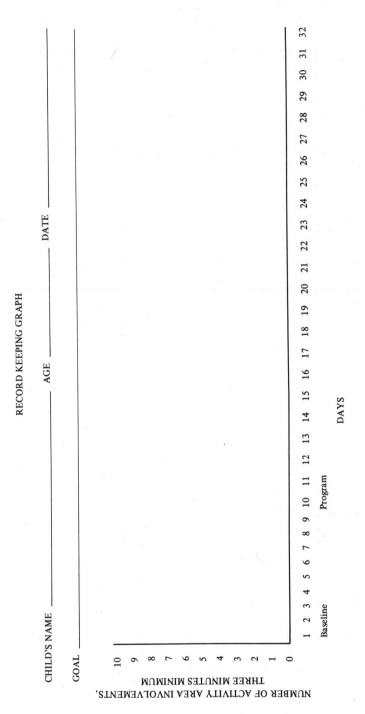

CHAPTER 36

Infrequent Large-muscle Activity

"Come on, Marianne, I'll push you on the swing!" Four-year-old Marianne shakes her head vigorously. She says, "I don't want to," and quickly turns toward the classroom entrance to the playground. There she stands by the door, pressed against the wall. The teacher who offered to swing her approaches Marianne a few moments later. "What would you like to do, Marianne?" she asks. "I wanna go inside," answers Marianne. "Well," says the teacher, "it's time to play outside now. You can slide or climb or swing or ride a tricycle. Would you like to do one of those things?" "No," she says again with a vigorous shake of the head. "Well," sighs the teacher, "how about a story? Shall I get a book and read to you?" "Okay." Five minutes later Marianne and the teacher are still sitting on the grass reading. This incident is a common one at the Head Start Center. Marianne has steadfastly refused to use any large-muscle equipment during the half year she has been at the school. She enjoys and participates in other activities freely.

STATE THE BEHAVIOR

The child engages in few large-muscle activities such as climbing, swinging, and riding a tricycle.

OBSERVE THE BEHAVIOR

Take a few days to observe the child's large-muscle activity. You should gain insight into the circumstances under which she refuses to participate in large-muscle activities.

A. What does the child do during large-muscle activities?
- The child engages in quiet activity such as reading a book
- The child engages in activities that require potentially little use of large muscles, such as sand or water play

- The child sits and watches other children at play
- The child frequently expresses a desire to do something else

B. What large-muscle equipment does the child avoid?

- All equipment
- Climbing equipment
- Swings
- Slides
- Large building materials
- Woodworking
- Any equipment that requires climbing to a height
- Any equipment that involves fast movement

C. What is the child's relation to other people during large-muscle activities?

- The child talks freely to others
- The child plays with other children in games and activities not involving large-muscle equipment
- The child seeks out adults
- The child avoids adults
- The child avoids children
- The child plays selectively with one or a few other children
- The child plays only with boys
- The child plays only with girls

Use the information you gain from these informal observations to help you plan an approach to help the child.

EXPLORE THE CONSEQUENCES

One of the objectives of early childhood education is to enhance large-muscle development. This is done by providing a variety of activities and equipment to encourage stretching, climbing, pushing, pulling, pumping, crawling, balancing, reaching, running, jumping, digging, and sliding. Such equipment is traditionally found in outdoor play areas or gymnasiums. The equipment includes slides, swings, a variety of things to climb on and over, sand and sand tools, tricycles, wagons, teeter-totters, and movable boards and crates for flexible building possibilities. When outdoor play is not part of a program because of space limitations and a gym is not available, the indoor environment may be modified to include large-muscle activity. Usually children welcome the chance to participate in large-muscle activities, and use the equipment with great enjoyment.

Occasionally, however, a child refuses to use large-muscle equipment. A refusal is usually based to some extent on fear. This child loses the chance to exercise her muscles. She also misses activities that are vital to development of increasing body control, eye-hand coordination, and eventual skills like reading and writing. Involvement in large-muscle activities during early childhood has widespread effects.

Teachers recognize the importance of large-muscle activity. They are concerned when a child consistently fails to participate. They may show this concern by spending time with the child, encouraging her to use the equipment. Unless such measures are systematically carried out over a period of time, they only serve to strengthen the child's unwillingness to try. As long as the child does not use the equipment, she receives considerable adult attention. Giving attention when the child will not use the large-muscle equipment reinforces this behavior.

CONSIDER ALTERNATIVES

Consider whether one of the following suggestions might provide a solution to increase large-muscle activity.

- The equipment in the play yard might not be appropriate for the children. A child may be reluctant to use equipment because the steps or rungs are too far apart, the slide is too steep, or the swing seats are up too high. Preschool children need a challenge. Equipment should be carefully selected to provide challenge without hazard. Observe all the children in the play area. If many experience difficulty with the equipment, evaluate its appropriateness. Make the necessary changes.
- The child might have a perceptual problem or developmental delay that causes reluctance to use large-muscle equipment. Observe the child to look for frequent and unaccountable clumsiness. The child may be suffering from a vision problem, poor motor control, or another kind of perceptual difficulty. If your observation supports your concern, talk with the parents and suggest they have their pediatrician examine the child.
- The child's unwillingness to use large-muscle equipment may be based to some extent on fear. Talk with the child and discuss her reluctance to participate. You may learn why the child does not want to use the equipment. If her reasons are based on fear, help the child to overcome her fear.

If none of these suggestions serves as a solution to the problem, then start the following program.

STATE THE GOAL

The goal is for the child to use large-muscle equipment a minimum of five times per play period.

PROCEDURE

The basic strategy to increase participation in large-muscle activities involves three simultaneous steps:

- Systematically help the child overcome her fears and gain confidence in using large-muscle equipment.
- Reinforce all use of large-muscle equipment.
- Ignore nonparticipation in large-muscle activities.

Definition

Infrequent large-muscle activity involves the child's reluctance to use large-muscle equipment such as slides, swings, and climbers. Frequent large-muscle activity involves free and confident climbing, swinging, and sliding on equipment, at a rate of at least five times per play period.

Baseline

For three play periods, observe the child for the purpose of gathering baseline data. Each time the child uses a piece of large-muscle equipment, mark it down on paper. At the end of each play period, record the total on the Record Keeping Graph. To measure usage, count only those instances where the child uses the equipment as it is meant to be used. For example, the child should not just sit on a swing, but should pump or be pushed so the swing moves in an arc of at least forty-five degrees. On the slide the child should come down freely rather than holding a teacher's hand or the sides. On the climber she should climb at least three feet above ground level. All of the teachers need to discuss and define usage as it best fits the play area and equipment.

Program

After gathering baseline data, begin the following program. All teachers should be aware of the procedures and follow them consistently.

Systematically Help the Child Overcome Her Fears and Gain Confidence in Using Large-Muscle Equipment. If the child's reluctance is focused only on one piece or type of equipment, use that equipment in carrying out the following procedure. If she does not use any equipment, start with a climber, preferably one that is not too high and has a short distance between rungs. Decide on a period of time to implement the program. For instance, use the first fifteen to thirty minutes of each play period. Use the following process of *successive approximations* — reinforcing these steps which come closer and closer to the desired behavior:

1. At the beginning of the play period take the child by the hand and move toward the climber. If she shows anxiety at being near the equipment, stop a few feet away. Sit or stand at that spot and converse with the child. Expect to be stationed at this spot for a couple of weeks. If the child moves away, accept the fact. No other teacher should pay attention to the child while she is not near the climber unless she is playing on another piece of playground equipment. Giving attention depends on the child being near the climber. If the child returns, talk with her and pay ample attention. Do not, however, discuss the need for her to use the equipment.

2. Once the child consistently spends at least half the designated time near the climber, station yourself right next to the climber. Now pay attention to the child only when she is right next to the climber. Ignore her at any other place. Again, all the other teachers should ignore her when she is not next to the climber.

3. It should not take long for the child to be spending time next to the climber. When she does this for at least half the play period, again change the condition for attention. Now give the child attention only when she touches the climber. You may have to place her hand on the climber the first few times. Encourage and praise her when she holds any part of the climber. Focus particularly on the next rung she would hold if she were to climb on the equipment.

4. Once the child touches the climber without help from you, at least five times during the play period, again change the condition for reinforcement. This time pay attention to the child only when her entire body is on the climber and off the ground. Even if she is only one inch from the ground, praise her. At first, you may have to pick her up and hold her on the lowest rung of the climber. Be encouraging and supportive, and reinforce her enthusiastically. Do not compare her to other children with comments such as, "See, he can climb to the top. Why can't you?" Accept the child's individuality. Let her know that you are proud of her accomplishments even if they do not match those of the other children.

5. When the child consistently climbs onto the climber by herself at least five times during each play period, move on to a new step. Expect the

child to climb higher, at least eighteen inches off the ground. At first you may have to give verbal encouragement and perhaps physical help. Once the child begins this move unassisted, give attention only when she climbs to that height.

6. When the child consistently and independently climbs to eighteen inches at least five times per play period, move to the next step. From this point, plan the steps according to the equipment. The number of additional steps depends on the height or complexity of the material as well as the progress of the child. The final step involves the child's unassisted and free use of the climber at least five times per play period.

7. It is quite likely that the child's newly acquired ease in climbing will extend to other pieces of equipment. If at any point in this process you notice the child approaching and using the swing, slide, or other climbers, encourage her. If the child has not begun using other pieces of equipment by this time, plan a similar but simplified approach. It is very likely that within a few days the child will be using other equipment freely and unassisted.

8. Once the child is at ease and uses all playground equipment at least five times per day, the child has achieved the goal. Gradually decrease the constant attention you have been giving. Eventually reinforce her at about the same rate as you do other children when they use large-muscle equipment.

Reinforce All Use of Large-Muscle Equipment. The previously outlined steps give detailed instructions for the teacher who will be stationed near the climber. The role of the other teachers on the playground is equally important. They help the child reach the goal by supporting the actions of the lead teacher. They should be aware of the child's movements when she is away from the climber. If at any time the child is on or near other large-muscle equipment, they should reinforce such behavior.

Ignore Nonparticipation in Large-Muscle Activities. During play periods, teachers must ignore all behaviors not related to using the large-muscle equipment. Give no reinforcement to other activities. Ignoring focuses the child's activity toward the large-muscle equipment. If attention is given when the child is doing anything other than approaching or using equipment, the wrong reinforcement is given. As soon as the child reaches the goal, the ignoring is ended. The child should receive attention for large-muscle activities in the same way other children do.

Continue Graphing the Behavior. As the program is being implemented, count only the number of times the child uses the equipment independently. Use the Record Keeping Graph. Do not count being near, touching, or only partially using the equipment. Draw a vertical line after baseline and record the total of each play period.

Maintenance

Give intermittent praise when the child uses large-muscle equipment. If the child occasionally refuses to use the equipment for any reason, simply ignore any behavior other than participation in large-muscle activities.

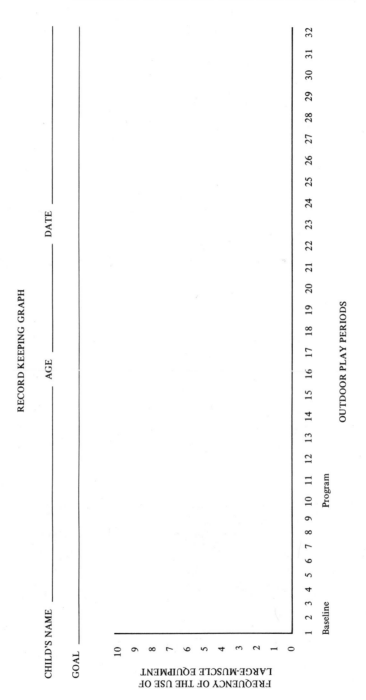

RECORD KEEPING GRAPH

CHILD'S NAME _____ AGE _____ DATE _____

GOAL _____

FREQUENCY OF THE USE OF
LARGE-MUSCLE EQUIPMENT

10
9
8
7
6
5
4
3
2
1
0

1 2 3 4 5 6 7 8 9 10 11 12 13 14 15 16 17 18 19 20 21 22 23 24 25 26 27 28 29 30 31 32

Baseline   Program

OUTDOOR PLAY PERIODS

CHAPTER 37

Infrequent Dramatic-Play Participation

Four-year-old Chip has had little interaction with other children. His enrollment in the nursery school eight months ago was his first departure from an adult world. Chip is quiet, polite, and intelligent. He interacts well with his peers, although with some reserve. He approaches activities with interest and is willing to try most new experiences. However, teachers are unsuccessful in getting Chip interested in dramatic-play activities. Chip firmly refuses to be drawn into any play in which he has to assume a role other than that of himself. In other areas of the class environment, he also shows a reluctance to engage in imaginative situations. He insists that he is riding a tricycle, not a car, when children turn the bike path into a "freeway." The teachers feel uncomfortable with Chip's literal views on life. They worry that he is missing something.

STATE THE BEHAVIOR

The child rarely or never participates in dramatic-play and role-playing activities.

OBSERVE THE BEHAVIOR

Observe the child for a few days to gain some insight into the behavior.

A. In what activities does the child engage at school?
- Nonsocial activities
- Social games which are relatively structured (like Lotto)
- Manipulative games and materials
- Blocks
- Art
- Clay
- Collage

- Reading books
- Woodworking
- Sensory activities
- Basically small-motor activities
- Basically large-muscle activities
- A combination of large- and small-motor activities

B. How does the child interact with others?
  - The child freely talks with adults
  - The child talks with children
  - The child avoids other children
  - The child interacts with only one child or a few others
  - The child interacts mostly when an adult is present
  - The child takes initiative in interactions
  - The child responds when others initiate interaction
  - The child is passive in communications with others
  - The child is aggressive
  - The child is assertive

C. Carefully listen and record what the child says, either to peers or to himself, when he is engaged in activities.

These informal observations should enable you to help the child take a more active part in dramatic play.

EXPLORE THE CONSEQUENCES

One of the goals of early childhood education is to teach the child about the world around him and the people in it. The child learns partly by observation about who people are, what they do, and how they act and react. Passive observation is not enough. The child has to assimilate information by making it a part of him. This the child does through role playing. He not only plays a role, he becomes it. In dramatic play the child takes on a role and is the mommy, the mail carrier, the grocer, the baby, or the gas-station attendant. He takes what information he has about the role and shapes it according to his perceptions and perspective. Role playing is a vital part of the early years; it facilitates socialization of the child.

Children role play naturally. Children begin with fairly simple interpretations when they are still very young (for instance, rocking a doll, turning an imaginary steering wheel). They progress to more elaborate and complex dramatic play involving many roles and interactions. A child who does not participate in dramatic play should be encouraged to do so. Teachers should refocus their attention to this child to encourage dramatic-play participation. If a child is given attention when he does not role play, he has no incentive to engage in it. When gaining the attention of adults depends on role playing, the child will be directed into this activity.

CONSIDER ALTERNATIVES

Consider whether one of the following suggestions provides a solution to the behavior.

- Role playing can take place in all areas of the classroom. It is not limited to the dramatic-play area. A child may never enter the dramatic-play section of the room but still engage in a great deal of role playing. Listen to the child as he talks with friends as well as when he plays alone. Making motor sounds as he runs a block across the floor, stopping his tricycle to get "gas," and putting together Tinker Toys® to simulate a swing are signs of potential or actual role playing.

- Children often use props to help them in role playing. The preschool classroom contains many items that encourage assuming specific roles such as dress-up clothes, dolls, grocery items, and trucks. Role playing helps children assume a sex-appropriate identity. Most preschool teachers are conscious of encouraging this in a nonstereotyped way. A child may feel that the available props do not meet his interests and therefore avoids the dramatic-play area. It may be that the dramatic-play area is solely feminine in the sex-typed materials that are provided. If this is the case, add some hats, boots, men's shoes, ties, and men's jackets to the purses, dresses, and high heels. Provide props that encourage role playing of various occupations. Supply props to encompass all the children's interests.

- Examine the variety that the dramatic-play area offers. Change the area periodically to stimulate new ideas and play. A child may avoid the dramatic-play area because it is overly familiar to him. Occasionally add new props to the existing area, or change it into an airport, a restaurant, a barber shop, a campground, or a grocery store.

- Dramatic play is a spontaneous activity that requires blocks of unstructured time during which children are free to select activities. If children are not given the time and freedom to carry out role-play situations, they do not fully develop this activity. Plan time blocks of at least forty-five minutes, at least three times during a full-time program, and at least once during a part-time program. During these times, provide activities and materials from which children can make choices.

- Because dramatic play is often social, involving more than one child, a shy child may participate little in such activities. If this is the case, Chapter 33 (Nonparticipation in Social Play) may be helpful.

If none of these suggestions provides a solution to the problem, continue to the following program.

STATE THE GOAL

The goal is for the child to participate in spontaneous dramatic-play and role-play activities at least twice per day (each for a minimum of five consecutive minutes).

PROCEDURE

The approach to involving the child in more dramatic-play activities will include four simultaneous steps:

- Provide many opportunities for role play within the environment.
- Give reinforcement for role play during free choice activity times.
- Give selective reinforcement.
- Systematically involve the child in role-play situations.

Definition

Infrequent dramatic-play participation involves the child's reluctance to assume a role other than himself in a play situation. Participation in dramatic-play activities means that the child freely joins in role-playing activities and willingly assumes a role other than himself.

Baseline

Take three days to gather baseline data. Watch for all instances of role playing in which the child assumes the role of another person. Whenever you see the child engaged in such play, keep track of the amount of time he spends there. Include outdoor play in the count, if this is feasible. For each separate instance, write the amount of time on paper. At the end of the day record the number of role-play situations in which the child was involved for more than five minutes. Use the Frequency Graph at the end of this chapter. Then, average the times spent in *all* role-play situations and record this average on the Duration Graph at the end of this chapter.

Program

After gathering baseline data, begin implementing the following program. All teachers should consistently follow the procedures for maximum effectiveness.

Provide Many Opportunities for Role Playing within the Classroom and the Curriculum. Classroom materials and room arrangement can encourage and facilitate dramatic play. Examine the room carefully. If the room arrangement has been the same for more than two months, consider rearranging it. Make the dramatic-play area more prominent and appealing. Add new props to the area. Additions to the dramatic-play area can be inexpensive, such as old hats, shoes, clothing items, kitchen utensils, and food containers. The addition of a large, sturdy cardboard box can also stimulate imaginative play. The outdoor play area can be made more conducive to role play through such props as traffic signs, a length of hose for a gas station or fire department, or a blanket thrown over a climber to make a house.

The curriculum can encourage more dramatic play by providing many opportunities to create and take on roles. If your curriculum revolves around a theme, plan dramatic-play activities related to that theme. For example, children can become astronauts, zoo keepers, pilots, doctors, or beauticians, according to your current theme. You could even convert the entire classroom into a home if your theme revolves around the family. Include centers and activities related to cooking, laundering, cleaning, dressing, and other family-related activities. Another way to include more dramatic-play opportunities is through individual activities. Add block people and animals to the block area, or plan craft activities where the children can make a variety of puppets. You may also provide movement activities that suggest new roles.

Reinforce Role Playing. Keep careful watch on the child during free choice activities as well as during outdoor play. Whenever the child approaches or watches other children engaged in role play or participates in role play, reinforce this behavior. Verbal praise, a smile, your presence, suggestions, or your involvement provide reinforcement. Let the child know that you approve of his behavior. As the child increases involvement in dramatic play over a period of time, focus reinforcement on instances when the child actually engages in role playing. When the child regularly participates in dramatic play, gradually decrease the frequency of reinforcement until you are giving it at the same rate as to the other children.

Give Selective Reinforcement. While trying to increase role playing, give selective reinforcement. Minimize the attention you give to the child when he is engaged in other activities. Be careful, however, not to be harsh in implementing this measure. As the child engages more in role play, gradually increase the attention you give him for participating in other activities. Do not discourage his enjoyment of other areas in the classroom.

Systematically Involve the Child in Role-Play Situations. The child may increase involvement in role play on his own because of selective reinforcement and increased opportunities through classroom arrangement and curriculum. For the first week of this program, use only the preceding three steps. If, by the end of the week, you begin to note an increase in either or both of the Record Keeping Graphs, continue with those steps. If environmental changes and selective reinforcement do not bring about change, begin the following steps to systematically involve the child in role playing:

1. Take the child by the hand and lead him to an area where children are engaged in dramatic play. Stay there with him for two to three minutes, watching the children. Verbalize what the other youngsters are doing. Insert praise into the conversation. Say, for instance, "Look, the daddy just came home from work. See his lunch pail? It looks as if the brother and sister are setting the table. Here comes the mommy now, too. Oh, Larry is barking. He must be the dog. Larry, you're a wonderful dog!" Encourage the child to verbalize what he observes.

   Do this step once during each free choice activity. Continue it for several days, or until the child appears comfortable in watching other children engage in dramatic play.

2. Next, begin as you did in the previous step. After one or two minutes of observing, tell the child that you and he are going to join the group. As you observe the play, be aware of the following:

   - What role can the child assume in this dramatic-play situation?
   - What will make the child a welcome addition to the play?
   - Is there a prop the child can contribute to make him a more desirable participant?
   - What role can you assume?
   - How can you use your role to make the child more welcome as a participant?

   You and the child might join in the dramatic-play situation in the following way. Quickly find a prop (a grocery container or even a block) and hand it to the child. Take him by the hand and knock on a nearby surface. Say, "Hello. We're here for dinner. We brought a cake for dessert." Help the child place his prop on the table. Ad lib as appropriate to the situation. Encourage the child to participate and let the other children continue their play in the way they prefer. Your role is to not take over, but to blend in as a facilitator.

Continue this step over a period of time until the child participates in role-play situations freely, with your help.

3. Continue leading the child to dramatic-play situations. Withdraw your support gradually. Take a less active role in the play, while continuing to praise the child and the others for their imaginativeness. You should eventually need to take on no more than an observer's role, while the child participates.

4. By this time the child should engage in spontaneous dramatic play at times other than when you are with him. The Record Keeping Graphs should tell you if this is happening. When the child meets the goal you have set, begin gradually to decrease your role. Lead him to dramatic play every other time, then every third time, and so forth. Eventually the child should be participating freely and spontaneously in the same way the other children do.

Continue Graphing the Behavior. Keep track of the duration of role-play involvement, and record the average duration and number of role-play situations that last more than five minutes on the graphs. Count only spontaneous situations, not ones to which you lead the child. Draw a vertical line after baseline to distinguish it from the child's progress after starting the program. Draw a vertical line after the first week if you decide to use the systematic procedure to involve the child in dramatic play.

Maintenance

Once the child freely engages in dramatic play, he should continue on his own because it offers intrinsic satisfaction. When the child feels comfortable with role playing, he participates in it at his own pace. There may be days when he engages in a great deal of dramatic play, and other periods when he leaves it because his attention and energies are focused elsewhere. The child need not engage in role playing on a daily basis, but when it is right for him. He should do so freely.

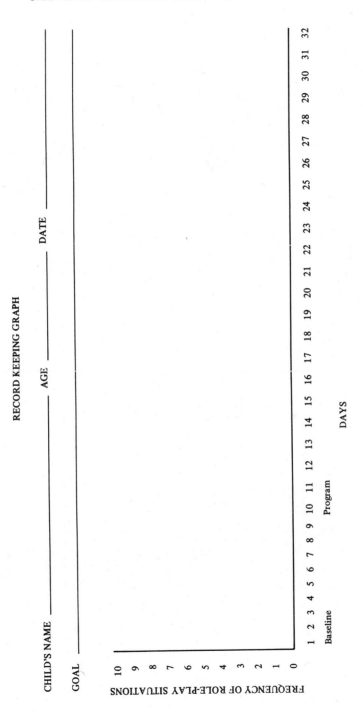

RECORD KEEPING GRAPH

CHILD'S NAME

GOAL

AGE

DATE

FREQUENCY OF ROLE-PLAY SITUATIONS

10
9
8
7
6
5
4
3
2
1
0

1 2 3 4 5 6 7 8 9 10 11 12 13 14 15 16 17 18 19 20 21 22 23 24 25 26 27 28 29 30 31 32

Baseline

Program

DAYS

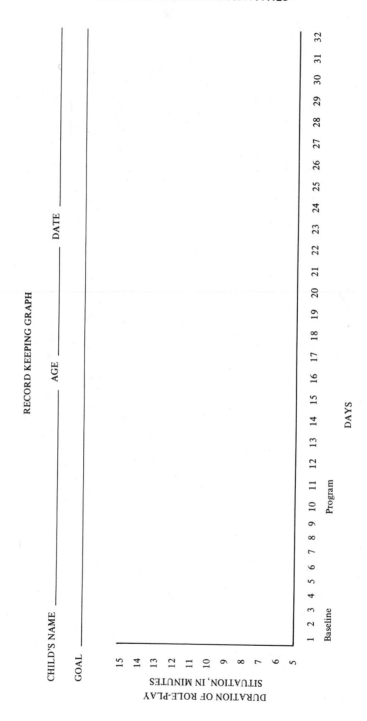

RECORD KEEPING GRAPH

CHILD'S NAME _____   AGE _____   DATE _____

GOAL _____

DURATION OF ROLE-PLAY SITUATION, IN MINUTES

15
14
13
12
11
10
9
8
7
6
5

1 2 3 4 5 6 7 8 9 10 11 12 13 14 15 16 17 18 19 20 21 22 23 24 25 26 27 28 29 30 31 32

Baseline   Program

DAYS

CHAPTER 38

Talking Infrequently

"What is it you want, Noah?" Mr. Parker gets increasingly frustrated with five-year-old Noah's tugs at his shirt and grunting sounds. Finally Noah succeeds in pulling Mr. Parker to the shelf. Noah points upward. "You want something from the shelf, Noah?" Noah eagerly nods his head. After several tries, he conveys that he wants the stapler. Mr. Parker, handing it to Noah, says, "Why didn't you tell me what you needed, Noah?" Noah says nothing, and walks to the table. He staples together several drawings, carefully writes his name on the cover, and takes the book to Mr. Parker. "Say, that's neat, Noah!" Mr. Parker looks through the drawings and comments on them as Noah stands by, smiling. A little while later Noah sits quietly at a table near several children working together on a game. He turns his chair to get a better view of the teachers as they move about the room, talking to and working with the children. One of the teachers sees Noah watching her. After a few seconds she goes to him. She spends several minutes by Noah, talking to him and trying to coax him to talk. Noah obviously enjoys the attention but remains quiet. The teachers know Noah's language ability is quite adequate because they have heard him chatter with his mother. When he is at school, however, he steadfastly refuses to talk. The teachers are resigned and now seldom try to involve him verbally.

STATE THE BEHAVIOR

The child talks infrequently to peers or teachers while at school.

OBSERVE THE BEHAVIOR

Spend a few days observing the child to learn what you can about his infrequent verbalizations.

A. How does the child communicate his needs and wishes?

- The child talks when he needs to
- The child never talks
- The child uses sign language (i.e., pointing) to communicate
- The child tries to find his own solution to problems rather than ask for help
- The child cries if he needs something
- The child leads an adult to what he wants
- The child asks for his mother or father when he wants something

B. How does the child react when spoken to?

- The child answers
- The child turns away from the person addressing him
- The child responds nonverbally, such as by nodding
- The child responds by smiling
- The child reacts in a distressed way
- The child responds verbally or nonverbally to only one person or a few people such as a trusted teacher or a special friend

C. What does the child do while at school?

- The child joins freely in planned activities
- The child is reluctant to participate
- The child engages only in nonsocial activities
- The child joins activities when an adult is present
- The child engages in parallel play
- The child goes off by himself to play
- The child seems to enjoy blocks, manipulatives, sensory activities, art, housekeeping activities, games, books, or music

D. Note how the child communicates with his parents when he is brought to school and picked up at the end of the day.

Such observations will give you some insight into the child's behavior so you can help him verbalize more frequently, or at least more freely.

EXPLORE THE CONSEQUENCES

Communication is one of the most important things learned during early childhood. The process of learning to communicate begins in early infancy. The baby has needs which he makes known through crying and movement. As he grows older, he begins to coo and gurgle. At the same time he hears language and experiences nonverbal communication which begin to take on more meaning as he progresses. After the first birthday, formal language usage becomes more prevalent as the child learns, understands, and speaks words that other people use. Soon he is expected to make himself understood by speaking the language of those around him rather than by nonverbal means. By two and a half, most children have a sizable vocabulary and are capable of communicating with people outside the family.

When a young child fails to communicate verbally, one is never sure what the child has understood. More seriously, the child's ability to gain fully from his experiences is impaired. For these reasons, a child who rarely or never speaks is of concern to the preschool teacher. Failure to speak may be caused by one of two factors. The child may be physically unable to speak, or the child may be unwilling to speak. In the former case, medical and remedial help must be sought. This chapter addresses an unwillingness to speak. When a child is able but unwilling to speak, he needs help to overcome his reluctance. Teachers must pay careful attention to the child's nonverbal ways of communicating. If teachers respond to the child when he communicates without spoken language, they reinforce his nonverbal communications. Also, the child is not encouraged to speak.

CONSIDER ALTERNATIVES

Carefully consider the following suggestions. One of them might provide a solution to the problem.

- Check for physiological causes for the child's unwillingness to speak. A hearing problem can cause slow language development. Conduct a simple test by making a variety of noises behind the child and checking his responses. If you feel that he might have trouble hearing, encourage the parents to consult with their physician for further testing. Besides hearing difficulties, the child's lack of language might be caused by a throat or mouth abnormality or by brain damage. A physician should examine, diagnose, or refer for diagnosis, and recommend steps to correct the problem.
- Preschool teachers should be gentle and soft-spoken. Sometimes, however, some of the adults in a classroom can be overpowering to young children. Carefully consider how the adults are interacting with the children and whether their behavior is intimidating to some of the youngsters. A child may react with silence if he perceives the adults in an overpowering role. If you conclude that the child speaks infrequently because of the adults, the teachers as a group need to discuss the problem and consider ways to improve it. A quieter, slower-paced, and less

demanding approach by the adults may encourage the child to speak more frequently.

- A child from a non-English-speaking or bilingual family needs extra help and encouragement in learning English. If such a child is reluctant to speak, plan a systematic approach. Involve the other children in the class to help him gain proficiency in English.

- A child with a speech impediment may be discouraged from speaking freely because others have trouble understanding what he says. Such a child should receive treatment from a speech therapist. The therapist should give guidance to the preschool staff on how best to help the child. Cooperation among all adults who are around the child will help the child reach the goals set for him.

- Sometimes children speak infrequently because they have little need to do so. A child whose every need is anticipated and met by parents, grandparents, older siblings, and others during his early development may not speak because it has never been necessary. If, from discussions with the parents, you conclude that this is the case, and you have ruled out a physiological problem, use the program outlined in this chapter. Encourage the parents to use it as well.

- Consider the child's developmental level. Some two-year-olds are not yet proficient in language usage and use a variety of verbal and nonverbal ways to communicate. A two-year-old who tries to communicate through language, even if not always successfully, gains language skills very quickly. Within a few months the child should be much more competent. If a three-year-old does not communicate effectively, there is cause for concern. A physiological problem or a developmental delay should be considered before the program outlined in this chapter is applied.

- The child may speak little because his vocabulary is limited. In such a case plan a systematic approach to expand vocabulary and reinforce new word usage. Use books, word games, picture cards, magazines, and other appropriate means to work with the child individually or in a small group. Gear other activities to achieve vocabulary expansion as well. Many of the suggestions in this chapter should help you reach your goals for the child.

If none of these suggestions provides an answer to the problem, proceed to the following program to help the child increase verbal communications.

STATE THE GOAL

The goal is for the child to use verbal communications freely — to ask questions, answer questions, and make observations and comments. The child should initiate and respond to a minimum of twenty verbal communications of one word or more per hour.

PROCEDURE

The basic strategy to increase verbalization involves two simultaneous steps:

- Encourage and reinforce speaking.
- Do not reinforce nonverbalization and nonverbal attempts to gain attention.

Definition

Infrequent talking means that the child refuses or is reluctant to ask or answer questions, or to otherwise speak verbally like other children of his developmental level.

Baseline

Establish a baseline with which to compare later progress. Select one hour during the day (or two half-hour periods) when the children are free to select activities and are free to talk as they want. Do not use group periods when children are expected to listen quietly while others speak. Watch the child carefully during this hour and count all verbalizations, whether they are initiated by the child or are in answer to someone else's question or comment. Count all verbal utterances of one or more words, not just sounds. (Exception: If part of your concern is that the child only speaks in one-word communications such as yes and no, then change the goal to include only sentences of two or more words.) At the end of the hour, record the total on the Record Keeping Graph.

Program

After collecting baseline data, begin this program. All teachers should follow this procedure consistently.

Encourage and Reinforce Talking. To get the child to talk, you must convey to him that you expect him to talk. Reinforce him when he does speak. There are a number of ways of doing this.

1. If the child speaks occasionally, be alert to such instances and reinforce him as quickly as possible. If the child's verbalization is not a question, respond with attention, enthusiasm, and praise, as appropriate.

2. If the child asks a question, answer or provide the child with what he asked for if possible. Convey to the child that he is getting the desired response through talking. Having his wishes consistently granted when he speaks reinforces the fact that talking can be effective and rewarding.

3. If the child speaks only in monosyllables, encourage him to expand his verbalizations. If the child who wants a truck from a shelf points and says "That," insist that he describe what he wants. Say, "Tell me what you would like." If he again tells you "That," respond: "Tell me what 'that' is." If necessary, model a sentence for the child and have him repeat it. This step ensures that the child knows the name of the item he desires. If you consistently expect the child to tell you precisely what he wants or needs before you satisfy his desire, he will begin to use language more spontaneously. Since you expect precise language usage from the child, be sure that you are exact in your verbalizations also. Avoid vague words such as *those, over there, this,* and *stuff.* Use the most exact word available for what you want to say. Do not say, "Put that stuff over there." Say, "Put the game on the shelf next to the window."

4. Look for activities and events that the child particularly enjoys. During or soon after these have taken place, talk about them to the child. If he is intrigued by a fire engine that has stopped outside the school, ask, "What do they use those ladders for?" Encourage the child to respond and reinforce his response through your interest, praise, and attention.

5. When the child is engaged in activities, sit near him to encourage talking. Children's artwork provides an excellent opportunity for discussion. You can talk and ask questions related to the colors, textures, shapes, techniques, and media the child is using. Make your attention and praise contingent on verbal responses rather than on the child's art. If the child responds verbally, continue giving attention. If he does not respond verbally, withdraw attention.

6. If the child speaks to neither adults nor to other children very often, begin with encouragement of interaction with adults. Use some of the techniques previously described. Once the child starts to speak more freely with teachers, expand your efforts to include other children. Read the suggestions for increasing peer interaction in Chapter 33 (Nonparticipation in Social Play) and Chapter 37 (Infrequent Dramatic-play Participation). Use appropriate techniques to get the child into verbal interaction with other children.

7. When you make attention contingent on the child's talking frequently, the child should soon begin to verbalize more often. Increase your expectations as the child's frequency of talking increases. At first, you may

be satisfied with a word or two. Later, expect the child to say more before you give praise and attention.

Do Not Reinforce Nonverbalization and Nonverbal Attempts to Gain Attention. While encouraging and reinforcing talking, ignore nontalking. Children enjoy attention and conform to expectations when attention is given selectively to reinforce certain behaviors. To increase talking, give attention selectively to times the child talks. Provide ample opportunity for verbal interaction. To ensure that attention is given selectively, be careful to not provide it when the child does not talk. The following points clarify how to implement this step:

1. If the child asks for something in a nonverbal way such as by pointing, gesturing, or grunting, say, "You have to tell me what you want." If the child tells you in words, give him what he asks for and praise him. If he does not, say, "I'm sorry, but I cannot help you until you tell me in words what you would like." Wait about ten seconds without saying anything more, then turn away and move elsewhere. Insist on verbal requests. If you give the child what he wants when he does not verbalize his desire, you reinforce nonverbal communication by allowing the child to successfully get what he wants without asking for it.

2. If you see the child seeking attention, do not give it. He may stand or sit in a corner, not involved in an activity, and watch you, hoping to gain eye contact. Do not go to him to talk. If the child comes to you, look at him expectantly and let him talk first. If he talks, reinforce him with your attention. If he says nothing for about fifteen seconds, walk away. Do not communicate displeasure in your manner. Simply convey that if he has nothing to say, you will go elsewhere.

3. Structure situations to encourage talking when the child is engaged in an activity. If the child is busy at an activity, go to him and sit nearby. Be silent for ten or fifteen seconds. If the child says nothing, begin a simple conversation. Comment on what he is doing, then ask a question. For example, say, "You're painting your picture in the same color as your sweater. That's nice! Do you see anything else in the room that is red like your sweater and your picture?" Be sure that the question you ask is simple and nonthreatening. Your objective at this point is not to stimulate thinking as much as it is to stimulate talking. If the child does not answer, prompt him. "Look over by the block shelf. What is Angie wearing that is red?" Any answers you get should be praised with comments such as, "It makes me so happy when you talk to me!" If the child refuses to speak, move away. Try to prompt and encourage verbalization by initiating conversations at appropriate times. If the child does not respond, withdraw your attention.

By ignoring nontalking you insist that the child verbalize before you give him the attention he wants and needs. Such selective reinforcement helps you meet your goal.

Continue Graphing the Behavior. Each day, continue counting the number of verbalizations and record the total on the Record Keeping Graph. Draw a vertical line after baseline to differentiate between the before- and after-program data. This graph illustrates progress toward your goal.

Maintenance

Once the child reaches the goal and talks more freely, continue reinforcing him for his behavior. His verbal requests and questions should be answered promptly and satisfactorily whenever possible. Also let him know periodically that you are pleased to talk with him. Continue to ignore nonverbal attempts at communication.

RECORD KEEPING GRAPH

CHILD'S NAME _____ AGE _____ DATE _____

GOAL _____

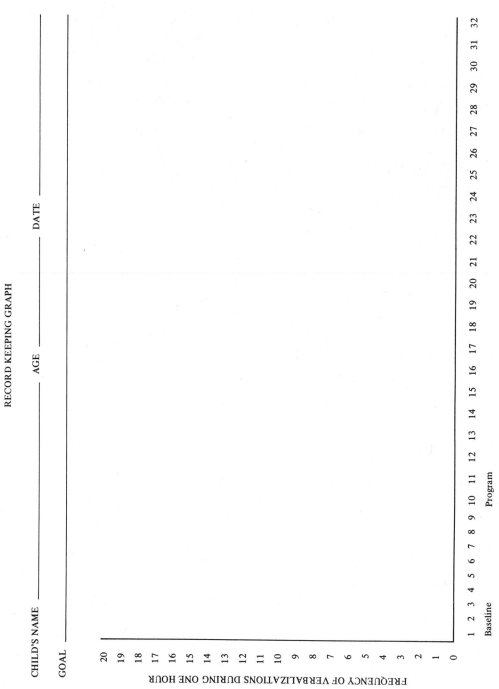

FREQUENCY OF VERBALIZATIONS DURING ONE HOUR

20 19 18 17 16 15 14 13 12 11 10 9 8 7 6 5 4 3 2 1 0

1 2 3 4 5 6 7 8 9 10 11 12 13 14 15 16 17 18 19 20 21 22 23 24 25 26 27 28 29 30 31 32

Baseline Program

DAYS

CHAPTER 39

Short Attention Span

Rosie, aged three and a half, gets up from the circle with the other children. It is time to move into activity time. Mrs. Peralta just told the children what activities are available to them. The other teachers set out the materials for the activities. Some children stand still and look around briefly. Others move toward a specific interest area. Rosie rushes toward one of the tables with a big smile on her face. She picks up a pair of scissors and a magazine. She snips into the cover; she then opens the magazine and cuts a corner off the first page. As the teacher tells the children that they will be looking for pictures of animals to cut out, Rosie puts down her scissors and leaves the table. She moves to the sand table where two boys are filling and emptying plastic cartons. Rosie looks around, finds an empty juice can, and begins to scoop sand into it. Halfway through she drops the can and walks away from the sand table. Mrs. Peralta walks up to Rosie and says, "Rosie, you need to find something to do. Would you like to play in the doll area, make scrambled eggs in the cooking corner, or play with the blocks?" "I want to make an egg," answers Rosie enthusiastically. She is led to the area where several children are cracking, scrambling, and stirring eggs. The teacher in charge smiles at Rosie and begins to explain what needs to be done. Rosie has already picked up an egg and cracked it. Unfortunately, she had no bowl under her egg. As the teacher turns for a sponge and water, Rosie leaves. Mrs. Peralta again notices Rosie and talks to her about finding something to do. As the activity time continues, Rosie flits from one activity to another, but never stays in any one area for more than a few seconds. By the end of the period, she has left a trail of unfinished puzzles, undressed dolls, unread books, and other barely touched activities. This is typical. The teachers hope that catching her when she is not busy will help her focus her attention. This does not happen.

STATE THE BEHAVIOR

The child has a short attention span and does not attend to any task for very long.

OBSERVE THE BEHAVIOR

Spend a few days observing the child to gain more insight into the behavior.

A. In what activities does the child spend the most and the least time?
- Blocks
- Dramatic play
- Art
- Crafts
- Manipulative materials
- Sensory activities
- Water play
- Sand
- Books
- Science
- Cognitive games or activities
- Activities where a teacher is present

B. How does the child approach and first engage in activities?
- The child reluctantly joins in activities
- The child eagerly joins in
- The child observes briefly to see what is happening
- The child listens to adult instructions if these are given
- The child does not listen to adults directing the activity
- The child selects the activity closest to her
- The child participates in any type of activity
- The child participates selectively in a limited number of activities
- The child selects activities in which there is considerable physical movement rather than quiet ones (such as, blocks rather than books)
- The child stands rather than sits at activities where the other children are seated

C. How does the child leave activities?
- The child's attention is caught elsewhere and she walks away
- The child rushes through the activity, completes it, and walks away
- The child leaves activities unfinished and rushes away
- The child leaves activities before even beginning them
- The child claims she cannot accomplish the task at hand and walks away
- The child resents being called back by a teacher (to finish or clean up)
- The child returns if the teacher asks

Use the information from these observations to gain better understanding of how the child engages in activities and for how long.

EXPLORE THE CONSEQUENCES

The process of learning requires that a young child observe, manipulate, change, and try out objects, events, and human reactions. Learning does not take place fully if the child is not able to spend time gaining some understanding of the world around her. It is fairly common in a preschool setting to find at least one youngster who has trouble focusing on any task for more than a few seconds. The child who has a short attention span never really becomes involved in an activity and never really learns all she could from classroom activities. This is of concern to teachers. The child is not gaining what she could from her school experience. She is not learning one of the skills prerequisite to success in elementary school — the ability to focus attention and complete a task. Teachers find short attention spans disruptive because they disturb classroom routine and the other children's work. Teachers may react by trying to stop the child as she flits about the room. The child receives more attention for her restless behavior than for the times when she participates in activities. The negative aspects of the child's activity level are reinforced instead of the positive aspects.

CONSIDER ALTERNATIVES

Before deciding that the problem stems from the child's short attention span, carefully consider the following points.

- A child's attention span is related to the child's age and developmental level, among other things. Attention span increases with age; adult expectations must be realistic. Very young preschoolers are busy people. It is natural for them to move quickly from one activity to another. Therefore, curriculum plans for a class of two-year-olds and young three-year-olds should include very short group activities, enough available options during free choice times, and fairly frequent schedule changes.

  While young preschoolers change activity involvement frequently, they also have the ability to become engrossed in and concentrate on what they are doing. Young preschoolers do not lack concentration, but for them the periods of concentration last a shorter time than with other children. As preschoolers grow older, they become increasingly more able to attend to a task for longer periods of time. It is typical for a two-year-old to focus on an activity for two or three minutes, then lose interest. A five-year-old should be able to concentrate for fifteen or twenty minutes with no trouble. Take into account, however, the nature of the activity. Some activities hold children's attention more than others.

- Examine the age-appropriateness of the activities offered for the children. A child may not participate for very long in activities because they are not of interest to her. Be sure to provide a wide range of activities to meet the interests and needs of all the children.

- In recent years many children have been labeled hyperactive. There has also been a great deal of criticism about the overuse and overdiagnosis of this affliction. As a preschool teacher, you should be aware of the clinical signs of *hyperactivity,* or *hyperkinesis.* Be aware, also, that young children must be assessed accurately. Preschoolers are very active, but this natural activity is not the same as hyperactivity. Be careful not to confuse the two.

Following are some symptoms of hyperkinesis. If you feel that a child truly fits these, discuss your concerns with the parents and ask them to consult with their physician.

Excessive Activity Level. The child is constantly in motion, never still and always fidgeting. She is unable to settle down for long.

Short Attention Span. The child finds it hard to stick to an activity for more than a few moments. She is also easily distracted if she is involved.

Demanding of Attention. The child's demands for attention are constant. Even when such attention is given freely, she always seems to expect more.

Impulsiveness. The child usually acts on what she wants at the moment without consideration for consequences. Her judgment is often poor.

Coordination Problems. The child may have trouble with fine motor control, evident through difficulty with coloring, cutting, or buttoning. She may also experience difficulty in eye-hand coordination and balance.

Discipline Problem. The child has difficulty accepting and following rules. She often acts stubborn, negative, and disobedient. Discipline techniques seem unsuccessful.

Domineering Behavior. The child often is bossy, and wants to make group decisions and decide what everyone will do. She may also tease and annoy other children.

Emotionality. The child tends to have unpredictable mood swings. She is happy and exuberant one minute, and impossible to cope with the next. She may react irritably and angrily to frustrating situations.

It is important to keep in mind that these characteristics appear in most children at one time or another. It is the intensity, persistence, and excessive presence of such traits that may be indicative of hyperactivity.*

- Another physical reason for a child's short attention span may be related to nutrition. The child may not have eaten an adequate breakfast, and as a result is prevented from full participation in classroom activities because of hunger. Or a child may have an allergy or sensitivity to certain foods which cause hyperactive symptoms. Food allergies manifest themselves in many ways, such as a rash, crankiness, and swollen eyes. Some allergies may result in the child's inability to concentrate. If you suspect that the child is affected by what she eats or does not eat, meet with the parents. Share your concerns with them, and suggest consultation with their doctor.

- Consider whether the environment itself may be so distracting to the child that it causes the short attention span. Excessive noise, poor room arrangement, and poor traffic patterns within the room may distract the child. If so, consider changes that will facilitate rather than hinder concentration by all children.

If none of these suggestions decreases the behavior, continue to the following program.

STATE THE GOAL

The goal is for the child to attend to activities as long as other children of the same developmental level. This varies according to the age and development of the child. The child should attend to at least one-fourth of the tasks in which she engages. Two-year-olds should attend for two minutes; three-year-olds for five minutes; four-year-olds for ten minutes; and five-year-olds for fifteen minutes.

*From Paul H. Wender, MD. *The Hyperactive Child: A Handbook for Parents.* New York: Crown Publishers, Inc., 1973.

PROCEDURE

To increase attention span, use these steps:

- Make the environment as conducive to concentration as possible.
- Provide a quiet place where the child can get away from the noise, activity level, and stimulation of the classroom.
- Systematically reinforce the child for attending to activities for increasingly longer times.
- Ignore nonproductive activity.

Definition

Short attention span is a behavior in which the child attends to activities for a shorter period of time than other children of the same developmental level. This may be demonstrated by such behaviors as an inability to sit still, difficulty in focusing on what she is doing, distractibility when she is engaged in an activity, and frequent difficulty in finishing projects.

Baseline

It is important to know how long, on the average, the child attends to activities. Select one hour (or two half-hour periods) per day when the children have access to a variety of activities. This same time should be used for all observations. Keep available a pencil and paper, and a watch or clock with a second hand. For the selected hour, observe the child's movements. Every time she begins an activity, note the time and watch her closely. When she abandons the activity, again note the time. Write down how long she remains in each activity. At the end of the selected period, average the time spans of all activities and record this on the Record Keeping Graph. Gathering this information for three days provides a baseline with which to compare later progress.

Program

After gathering baseline data, begin the following program. All teachers should follow this program consistently.

Make the Environment as Conducive to Concentration as Possible. There are a number of specific ways to make the classroom environment supportive of concentration by the children.

1. Spend some time simply listening to the class. Are there unnecessarily loud noises? Do voices carry and reverberate more than they should? Are

there frequent crashing and bumping sounds? If these noises are present, carefully examine the room for ways to decrease them. There should be a carpet in the block area and in other active areas, such as housekeeping. Dividers between different areas of the room, pictures on the walls, and drapes or curtains at windows help to absorb sound. If noises come from outside the class, keep doors and windows closed when possible.

2. Room arrangement can help children concentrate. Separate quiet and noisy areas. The book section should not be next to the block area, for example. Use dividers to separate interest areas. Create an air of privacy for the children working in the various areas. This decreases distraction from totally unrelated activities. Arrange the room so that traffic patterns do not interfere with activity centers. Children should not have to cut through the middle of any area to reach another one.

3. Be sure that the curriculum is age-appropriate and stimulating. Introduce some new materials, new media, and new activities if you find that children seem to be losing interest. Consult one of the many preschool curriculum and activity books for ideas.

Provide a Quiet Place Where the Child Can Get Away from the Stimulation of the Classroom. A child may have trouble attending because the level of stimulation in that class is, at times, overwhelming to her. A group of children who are busy, productive, and engaged in a number of activities can be noisy and active. Although such an environment is generally considered appropriate for preschoolers, it may prove to be too much for some children, who are very sensitive to external stimuli, to handle.

One way to help is by giving the child the opportunity to remove herself from the class. It is important that the child be the one who decides when she is overstimulated and needs to leave the class. Find a quiet, less stimulating area, either inside or out of the classroom, where the child can go when she feels the need for decreased stimulation. An area in the classroom could be a large cardboard box with some throw pillows and one or two simple activities inside it. Alternately, an area of the room could be partitioned off as the "quiet" area, and rules could stipulate that only one child at a time be allowed in this area. Whatever area in the room is used, however, the teacher needs to ensure that in it there is a decreased level of stimulation from external noise and activity.

If the designated area is outside of the classroom, both teachers and the child must understand and agree on the parameters of this technique. First, the staff must agree that the area is appropriate, safe, and always staffed. The way from the classroom to this area needs to be direct and safely reached; otherwise, an adult will have to accompany the child. Going to this area is not a punitive action, and should never be considered so by any adults (teachers, secretary, cook, parents) or the child. For her part, the child must let one of the teachers know before she leaves the room. She may not go to any area other than the one designated.

When the child has the opportunity to recognize that she feels overly stimulated by the environment and remove herself from it, she is given the chance to control her environment and her behavior. At the same time she must fulfill her obligation to go only to the designated area and let a teacher know, if that area is outside the classroom.

If you decide that a child needs the opportunity to remove herself from the stimuli of the class as a method of controlling overactive behavior, you need to discuss this procedure with all who are involved. This includes the staff, the person whose office the child will go to, the child's parents, and the child herself.

Systematically Reinforce the Child for Attending to Activities for Increasingly Longer Times. Children enjoy attention. Give your attention selectively to increase the child's attention span. First, estimate the average time the child spends at activities. To get this figure, average the information you have from the baseline days.

1. When you begin this program, give guidance and frequent reinforcement to the child as she selects and remains with activities. As often as you can (but at least five times per day) go to the child as soon as you see that she has selected and started an activity. Give her immediate reinforcement. Say, for instance, "That's a pretty puzzle. I'm glad you're working on it," or "You can make such great patterns with these blocks!" Sit next to or stay by the child as she works and give periodic reinforcement.

   Time your reinforcement according to the baseline average you computed. For example, if the child attended for an average of thirty seconds during baseline, reinforce her approximately every thirty seconds as she engages in an activity. Praise and encourage with words, smiles, hugs, hand clapping, and any other reinforcement to which the child responds.

   Stay with the child until she leaves the activity on her own. Do not stop her from leaving or coax her to stay. Offer the child help if you see she gets frustrated with what she is doing. Be sure your assistance is minimal. You might want to direct the child to appropriate activities if she tends to select ones that are too difficult for her. Say, for instance, "That puzzle is very tricky. This one with the ducks should be a little easier. Let's try it."

2. When the child regularly stays with the activity for at least three times as long as during the baseline average (one and one-half minutes if the baseline average was thirty seconds), increase the time required for reinforcement. Try expecting fifty percent more time to elapse before you give praise

(e.g., forty-five seconds if the baseline average was thirty seconds). Approach the child as soon as you note her starting an activity and give immediate reinforcement. Continue praising and encouraging at the new, increased time interval. Try to give this individual attention as often as possible, but give it at least five times during each day.

3. As the child stays with activities for longer time periods, gradually increase the interval between reinforcements. If you note a reversal, with the child participating for consistently less time than she has been, increase your reinforcement rate. Your objective is success. If the child has difficulty, change what you are doing so you are again helping the child lengthen her attention span.

4. Keep the final goal in mind. By the time the child is engaging in activities for the minimum time, in at least one-fourth of all activity involvements, your rate of reinforcement should be considerably decreased. Eventually, the child should engage in activities for appropriate lengths of time with only periodic reinforcement from adults. Such reinforcement should be given and continued at about the same rate as to the other children.

Ignore Nonproductive Activity. As you reinforce the child for desired behavior, also let her know which behaviors are not acceptable. Because children want and need attention, they continue engaging in behaviors that earn them attention. They eventually discontinue certain behaviors when they consistently do not get attention for them. In this case, the child has been reinforced by the teacher's reactions for short attention span and nonproductive activities. To withdraw that attention, ignore the child when she is not engaged in an activity. This means not talking to, looking at, or in any other way indicating your concern with the child's behavior. Whenever the child moves from area to area in the room, abandons activities which are scarcely started, or sits by without engaging in activity, ignore her. As soon as she begins an activity, give her appropriate attention.

Continue Graphing the Behavior. Continue measuring and recording behavior so you can keep track of progress and move on to the next reinforcement step at the right time. Continue measuring the duration of activity involvements for the selected hour. Transfer the average time onto the Record Keeping Graph. The final goal stipulates that the child must participate for a minimum time in at least one-fourth of the activities she begins. To calculate this, place the durations for one day in order from longest to shortest. Take the average of just the top fourth. You now have two measures: the average of all the activity durations, and the average of the top fourth of the longest durations. The latter will, of course, be the higher line on the graph. This method is illustrated by the following example.

If the selected (one hour) data for one day shows 8 involvement durations of 30 seconds, 10 seconds, 50 seconds, 25 seconds, 70 seconds, 45 seconds, 20 seconds, and 30 seconds, the average is computed as follows:

$$\frac{30 + 10 + 50 + 25 + 70 + 45 + 20 + 30}{8} = \frac{280}{8} = 35 \text{ seconds}$$

One-fourth of 8 measures is 2. The top 2 measures are 50 seconds and 70 seconds. The average is computed as follows:

$$\frac{50 + 70}{2} = \frac{120}{2} = 60 \text{ seconds}$$

On the graph, these two figures for the same day would be shown as illustrated.

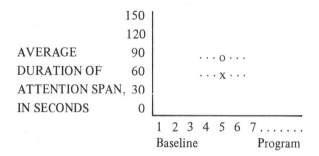

The rows of dots (. . .) indicate that the points on the graph for the one day should be continuous with the measures of the previous and following days.

On your Record Keeping Graph differentiate between the two lines. Mark the total durations averages by x's connected by a solid line. Mark the top one-fourth durations averages by o's connected by a broken line.

Maintenance

Once the child engages in activities at about the same rate as other children of the same developmental level, she should be motivated by intrinsic enjoyment of the activities rather than by adult reinforcement. Continue assessing the environment to ensure that it is conducive to attention and concentration. Provide periodic reinforcement to the child for engaging in and successfully completing activities. Reinforce at about the same rate as for the other children in the class.

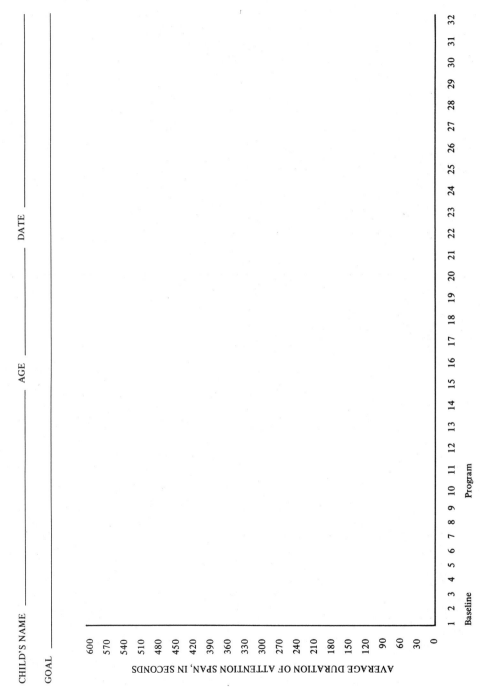

RECORD KEEPING GRAPH

CHILD'S NAME _____   AGE _____   DATE _____

GOAL _____

AVERAGE DURATION OF ATTENTION SPAN, IN SECONDS

600
570
540
510
480
450
420
390
360
330
300
270
240
210
180
150
120
90
60
30
0

1 2 3 4 5 6 7 8 9 10 11 12 13 14 15 16 17 18 19 20 21 22 23 24 25 26 27 28 29 30 31 32

Baseline   Program

DAYS

SECTION 6
EATING
BEHAVIORS

CHAPTER 40

Finicky Eating

All the children in the class of three-year-olds wash their hands and sit down at the tables for lunch. Jason surveys the contents of the serving dishes, points at the macaroni and cheese, and says, "I don't want any of that." Mr. Barton replies, "But Jason, that's really good. You'll like it. Everyone loves macaroni and cheese!" Jason shakes his head and reaches for the milk. He pours himself a cupful, finishes it, and fills his cup again. Meanwhile, he lets carrot and raisin salad, green beans, and macaroni pass him by. Mr. Barton notices Jason's empty plate, gets up, and serves a little of each food to Jason. Jason pushes his plate back, saying, "I hate that stuff," and finishes his second cup of milk. When he reaches for the pitcher for more milk, Mr. Barton takes it away, saying, "You can have more milk when you've tasted your food." Jason protests and begins to cry. Another teacher glances at Jason, walks to the table, and says, "What's the matter?" Mr. Barton explains, while Jason continues to sob. The two teachers briefly confer, then Mr. Barton asks, "Will you try your lunch if I give you some more milk, Jason?" Jason eagerly nods his head and more milk is poured in his cup. He greedily drinks more than half; then Mr. Barton puts the cup down and says, "Hey, Jason, remember our bargain?" Jason picks up his fork and pushes some carrots and raisin salad around on his plate. He puts some food on his fork, then lets it drop off. Next he pushes the macaroni and cheese around. Mr. Barton, who has gone back to his own seat, notices that the food has been moved and says, "Good, Jason. Keep eating." Jason puts down his fork, finishes his milk, and pours himself more. Several times, Mr. Barton reminds Jason to eat some more, then finally says, "You won't get your dessert until you eat your lunch, Jason." When the other children finish their meal and throw their paper plates in the garbage, Jason throws his full plate away. He has a dish of ice cream and gets seconds when those are offered.

STATE THE BEHAVIOR

The child is a finicky eater, unwilling to eat or even try many foods.

OBSERVE THE BEHAVIOR

Spend some time observing the child so you can gain a better picture of his eating patterns.

A. What foods does the child refuse to eat?
- Raw fruits or vegetables
- Cooked fruits or vegetables
- Meats
- Grain products (bread, cereals) or pastas
- Mixed foods, such as casseroles
- Dairy products (eggs, milk)
- Juices
- Sweets
- Sandwiches
- Soups

B. What foods does the child enjoy eating?
- Sweets
- Juices
- Dairy products (eggs, milk)
- Sandwiches
- Soups
- Fruits
- Bread
- Meats
- Grain products or pastas
- Raw vegetables
- Cooked vegetables
- No foods

C. How does the child express his finicky eating habits?
- The child sits quietly without eating
- The child verbally expresses his dislike for some foods
- The child makes faces or noises at certain foods
- The child shows distress when certain foods are on his plate
- The child cries
- The child tries to remove food from his plate
- The child tries to give his food to other children
- The child holds food in his mouth for long periods of time
- The child plays with the food
- The child tries to throw food on the floor or in the garbage can
- The child complains that something is wrong with the food

D. What happens when the child exhibits this behavior?
- The child eats very little
- The child eats selectively
- Teachers talk to the child about the need to eat
- Teachers coax the child
- Teachers spoon-feed him
- The child is often the last to finish meals
- The child usually has leftovers from his meal
- The child eats dessert but he does not finish the main part of the meal
- The child talks often during meals
- The child talks rarely or not at all during meals

Use the insights you gain from these observations to help the child acquire better eating habits.

EXPLORE THE CONSEQUENCES

Eating is a fundamental human need and activity, one that most children enjoy. Eating is much more than an activity for mere survival. It is a sensory experience, a social experience, an emotional experience, and a source of learning. It is very much tied to the essence of children's feelings of well-being. Children's eating patterns develop from earliest infancy and are shaped by many experiences. Some babies are enthusiastic eaters right away. Their parents expect good eating behavior, and these children easily develop it. Other infants may worry their parents because they are collicky, allergic to some foods, or difficult to feed. Such babies may or may not develop into finicky eaters. Continuing experiences with food and eating contribute to shaping later eating habits. If a child is considered to be a delicate eater, he probably will be one. In subtle ways, this behavior is shaped as parents show worry over the way he eats, are concerned about how illness affects his eating behavior, and coax him to "try just a little." By the time the child reaches preschool, eating habits are well established, and the child may soon have teachers reinforcing the habits. If a preschooler sits at lunch dawdling and not eating, a teacher inevitably attends to this behavior. If teachers continue to attend as the child continues in his finicky eating, such behavior is reinforced.

CONSIDER ALTERNATIVES

Consider whether one of the following suggestions might help the finicky eater.

- Eating is very much affected by environment. When the atmosphere surrounding meals is pleasant, eating is more enjoyable. Examine how meals are conducted. Tables should be attractively set. Conversation should be lively, though low-keyed. Soft background music may also help make meals more pleasant. A relaxed atmosphere may help the finicky eater focus on a wider perspective than his feelings about the food.
- Be sure the food that is served is appropriate for preschoolers. Young children usually enjoy plain, unmixed foods. Avoid highly seasoned dishes. Include foods that look and feel attractive. Color and texture variety should be considered in meal planning and preparation as much as nutritional value. It is good to introduce new foods to young children, but most of the time familiar items should be served. Do not introduce more than one new food at a time. Menu planning guides for preschoolers are available through the federal government, through many local agencies, and from commercial books on the topic. Consult such guides for menu ideas.
- Menu planning guides can also be of value as you determine how much food to serve. Portions should be realistically planned so there is enough for everyone, but so that servings do not look overwhelming. It is often a surprise to teachers when they realize how little preschoolers eat and how small serving sizes should be. Children can always have seconds.
- A finicky eater may eat better if he feels more control over what he is required to eat. Therefore, serve food family style so children can help themselves. Provide small serving dishes at each table or for each group of six or eight. Allow children to take what they feel they can eat. You may want to set some guidelines for meals to help make this process run more smoothly. Children can certainly be involved in setting rules. You might want to suggest rules, such as "Take only what you can eat because you can always have seconds" or "Take at least a small taste of everything." When children are given control over how much food they should take, they are more likely to eat the food without fuss. Such a self-serve arrangement also encourages antonomy and fosters independence.
- Children tend to be more interested in food they help prepare. Plan periodic cooking experiences, especially ones where the food is later eaten at a meal. Mealtime conversation can then center on what part each child had in preparing the dish. Children usually feel a great deal of pride in their contribution to meals.
- When a new food is served, avoid introducing it to the children during the meal. Instead, prepare them for accepting the new item by discussing it earlier. Such an introduction can become part of the curriculum. For example, rather than allowing a dish of broccoli to just appear at lunch, plan activities related to the dish earlier in the day. Include a discussion

of broccoli during group time to explore its looks, texture, smell, parts, and name. Discuss how it is grown. You may add plastic broccoli to other play food items in the dramatic play area. Broccoli can also become part of a Bingo-type game, a classification activity, or a cooking experience. If the children have some experiences with this vegetable before lunch, they are more receptive to trying it when they see it at lunch.

Consider these suggestions as you try to change the child's finicky eating pattern. They may suffice in the case of a child who is somewhat fussy in what he eats. If a more systematic approach is needed to handle the problem, then move on to the following program.

STATE THE GOAL

The goal is for the child to be more accepting of foods and to at least taste each of the foods served at a meal.

PROCEDURE

The basic strategy to decrease finicky eating includes four simultaneous steps:

- Make the mealtime environment pleasant and conducive to good eating.
- Reinforce appropriate eating behavior.
- Put stars on a chart for tasting all items on the menu.
- Ignore all signs of finicky eating.

Definition

Finicky eating means that during meals the child engages in such behaviors as refusing to eat many foods, dawdling over his food, playing with his food, not swallowing his food, and in other ways displaying poor eating behaviors. The teachers, as a group, should discuss and list all the specific behaviors to be considered as finicky eating.

Baseline

Take three days to gather baseline data with which to compare later progress. Since the goal contains two separate parts, two types of data should be gathered. One is related to the number of menu items tasted, and the other is related to the number of behaviors defined as finicky eating. Decide on the meal during which eating is to be observed and measured. Lunch will probably be the most appropriate meal to use. Snacks, breakfast, or dinner may also serve the purpose. A teacher must sit next to the child and observe him carefully throughout the meal. For the first measure, count the number of different menu items or lunch box items. Keep track of how many the child tastes. Compute a percentage at the end of the meal and record it on the first of the Record Keeping Graphs (Percentage of Food Tasted). If at lunch the menu consists of a piece of chicken, potato wedges, tossed salad, carrot sticks, grapes, and milk (six items), and the child tasted the chicken, potatoes, and grapes (three items), then record fifty percent on the graph. The percentage is computed as follows:

$$\frac{\text{Items Tasted}}{\text{All Menu Items}} \times 100 = \frac{3}{6} \times 100 = 0.5 \times 100 = 50\%$$

For the second measure, simply count the number of behaviors that fit your clear definition of a finicky eater. Keep a pad of paper and a pencil with you and unobtrusively mark down each time the child engages in such a behavior. For instance, count each statement of rejection or dislike of a food as one behavior (such as, "I don't want to eat that"). Consider dawdling as two or more minutes without eating. Go through the list of behaviors that the teachers as a group specified and define more exactly how they should be measured. At the end of the meal record the total on the second Record Keeping Graph (Total of Finicky Eating Behaviors).

Because finicky eating is very likely a problem behavior at home also, be sure to discuss your concerns with the parents. You might gain some insights into the child's early eating behavior. Similarly, you can share your observations with the parents. Discuss your plans for changing finicky eating. The program will be more effective if it is implemented at home as well as at school. Keep in frequent touch with the parents during the program so you can exchange information and provide mutual encouragement and help.

Program

Once baseline data have been gathered and you have conferred with the parents, you are ready to begin. All teachers should be fully aware of the program and implement it at all meals, even though daily counting is done at only one meal.

Make the Mealtime Environment Pleasant and Conducive to Good Eating. There are a number of ways in which meals can be made more enjoyable. Implement as many of the following suggestions as are appropriate:

1. The classroom environment should be neat and orderly before meals begin. Schedule a cleanup time just before meals so that the room is put back in order before the children begin to eat. When unfinished games, toys, and materials are left lying about, there is the potential for a great deal of distraction. Avoid this by making sure everything is in its place before the meal.

2. Make the table attractive. Table settings should be neat, not haphazard. If children set the table, spend time teaching and discussing the proper way to lay out plates, cups, napkins, and utensils. Placemats and centerpieces also add to the attractiveness of the table. Children can make placemats and centerpieces during craft activities. Each child's personalized placemat can be made more durable by covering it with clear plastic adhesive or by laminating it.

3. Food should be served attractively. Serving dishes should be of a proper size for ease of handling. Food should be selected and arranged for color, shape, and texture appeal as well as for nutritional value.

4. Select food that is familiar and appealing to the children. Periodic discussions to find out what dishes children particularly like can be helpful. You might ask the child who is the finicky eater what foods he enjoys, and incorporate them into the menu.

5. Do not treat dessert as a reward or treat, but rather as part of a meal. Dessert, like all other parts of the menu, should contribute to the total nutritional value of the meal. Since highly sugared foods are often of little nutritional value, avoid them. Fruit or milk products make satisfactory desserts. Do not offer dessert as a reward for eating the rest of a meal. Since dessert is nutritious, it should not be withheld. You might even consider putting dessert on the table with the other food items at the beginning of the meal so the children may eat it as they wish. There is no hard and fast rule that dessert must be eaten at the end of the meal.

6. Engage in friendly mealtime conversation. Avoid dwelling on table manners and eating behavior too much. Instead talk about whatever interests the children. Encourage children to talk with each other as well as with you. Mealtimes should be happy and relaxed. Pleasant conversation contributes to this atmosphere.

7. Periodically introduce new foods into meals; however, do this only after the children have the chance to familiarize themselves with each one. The more children understand the food before it is served, the more likely they are to accept it. Provide an opportunity to see, smell, feel, and manipulate the new food. Incorporate such introductions into planned activities on the day the food is served.

8. Your informal observations indicate which foods the child enjoys and which foods he dislikes. Pay particular attention to foods he generally rejects. Introduce new but related foods in learning activities. For

instance, if the child generally refuses to eat fruit and you plan to have honeydew melon for lunch, incorporate honeydew melon into the curriculum. Allow children to feel its smoothness and weight, guess at its inner color and texture before you cut it, smell and taste its flesh, observe and discuss its seeds, and classify and seriate it in relation to other foods. Use the seeds in a collage, and paint at the easel with colors matched to the honeydew. The more the child knows about the honeydew before it appears on the lunch menu, the more likely he is to taste and enjoy it. Be sure you let parents know that the children experienced a new food that day.

9. Plan frequent cooking and food-related activities for children to experience where foods come from and how they are made. It is hard to relate hamburger to a cow, french fries to potato plants, or spaghetti to wheat and tomatoes. Children can begin to understand some of the origins of food through field trips, gardening projects, and cooking activities. If your outdoor play area and the weather allow, you might plant vegetables. Seeing seeds develop into plants which later are picked and processed can be very enlightening. For instance, few children know that catsup does not grow in a bottle on the store shelf. If you have gardening facilities, you can plant and pick tomatoes, and process some of them into catsup.

10. Plan periodic cooking experiences related to the finicky eater's dislikes. The child may be more likely to try a food he has helped to make because he has become familiar with it through his involvement. At the meal where this food is served, encourage him to talk about the item and his role in preparing it.

11. Eat meals with the children. Your behavior during meals serves as a model to the children.

Reinforce Appropriate Eating Behavior. In addition to the preceding steps for making mealtimes more pleasant, your behavior can let the child know that you approve or disapprove of how he is eating. Sit next to the child during all meals so you can respond to his behavior. Unobtrusively observe how the child eats. Whenever he is not engaged in one of the behaviors described as finicky eating, give reinforcement. You may do this in one of several ways. You can comment directly on his eating behavior by saying, for example, "You're eating so nicely today!" or "That's the way I like to see you eat!" You can also reinforce the child by talking with him, patting him on the shoulder, giving him a hug, or smiling your approval. As the child learns to eat well, continue to reinforce at least once per minute during the meal. When you count fewer than usual finicky eating behaviors for the meal just finished, tell the child again how pleased you are with him.

As finicky behaviors decrease, you can decrease direct comments about his eating behavior. Continue to engage in mealtime conversation with the child when he displays good eating behavior. At the same time, converse with other children sitting nearby.

Put Stars on a Chart for Each Meal in Which the Child at Least Tastes Every Item on the Menu. Since one of the two objectives of this program is to have the child taste each menu item, a star chart is used to provide incentive for this goal. Before beginning the program, make a chart similar to the one shown. Include all appropriate meals down the side.

CHILD'S NAME									
Date									
Snack									
Lunch									
Snack									

Talk to the child before the first meal on the day you start this program. Tell him that you are concerned about his eating behavior and that you really want him to at least take a bite of every item served. If the child has any allergies, substitute an appropriate item for the forbidden food. Show him the chart and some of the gummed stars you will use. Tell the child that you will sit next to him and will keep track of what he eats. Explain that if he has tasted each of the menu items, he may put a star on his chart at the end of the meal. Plan for success for the first few meals by serving items that the child enjoys eating.

During the meal, unobtrusively watch what the child eats. Do not comment on what he does not eat; reinforce lavishly when he does taste a food. Say, for instance, "You've tasted the milk, the meatballs, and the rice! I bet you're going to get a star today!" Combine reinforcement for items tasted with reinforcement for nonfinicky eating, as described.

Share daily progress with the child's parents by letting the child show them the stars he has earned.

Ignore Finicky Eating Behavior. This program is based on the assumption that inappropriate eating patterns are maintained because they have been reinforced by adults. It is important, therefore, to pay as little attention as possible to the behaviors you have defined as finicky eating. At the same time, reinforce appropriate eating behaviors. Never coax or urge the child to eat. Do not use bribes or threats.

1. Whenever the child engages in one of the finicky behaviors, withdraw your attention. Talk to another child or focus on your meal. Pay no attention to the finicky eater.

2. If the child tries to get your attention, such as by talking to you or tugging at your sleeve, turn to him and say, "I'll talk to you when you're eating again." Turn away in such a way that you can still watch the child without being obvious about it. As soon as he begins eating, pay attention to him.

3. If the child makes comments expressing dislike for the food, ignore them. If he tries several times to gain your attention by repeating the comments, say simply, "I heard you." Turn your attention elsewhere. Again, as soon as the child begins to eat properly, pay attention.

4. If the child is slow in eating, do not comment on this either. When most of the children have finished eating and the child still has food on the plate in front of him, casually ask, "Are you done?" If he says he is finished, have him put his dishes away. If he says he is not done, instruct him to clean up when he is done. Never force the child to sit in front of his food until he is done. This only focuses attention on the negative behavior and sets up a potential stalemate in which the child refuses to eat. You either have to back down from your stand or continue insisting that the child sit at the table.

5. If the child has eaten little during the meal and then tells you he is hungry a while later, do not lecture about his not having eaten. Also, do not provide any food. Simply tell him when the next meal will be. Say, for instance, "Snack will be after we've finished storytime and outside play. Then we'll all eat."

Continue Graphing the Behavior. Throughout the program, continue to compute the percentage of items tasted and to count the number of finicky eating behaviors. Use the same meal each day as you did during baseline. When you find that the child consistently tastes one hundred percent of the items served, begin to withdraw the star chart gradually. Start using it at every other meal, then at every third meal, and so on, until the child continues at least tasting every item served without being reinforced by the chart. Within a few weeks, you should achieve this end. Also gradually decrease frequent reinforcement for nonfinicky eating when the chart shows that these behaviors are consistently near zero. Because finicky eating is a long-established habit, it may take quite a while to reach the goal.

Maintenance

Once the child has stopped finicky eating behaviors and at least tastes every food on his plate, maintain these accomplishments. Continue selective reinforcement of good eating behavior and ignore any finicky behaviors. It should not be necessary to sit next to the child at all meals. Be sure to give him your attention as you do with all the children.

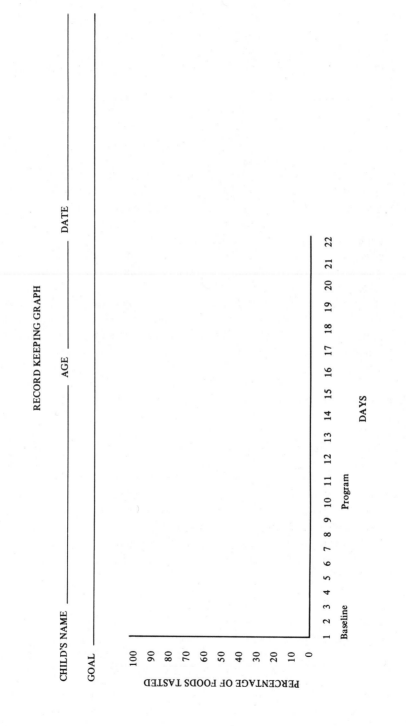

RECORD KEEPING GRAPH

CHILD'S NAME ———————— AGE ———————— DATE ————————

GOAL ————————

PERCENTAGE OF FOODS TASTED

100
90
80
70
60
50
40
30
20
10
0

1 2 3 4 5 6 7 8 9 10 11 12 13 14 15 16 17 18 19 20 21 22

Baseline   Program

DAYS

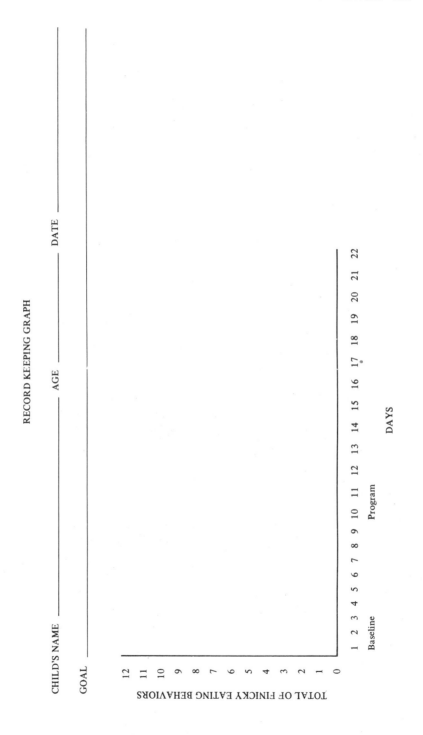

RECORD KEEPING GRAPH

CHILD'S NAME ——————————— AGE ——————— DATE ———————

GOAL ————————————

TOTAL OF FINICKY EATING BEHAVIORS

12
11
10
9
8
7
6
5
4
3
2
1
0

1 2 3 4 5 6 7 8 9 10 11 12 13 14 15 16 17 18 19 20 21 22

Baseline   Program

DAYS

CHAPTER 41

Overeating

During outdoor play, five-year-old Brenda sits on the grass. She plays with a doll and some clothes for most of the 45-minute period. At activity time, she finds a seat at a table and works with manipulative materials. At one point, she gets up and moves toward another table where a craft activity is underway. She sits there for the remainder of the hour. Several times she asks a teacher when it will be time for lunch. When the lead teacher announces that it is time to put everything away in preparation for lunch, Brenda stops her activity immediately and goes to the bathroom to wash her hands. She is the first in line to go to the lunch room. At lunch she eats three servings of mashed potatoes, two pieces of chicken, four rolls, and two helpings of dessert. The second dessert is from a neighbor who does not like chocolate pudding. Brenda did not touch the carrots and salad that were also part of lunch. Brenda's lack of activity and overeating worry the teachers and her parents. Brenda weighs 92 pounds.

STATE THE BEHAVIOR

The child eats more food than her body requires and as a result is overweight.

OBSERVE THE BEHAVIOR

Take a few days to observe the child's eating habits to gain greater insight into what foods and what circumstances are most closely related to overeating.

A. Of which foods does the child consume more than an average portion?
- All foods
- Sweets
- Bread products

- Meats
- Fruits
- Vegetables
- Mixed foods, like casseroles
- Dairy products

B. Does the child dislike or avoid certain foods?

- Vegetables
- Fruits
- Meats
- Mixed foods, like casseroles
- Dairy products
- Bread products
- Sweets

C. How does the child behave at meals?

- The child serves herself large portions
- The child usually asks for seconds or thirds of all or some of the menu items
- The child eats very fast
- The child eats slowly
- The child puts large amounts of food in her mouth at one time
- The child converses
- The child does not talk much
- The child talks about food
- The child seems happy

D. Does the child often bring foods from home, such as candy, cookies, or gum?

E. What specific events seem to be related to greater consumption of food?

- The child has been upset
- The child is rejected by another child or children
- The child is called names by someone
- The child is reprimanded by a teacher
- The child is frustrated in completing a task
- The child hurt herself
- The child is hurt by another child

F. What is the child's activity level like?

- The child engages in about as much activity as the other children
- The child engages in more activity
- The child engages in less activity
- The child engages primarily in sedentary activities in which she can sit
- The child runs and engages in other large-motor activities about as much as the other children
- The child avoids large-motor activity

Use these informal observations to help you gain a better understanding of the behavior.

EXPLORE THE CONSEQUENCES

An overweight or obese preschooler may have many areas of need. Extra weight poses a physical health hazard. The overweight child is likely to become an overweight adult and be much more vulnerable to cardiovascular disease, diabetes, and other illnesses. Such a child is also susceptible to social problems. Other children may make remarks about a child's obesity and leave the child out of group play. She is considered different. In school activities the overweight child is at a disadvantage. It may be difficult for her to physically keep up, since she is not as agile as her peers. She may run out of breath on walks, tire easily during movement exercises, and prefer sedentary activities to more active ones. Perhaps most serious is the damage that obesity causes to the child's self-esteem. She looks different. Her peers make fun of her.

Overeating may stem from many causes. Factors in one child's background may lead to a pattern of overeating, while in another child there is no such result. By the time the overweight child reaches the preschool years, she is already caught in the habit of eating more than she needs. She usually eats the wrong foods, such as sweets rather than a balance of foods. Eating is one of the most difficult activities to change because of its association with pleasure. If overeating is not changed during the child's younger years when adults still have considerable control over her food intake, it becomes increasingly difficult to alter it later. The preschool staff, in cooperation with the parents, can make a contribution to changing the child's eating style. This may help her lead a happier, more normal life.

CONSIDER ALTERNATIVES

It is generally easy to spot the obese overeater, but consider the following points as alternative explanations.

- When you have a child who is considerably overweight in your class, check for any medical reasons for the weight problem. Obesity due to glandular or other bodily dysfunctions is quite rare but needs to be carefully considered by the child's physician. Discuss your concerns with the parents. If they have not already done so, ask them to have their doctor give the child a thorough checkup to eliminate any possible medical cause for the obesity.

- You may have a child in your class who is not particularly overweight but who eats a great deal. Children's appetites respond to internal and external factors. A child may eat a large meal because she engaged in considerable physical activity before eating and worked up a good appetite. Perhaps she is in a growth spurt and her body requires more food intake. Also, the food and mealtime atmosphere may be so enjoyable that she eats more than usual. Consider the child's appetite in relation to her activity level. Remember that metabolism varies in different people.
- Consider a child's bone structure when judging weight. A child may appear large because she has a large skeletal frame rather than because she is overweight. Look at fat layers as well as overall dimensions.
- Young preschoolers sometimes are heavy because they have not yet lost their "baby fat." Toddlers and young two-year-olds often appear quite chubby for their height. Unless their heaviness is excessive or persists into the fourth and fifth years, do not worry about it.

If none of these points pertains to the child's situation, start the following program to deal with overeating.

STATE THE GOAL

The goal is for the child to decrease eating so she consumes no more food than her body needs, to eat a well-balanced diet each day, and to increase activity level so that she is active in at least one-half of the time segments counted.

PROCEDURE

The basic approach to dealing with overeating and to decrease weight involves five simultaneous steps:

- Discuss the proposed program and goal with the child each day.
- Monitor food intake at all meals.
- Stress a well-balanced diet.
- Reinforce appropriate eating behavior.
- Systematically increase activity level through an exercise program.

Be sure that the child has been seen by a doctor, that there is no medical reason for the problem, and that the doctor approves of the program you are going to implement.

Definition

Overeating is a behavior in which the child consumes more food than her body needs for proper functioning, resulting in obesity.

Baseline

It is important to gather some baseline data before beginning. First weigh the child. Ultimate progress will be gauged by a decrease or at least a lack of increase in weight. Record the weight on Graph A of the Record Keeping Graphs. Continue to weigh the child once a week, at about the same time of day, throughout the program.

Graph B deals with what and how much the child eats. Parents as well as teachers must collect the information for this graph on a daily basis. Ask the parents to keep track each day of what and how much the child eats outside of school and to bring you the list the following morning. Combine the list with your record of what and how much the child ate at school. Convert this information for Graph B. Keeping track of the child's intake is simple. Record everything the child eats for all meals and snacks. Estimate in tablespoons, cups, or other appropriate measures the amount she consumes. An example for breakfast might be as follows:

> 1 slice toast
> 2 soft-boiled eggs
> 1/2 cup orange juice
> 1 cup milk

When you have data for a full day, classify the food according to the five categories on the graph. The conversion table at the end of this chapter tells you how many servings of a given food the child had. Record the number of servings on Graph B. Your measures may not be absolutely accurate, but they will give you enough information to carry out this program. Using the above example of a breakfast, the totals to be recorded for that day can be converted into servings as follows:

> | 1 slice toast | = 1 serving, bread group |
> | 2 soft-boiled eggs | = 2 servings, meat group |
> | 1/2 cup orange juice | = 1 serving, fruit group |
> | 1 cup milk | = 2 servings, milk group |

Graph C, to be filled out only at school, deals with activity level. Select one hour or two half-hour periods when the children have ample opportunity to exercise. Outdoor play may be a good time. Observe the child once every minute so that you have a total of sixty observations by the end of the time. If you see the child engaged in any kind of exercise, give her a mark for that minute. *Exercise* is defined as any activity that stimulates the lungs and heart to work harder. It includes running, climbing, jumping, repeated bending, swinging, hopping, skipping, fast tricycle riding, and any other relatively strenuous activity that involves the whole body. If the child breathes hard during and after the activity, she is exercising. Do not include instances when the child is sitting, standing, or walking, even if her hands and arms are occupied. Record on Graph C the total number of observations during which the child engaged in exercise.

Program

This program is effective only if carried out with the cooperation of the parents. Unless the child eats less and eats the right foods at home as well as at school, efforts to change overeating are negated when the child is not at school. It may confuse the child. Schedule a conference with the parents to discuss the problem. If the parents agree there is a problem and indicate they will work together with the school on solving it, then continue with this program. It is important that parents and teachers work closely together and that they share the commitment to changing the child's eating patterns. This is not an easy task for the family, because it means changes in their food-related behavior as well. Do not rush this step. Spend as much time as needed to talk with the parents so that they fully recognize how difficult the task ahead will be. Explore the emotional and social changes this program brings about for the child and the family. When family eating patterns are affected, the change is not a simple one. Once you discuss all the ramifications of working on the child's eating problem, you are ready to begin.

After you talk with the parents and collect the baseline data, the rest of the program may be implemented. It is important that all teachers and the kitchen staff be aware of the program and cooperate in carrying it out. The success of getting the child to change her eating habits depends on the support of all the adults who provide the food.

Discuss the New Eating Program and Goal With the Child Every Day. Although adults essentially control the child's supply of food, it is important to enlist the child's help in implementing this program as well. Make a point each day of talking to the child for a few minutes about nutrition, relating your discussions to the program you have outlined for her. If the child brings up her overweight condition, use such comments as a starting point for your discussion.

Otherwise, set aside a time other than at meals to talk about food and eating. Choose topics that suit your knowledge and the child's understanding and interest level. The following are some suggestions:

1. **The need for a balanced diet.** Every day the child should eat something from the meat, bread and cereal, fruit and vegetables, and dairy products groups. Everyone needs a balance of these four types of food.
2. **Food as a body builder.** How the body and mind grow and develop is related to what is eaten. Eating proper foods in the right amounts is important to growth and development.
3. **Calories.** All foods give the body energy. Some foods have more energy, or calories, than others. If a person consumes more calories than the body uses, these get stored as fat in the body.
4. **Exercise.** The body needs food to get the energy to function. The more energy the body uses, the less there is left over to turn into fat. Some activities like running, climbing, and jumping use more energy than sitting or standing still.
5. **Snacks.** Snacks eaten between meals should contribute to the daily total intake. Some snack foods are more nutritious and have fewer calories than others.
6. **Junk foods.** Some foods are not good for people. If one fills up on foods that have little nutritional value, a person then eats less of the foods that the body really needs.
7. **Food and emotion.** Sometimes when people are upset they like to eat to make them feel better. It is better not to eat when upset.

Use these suggested topics or add others as appropriate. The point is to give the child information to help change her attitudes toward eating. As an alternative to talking individually with the child, incorporate nutrition concepts into the curriculum so that all the children benefit from them.

Monitor Food Intake at All Meals. Adults control what the child eats to a large extent. Exert that control to decrease eating and encourage consumption of balanced meals. Follow the suggestions listed and encourage the parents to do the same at home. At school, a teacher should sit next to the child at all meals.

1. Encourage small serving sizes. If food is served to the children on individual plates, be sure the serving is small. If children serve themselves from larger serving dishes, help the child take small portions. Rules help enforce your expectations. You may say, "Take one at a time. You may have seconds." If the child reaches for more than the limit you have set for the first serving, gently but firmly stop her. Tell her, "That's enough for now."

2. If the child has a small first serving, she can have a second small helping as well. This technique of dividing the food into two portions makes it appear like the total is more, and it encourages slower eating.

3. Frequently encourage the child to eat slowly, in direct and indirect ways. Tell the child to slow down, chew slowly, take smaller bites, and wait between bites. Indirectly you can encourage slower eating. Engage the child in pleasant conversation. Give her the chance to speak, listen, and laugh.

4. Small plates and utensils make food seem more abundant than it is. A small amount of food fills a small plate but looks meager on a larger plate. Small utensils encourage smaller bites.

5. Avoid foods with excessive sugar and fats. All children benefit from such a move, and the overweight child is particularly helped by this. Avoid sweet desserts. Fruit not only provides a satisfying alternative, but it also contains many of the vitamins and minerals children need. If you use canned fruit, look for the kind that is packed in water or its own juice, or drain off the syrup. If a recipe calls for sugar, decrease the amount. Also use less butter, oil, or shortening whenever possible. Drain the fat of such meat as hamburger, and broil rather than fry foods.

6. Never serve foods that contain "empty calories." Soft drinks, potato chips, candy bars, and similar junk foods have little or no nutritious value and contain a large number of calories.

7. Be aware of how much food preschool children need each day. Allow the child to take no more than the required amount for all meals and snacks combined. This requires close cooperation with the parents to ensure that the total intake is not excessive. Use the conversion table at the end of this chapter to help you determine how much food is contained in a serving.

As a rough guide, consider the following percentages of the total daily allowance for each meal:

Breakfast	– 20%
Morning snack	– 10%
Lunch	– 25%
Afternoon snack	– 10%
Dinner	– 25%
Evening snack	– 10%

You may not be able to completely control the child's intake in relation to needs. The preceding information provides a guide so that you are at least within a reasonable range.

Stress a Well-Balanced Diet. In addition to monitoring how much the child eats, you also need to keep track of what she eats each day to ensure a balance of foods. This should be coordinated with the parents.

The required minimum daily allowances for preschool children are as follows:

Dairy (milk) group	4 servings (2 cups)
Meat group	2 servings (2 ounces)
Fruit and vegetable group	4 servings
Bread and cereal group	4 servings

Reinforce Appropriate Eating Behavior. At all times, be alert to appropriate eating behavior and reinforce it often. Whenever the child eats slowly, pauses between bites, takes small bites, takes small servings by herself, refuses second helpings, or focuses on lower calorie foods, praise her. Tell her during and after the meal that you are pleased with her efforts to change her eating behavior. Be warm and enthusiastic in your praise. Also give attention by engaging her in conversation and listening.

Systematically Increase Activity Level Through an Exercise Program. Because exercise burns off calories and because overweight children are usually less active than children of average weight, encourage the child to be more active. Carry out a systematic program of large-motor activities to combine exercise with fun.

Each day the child is at school, plan an exercise period of at least five minutes per hour. This can be an individual or class activity, as appropriate. The objective is to get the child moving vigorously to burn more calories. Following are some suggestions for such activities.

1. Movement exercises can be designed to encourage stretching, bending, twisting, or any other type of motion that involves the whole body. Encourage the overweight child and if necessary help her to carry out the exercises as vigorously as possible. Preschool children enjoy movement exercises that involve use of the imagination (such as "Pretend you're a snake!" or "Let's be popcorn popping"). They also enjoy straightforward instructions (such as "Touch your toes" or "Hop on one foot"). There are many excellent movement ideas in preschool activity books and records.
2. Follow-the-leader activities can also be designed to encourage movement of all kinds.
3. Devise an obstacle course, either inside or outdoors, in such a way that children have to bend, crawl, jump, and climb.
4. There are many props that make exercise fun. Give the children balloons to keep afloat, hula hoops to twirl, balls to bounce and roll, kites to fly, or tires to roll. Provide opportunities for a great deal of movement.
5. If you have a slight incline or hill in your outdoor play area or near the school, play a game with the overweight child that requires her to run uphill (rolling a hoop, for example).

6. Run races. Set the boundaries and encourage the children to run back and forth. There's no need to name winners.
7. Provide movable outdoor equipment such as large cardboard boxes and plastic crates. Encourage the child to push and pull these items into place, climb them, and use them in other ways.

There are many other activities you can use. Provide a variety so the child maintains interest. If the child particularly enjoys an activity, repeat it. If she dislikes an activity, stop it. Exercise should be fun, not a chore. Your individual attention should be based on the child's activity level. If she stands still, ignore her. If she is active, reinforce her with your comments, praise, attention, and enthusiasm.

Continue Graphing the Behavior. Continue the record keeping you began during baseline. Draw a vertical line on Graphs B and C to distinguish behavior after the program begins from baseline behavior. Once a week, record the child's weight on Graph A. Continue to record combined school and home information on what and how much the child eats on Graph B. If the parents wish, include weekend data also. If they decide not to write down food intake over weekends, encourage them to continue their awareness of what and how much the child eats. Finally, continue observing and counting exercise segments for one hour per day to record on Graph C.

Maintenance

The main objective of this program is not weight loss. However, if the child eats no more than she should for her age and exercises regularly, her weight should decrease. Measure and record data related to the stated goals: eating appropriate portions, eating balanced meals, and increasing the exercise level so that the child is active for at least half the segments you count for Graph C. Remember, however, that eating behavior is hard to change and that the child needs your continued support and help to change it. Continue talking about proper nutrition periodically, and continue to reinforce appropriate eating behaviors frequently. If the child begins to monitor her own food intake, withdraw your role gradually. This may not be achieved until well after the child leaves preschool. Decrease the hourly exercise periods as the child maintains her own activity at a higher level. Once the child has lost some weight, she should be more inclined to exercise on her own.

CONVERSION TABLE FOR FOOD SERVING SIZES
FOR PRESCHOOLERS

MEAT GROUP: any meat, fish, poultry, eggs, peanut butter or other protein equivalent

One serving equals
- 1 ounce lean beef, veal, lamb, pork, poultry, fish, seafood, or variety meats such as liver, heart, or kidney
- 1 egg
- 1 frankfurter
- 1 ounce cheddar cheese (if it is not counted as a milk group food)
- 1/4 cup cottage cheese (if it is not counted as a milk group food)
- 1/2 cup dried beans or dried peas
- 2 tablespoons peanut butter

BREAD/CEREAL GROUP: whole grain or enriched bread or equivalent

One serving equals
- 1 slice bread
- 1 roll, muffin or biscuit
- 5 saltine crackers
- 2 graham crackers
- 1 ounce ready-to-eat cereal
- 1/2 to 3/4 cup cooked cereal, cornmeal, grits, rice, macaroni, noodles, or spaghetti

FRUIT/VEGETABLE GROUP: any fresh, canned or frozen fruit or vegetable

One serving equals
- 1/2 grapefruit
- 1 medium orange
- 1/2 cantaloupe
- 3/4 cup strawberries, blueberries, or other berries
- 1/2 cup orange juice, grapefruit juice, or blended citrus juice
- 2 wedges honeydew melon
- 2 tangerines
- 1 cup tomato juice or cooked tomato
- 2 medium raw tomatoes
- 1 cup cooked brussel sprouts, raw cabbage, cooked collards, kale, mustard greens, spinach, turnip greens
- 1/2 cup broccoli, chard, carrots, pumpkin, winter squash, sweet potato
- 5 apricot halves
- 1/2 cup potato
- 1 medium apple
- 1 banana
- 1 peach, plum, tangerine

(continued)

DAIR Y (MILK) GROUP: fluid, whole, skim, buttermilk, or equivalent

One serving equals
- 1/2 cup milk of any kind
- 1/2 cup yogurt
- 1/4 cup undiluted evaporated milk
- 2 tablespoons nonfat dry milk
- 1 ounce cheddar cheese (unless it is counted as a meat group food)
- 1/2 cup custard or milk pudding
- 1 cup cream soup made with milk
- 1/2 cup milk used on cereal
- 1/2 cup ice cream

JUNK FOOD GROUP: all empty-calorie foods such as potato chips, soda, candy, cakes, and other nonnutritive snack foods

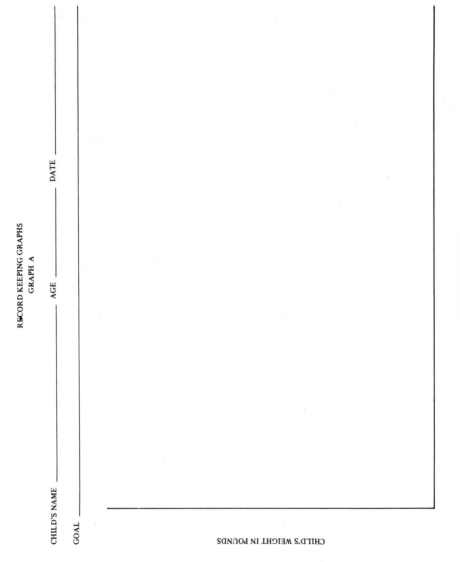

RECORD KEEPING GRAPHS

GRAPH A

CHILD'S NAME ——————— AGE ———— DATE ————

GOAL ————

CHILD'S WEIGHT IN POUNDS

DATES, BY THE WEEK

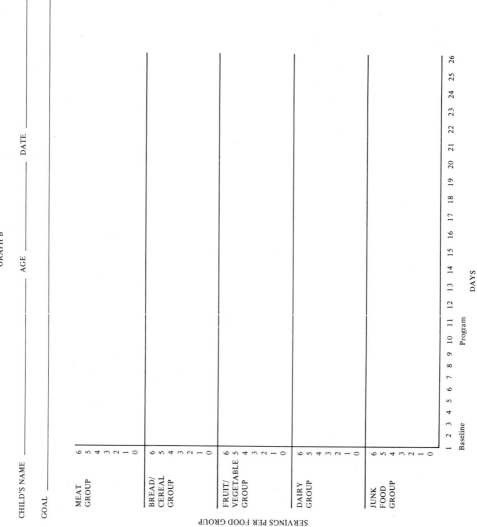

GRAPH B

CHILD'S NAME _____ AGE _____ DATE _____

GOAL _____

MEAT GROUP: 6 5 4 3 2 1 0

BREAD/ CEREAL GROUP: 6 5 4 3 2 1 0

FRUIT/ VEGETABLE GROUP: 6 5 4 3 2 1 0

DAIRY GROUP: 6 5 4 3 2 1 0

JUNK FOOD GROUP: 6 5 4 3 2 1 0

SERVINGS PER FOOD GROUP

DAYS: 1 2 3 4 5 6 7 8 9 10 11 12 13 14 15 16 17 18 19 20 21 22 23 24 25 26

Baseline   Program

GRAPH C

CHILD'S NAME _____ AGE _____ DATE _____

GOAL _____

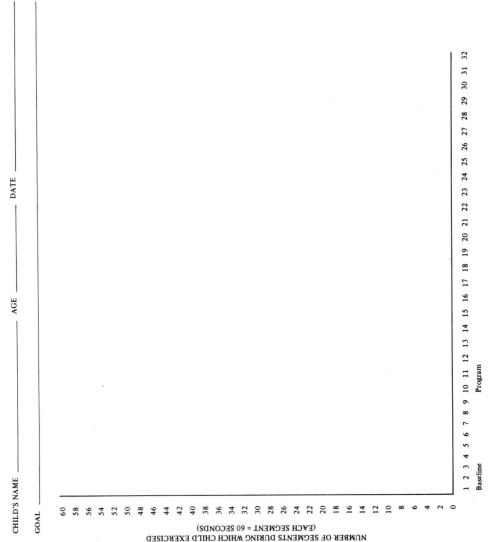

NUMBER OF SEGMENTS DURING WHICH CHILD EXERCISED
(EACH SEGMENT = 60 SECONDS)

Baseline   Program

DAYS

CHAPTER 42

Messy Eating

"Alicia, use your spoon!" Three-year-old Alicia turns to the teacher, her hand covered with potato salad. She tugs on her hair and leaves a smear of mayonnaise in the process. The teacher gets up in exasperation and wipes Alicia's hand, face, and hair with a napkin. "Now eat with your spoon, Alicia." Alicia looks at the spoon a moment, then uses it to mix the foods on her plate. Some of the food spills off the plate onto the table. The teacher gives Alicia a stern look, and Alicia uses her spoon to pick up a carrot stick. On the way to her mouth, the carrot stick drops onto her lap. Alicia picks it up, puts it in her mouth, and munches. She wipes at the food residue on her lap with her other hand. When dessert is served, Alicia uses her hand to eat the applesauce and drops muffin crumbs all over the table, herself, and the floor. The teacher who cleans up after lunch can always tell where Alicia has eaten; at no other spot is there so much food smeared and spilled on the table, chair, and floor.

STATE THE BEHAVIOR

The child eats in a messy manner, spilling food and soiling herself at meals.

OBSERVE THE BEHAVIOR

Take a couple of days to observe the child to gain a better understanding of how messy eating occurs.

A. What does the child do that results in messy eating?
- The child has problems getting food onto the fork or spoon
- The child twists the fork or spoon so food spills off
- The child does not always reach her mouth accurately with eating utensils

- The child eats with her hands, even if the foods should be eaten with a fork or spoon
- The child wipes dirty hands on her clothing, in her hair, or on someone else
- The child has trouble holding finger foods effectively
- The child knocks over drinks frequently
- The child spills food off the edge of her plate onto the table
- The child spills food in her lap or elsewhere on her clothing
- The child spills food on the floor
- The child plays with her food deliberately
- The child mixes food inappropriately on her plate (i.e., pours the catsup meant for the french fries onto the pineapple chunks)
- The child smears food around her plate or on the table
- The child spits out food

B. Is there a relation between what foods are served and how messily the child eats?

- The child is equally messy at all meals
- The child is more messy when liquid foods, such as soup, are served
- The child is more messy when soft foods, like spaghetti or mashed potatoes, are served
- The child is more messy with foods requiring a fork or spoon than with finger foods

C. Are there any times when the child eats very neatly, regardless of what is being served?

Use the information from these observations to help you change the behavior.

EXPLORE THE CONSEQUENCES

By the time a child passes her third birthday, she usually eats neatly. Spills and misses occasionally happen, especially with difficult foods. For the most part, however, the child eats properly and neatly. When a child has difficulty with eating, there can be one of three underlying reasons. The child could have a perceptual problem or developmental delay that prevents proper coordination. The child might be using messy eating as a way of gaining attention from adults and other children. Finally, messy eating may be caused by a combination of these two factors. A young preschooler who has problems with eating finds that adults give her considerable attention when she eats messily. When this repeatedly happens, the child may conclude that she can get even more attention by deliberately making a mess. Most likely she is correct. The messier her eating habits, the more adults react. It is easy for preschool teachers to reinforce messy eating by calling attention to the mess, scolding, or expressing concern. Combine nonreinforcement of messy eating with a systematic approach for teaching neat eating habits to overcome the problem.

CONSIDER ALTERNATIVES

Consider whether one of the following suggestions provides an answer to the problem of messy eating.

- A vision problem might be at the root of messy eating. Review your informal observations and see if the child has particular difficulty in scooping food on the spoon or fork and in reaching her mouth accurately. An optometric examination may reveal a visual impairment that can be corrected. If you suspect that such a problem is involved, discuss your concerns with the parents. Recommend that they consult their physician.
- Note how the child holds her spoon and fork and how she picks up finger foods. If a three-and-a-half or four-year-old uses her full fist, there is reason to recommend further testing.
- The child's age is important when considering how she eats. A young preschooler's coordination is not yet completely developed, and the child is not always adept at the mechanics of eating. Do not expect two-year-olds and young three-year-olds to eat neatly. By three-and-a-half and certainly by four, a preschooler should be able to eat neatly.
- Make sure that the environment is such that children are encouraged to eat neatly. Carefully prepared and served food, an attractive table setting, and a relaxed atmosphere convey your expectations for proper eating behavior from the children. When the table and food are presented haphazardly and with little care, you give the impression that you are not too concerned about neatness. In the eyes of the child, this may mean that messy eating is acceptable.
- Dishes and eating and serving utensils should be of an appropriate size for small hands. Provide plates and bowls that are lightweight and small, small sturdy cups, small, deep spoons, and small forks. These items should fit comfortably into the children's hands and should function efficiently.
- Be sure that food is served in the most appropriate container. For instance, a gelatin dessert can be hard to handle on a plate but is much easier to handle in a bowl, cut into small pieces.

If none of these suggestions helps the messy eater, continue to the following program.

STATE THE GOAL

The goal is for the child to eat neatly, use the appropriate utensils, and not spill food.

PROCEDURE

This program is designed on the assumption that messy eating is caused in part by an inability to eat neatly and in part by the attention such behavior brings from adults. The basic strategy includes several steps:

- Systematically teach proper eating skills.
- Reinforce appropriate eating.
- Ignore messy eating.

Definition

Messy eating is a behavior in which the child spills foods, plays with foods, and eats foods inappropriately. List all the specific behaviors you consider as messy eating.

Baseline

Take three days to gather baseline information. Gather data during lunch or at snack time, if lunch is not part of the program. Keep a pencil and paper with you as you observe how the child eats. Each time she engages in one of the behaviors listed in your definition of messy eating, unobtrusively mark it down on the paper. At the end of the meal, count the marks and record the total on the Record Keeping Graph.

Program

When you have baseline data, start the following program. All teachers should be aware of and carry out the procedure consistently.

Systematically Teach Proper Eating Skills. The way you implement this step depends on which specific behaviors the child engages in when eating. Following are two messy eating problems and ways to improve them. Use either or both of these as needed to change the child's behavior. Implement them simultaneously. You should sit next to the child at meals to carry out these steps.

1. **Problems getting food on the fork or spoon.** Food may easily be pushed off the plate or fingers may be used inappropriately if the child cannot get her food on the utensil. Scooping up food is a difficult skill to acquire. If the child has trouble with coordination, it is all the harder. You can help the child acquire the skills and give guidance in the process.

    First, be sure that the child knows which utensil to use if more than one is available. Many foods are easier to spear with a fork while others need a spoon. Some foods are unmanageable with a fork or spoon and require fingers. Before the child begins her meal ask, "Which foods will you eat with the fork?...Which ones with a spoon?...Which ones with your fingers?" Praise correct answers. Present a logical reason for how each food is to be eaten, whether the child's answers were correct or not. For instance, say, "Right. You eat the meat with the fork because you can spear it and pick it up more easily," or "It will be easier if you use your hand for the carrot sticks because you won't be able to pick them up with the spoon." Take only a few seconds for this.

    Second, be sure that the food is cut into bite-sized pieces. If food is in chunks that are too large, messy eating is inevitable. Foods like sandwiches should be cut into quarters for ease of handling.

    Third, show the child how to use bread, a roll, or other soft finger foods as an aid in scooping hard-to-catch foods on the spoon or fork. For instance, peas are much easier to capture if the utensil approaches them from one side and a piece of bread from the other.

    Fourth, guide the child's hand to show her how best to use the spoon or fork. Let her try on her own at first, but help if she fails to capture the food after two tries. Put your hand around hers and maneuver the utensil to get the food. Do this as often as necessary. Eventually the child acquires the feel for using utensils effectively.

    As the child becomes more adept at scooping up foods with the proper utensil, withdraw your help gradually.

2. **Problem getting food to her mouth without spilling.** Most spills occur somewhere between the plate and the mouth. If the child has trouble with this task, provide direct guidance.

    At first, take hold of the child's hand as she scoops the food on the utensil. Pause for a moment to make sure food and utensil are evenly balanced, then slowly guide them to the child's mouth. Verbalize the process as you help the child. Say, "First, we have to make sure that the food is on the spoon. Now let's make sure the spoon is straight. Now let's move the spoon very slowly to your mouth. We don't want to spill the food. Now it goes into your wide-open mouth. Close your mouth. Take the food off the spoon. Now the spoon comes out of your mouth and you can chew and swallow. See! You didn't spill one bit!" Guide the child and verbalize the steps as they happen for several days.

When you feel the child understands, try decreasing your guidance. Again guide the child's hand and verbalize the entire process, but remove your hand just before the spoon reaches the mouth. Tell the child that she will get the food into her mouth by herself, and praise her well for success.

When the child gets the food to her mouth with no spills for an entire meal, withdraw your guidance further. This time remove your hand about halfway between mouth and plate. Continue verbalizing what is happening and encouraging slow and neat eating.

Next, let the child go alone from plate to mouth after food and utensil are balanced. Then let the child balance the food. Finally, withdraw all physical guidance. Decrease and then stop the verbal comments gradually, as the child is able to remind herself of what needs to be done.

3. **Other messy eating behaviors.** Treat other messy eating behaviors in a way similar to the behaviors just described. Examine the behavior you want to teach, break it down into steps, and help the child acquire the process through direct guidance. As the child gains skill in the new behavior, withdraw your support.

Reinforce Appropriate Eating. During all meals, be alert to proper eating behavior and reinforce it lavishly. Whether it is a spontaneous behavior or a step you are teaching the child, let her know that you value neat eating habits. Tell her throughout the meal as well as at the end that she is doing a good job. Give praise according to her ability. At first you may reinforce only balancing food on the spoon (even if the food falls off the spoon afterward). Later, the child should be able to finish an entire meal with few spills, and you can gear your praise accordingly.

Ignore Messy Eating. If the child is messy because of lack of ability, continue helping her to learn the skills needed to eat neatly. Focus on small successes. If the child deliberately makes a mess by playing with or throwing food, deny the attention the child is seeking. Do the following when the child is deliberately messy:

1. Say, "No, you may not spit out milk." Use this statement as a warning with any specific messy behavior. Be sure the child hears you.
2. If the child continues this behavior, take any utensils the child may be using out of her hands, pick up her plate and cup, and remove these items. Be sure they are out of the child's reach.

3. Turn your back on the child. Do not look at her, talk to her, or otherwise react to her behavior. Ignore whatever she may do.
4. After one minute, put her plate, cup, and utensils back in front of her. Make no comments about the messy behavior.
5. Continue to help her eat neatly. Find a positive achievement to reinforce as soon as possible.
6. Repeat this procedure every time the child makes a deliberate mess with her food.

Continue Graphing the Behavior. Each day of the program, continue to count the number of messy eating incidents. Record these on the Record Keeping Graph. Draw a vertical line after the baseline data to distinguish it from the program data. When messy eating counts are consistently near zero, you have reached your goal. Expect that occasional accidents may occur.

Maintenance

Continue periodic reinforcement once the child has reached the goal. Give help occasionally if it is needed. If, at any time, the child reverts to deliberately messy eating behavior, ignore it in the way previously described.

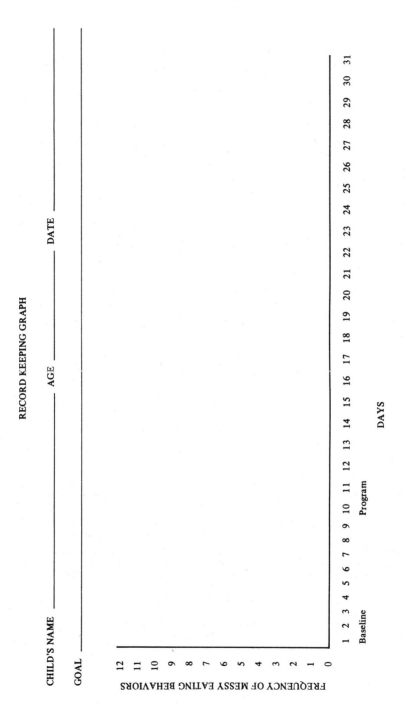

RECORD KEEPING GRAPH

CHILD'S NAME _____ AGE _____ DATE _____

GOAL _____

FREQUENCY OF MESSY EATING BEHAVIORS

12
11
10
9
8
7
6
5
4
3
2
1
0

1 2 3 4 5 6 7 8 9 10 11 12 13 14 15 16 17 18 19 20 21 22 23 24 25 26 27 28 29 30 31

Baseline   Program

DAYS

SECTION 7
MULTIPLE PROBLEM BEHAVIORS

CHAPTER 43

43

Dealing with
Multiple Problems

Sometimes a child presents not just one problem behavior but several. Such situations often become frustrating because it seems that too much effort is involved in bringing about changes. If your attempts to handle multiple problems in the past failed, those experiences probably reinforce the helplessness you feel in trying to deal with them now.

This chapter outlines a systematic approach to dealing with the child who has a number of problem behaviors. It is important that the staff as a whole follow the procedures suggested. Spend time in a staff conference to discuss the problems thoroughly, and decide on a specific approach. The time spent in planning a concerted effort will prove to be well spent when your program begins to take effect.

REVIEW THE BEHAVIORS THAT CONCERN YOU

List all of the child's behaviors that are of concern to you. Do not worry about listing them in order. Record your concerns on paper.

- Review the chapters in this text that deal with the problem behaviors on your list.
- Consider whether any of the problem behaviors are similar. One clue to similarity is that behaviors fall under the same general section heading in the Table of Contents.
- Consider whether any of the procedures for dealing with the problems are very similar.
- Check the behaviors to determine whether any of them are direct opposites. Often the decrease in one behavior leads quite naturally to an increase in another. Infrequent social interaction and hitting are behaviors that illustrate this point. As positive social interactions increase, negative social behaviors such as hitting should decrease. Another example involves concerns with infrequent participation in

activities and thumb sucking. Again, as the child increases participation in activities, thumb sucking should automatically decrease.

- Check whether any of the programs are primarily preventive. A preventive approach is largely based on change in the teachers' actions and reactions. Teachers become more aware of what the child is doing and act to stop the child if the child begins to engage in the misbehavior. Preventive methods are used either in combination with other techniques or are employed where the child's behavior is expected to stop soon on its own (biting by a two-year-old, for example). Most of the programs in this book are not preventive but use techniques that lead to direct behavior change in the child.

PRIORITIZE LISTED BEHAVIORS

Reorganize the behaviors you listed. Start with the behavior of greatest concern to you and the child's parents. Use the following criteria to decide on which behavior to deal with first.

- Any behaviors that lead to a direct hazard to the health or safety of the child or of other children should have first priority. Hitting and throwing objects at others are examples.
- The second most serious category includes behaviors that pose a severe threat to the self-esteem of the child or of other children. Examples are infrequent social interaction and shyness at group times.
- The third category includes other highly disruptive behaviors such as throwing tantrums and running in the classroom.
- The fourth category includes any behaviors that are an indirect health or safety hazard, such as breaking toys and flushing objects down the toilet.
- Include any other behaviors in the final category, such as wasting paper and baby talk.

As you prioritize behaviors, also keep in mind the magnitude of the behavior. The chapter on hitting, for instance, can include a wide variety of behaviors, from a light slap to a severe punch.

DECIDE ON THE APPROACH YOU WILL USE

Once you list, examine, and prioritize the inappropriate behaviors, you can decide what to do first. It is important that you do not try to do too much at one time. Focus on one or at the most two behaviors at a time.

- Begin with the most serious problem on your list. If you feel it is necessary, begin with two problems, combining the most serious with another from the top of your list. To do this, the two behaviors must fit one of the following categories:

  1. The two behaviors are very similar. The procedures can easily be combined.
  2. The programs for the two behaviors are very similar and can be combined easily.
  3. The two behaviors are direct opposites; as one increases the other automatically decreases.
  4. One of the programs utilizes primarily preventive action on the part of the teachers. Use such a preventive program at the same time you use another program only if you feel that you can handle both. For instance, if the first program you are going to implement requires your attention only at specific times, such as at group time or during meals, then you probably can handle it in combination with a preventive program. Remember, do not overreach your time, ability, and resources. Also, do not expect too much from the child at one time.

- When the one or two behaviors you start on are well under control, begin on the next behaviors on your list. Continue until you deal with all the inappropriate behaviors.

- Often, as one behavior improves, other behaviors also change without any specific intervention on your part. This may happen for several reasons. The child may establish a more positive relationship with the teachers and thus feel more inclined to do what is expected. Conversely, the teachers may find the child to be more pleasant and respond to the child more positively. The child's overall behavior may also improve because the program builds the child's self-esteem and self-confidence. The child may simply recognize that compliance with the requests of adults is not a bad thing particularly when adults reinforce such behaviors.

Keep these limits in mind when you deal with multiple problems. A systematic approach helps you eliminate undesirable behaviors. It takes time and effort to carry out several successive programs. In the long run, however, you save the time, energy, and frustration you would have spent dealing with misbehaviors. Most important, you help the child grow in the process of socialization. You help the child improve in relations with other people and in the child's feelings of self-worth.

Index